W9-DEO-212

SCHOOL AND BEHAVIORAL PSYCHOLOGY

Applied Research in Human-Computer Interactions, Functional Assessment and Treatment

SCHOOL AND BEHAVIORAL PSYCHOLOGY

Applied Research in Human-Computer Interactions, Functional Assessment and Treatment

by

H.A. Chris Ninness

Glen McCuller

Lisa Ozenne

Stephen F. Austin State University

KLUWER ACADEMIC PUBLISHERS
Boston / Dordrecht / London

Distributors for North, Central and South America:
Kluwer Academic Publishers
101 Philip Drive
Assinippi Park
Norwell, Massachusetts 02061 USA
Telephone (781) 871-6600
Fax (781) 681-9045
E-Mail <kluwer@wkap.com>

Distributors for all other countries:
Kluwer Academic Publishers Group
Distribution Centre
Post Office Box 322
3300 AH Dordrecht, THE NETHERLANDS
Telephone 31 78 6392 392
Fax 31 78 6546 474
E-Mail <services@wkap.nl>

 Electronic Services <http://www.wkap.nl>

Library of Congress Cataloging-in-Publication Data
Ninness, H.A. Chris.
  School and behavioral psychology: applied research in human-computer interactions,
  functional assessment and treatment / by H.A. Chris Ninness,Glen McCuller,Lisa Ozenne
    p. cm.
  Included bibliographical references and index.
  ISBN 0-7923-7975-6 (alk. paper)
    1. Educational psychology. 2. Human-computer interaction—Psychological aspects.
  3.Computer-assisted instruction. I. McCuller, Glen. II Ozenne, Lisa. III Title.
  LB1051 . N479 2000
  370.15—dc21

                                            00-058720

Contents

Acknowledgements

This book is dedicated to the memory of Don Whaley who inspired a generation of behavior analysts. In turn, our generation passes his torch to the next with the affirmation that he is alive in the behavior of his students. His gentle wisdom continues to radiate, generation after generation, in the evolution of human learning.

We gratefully acknowledge and sincerely appreciate the helpful comments provided by Cloyd Hyten and Sharon K. Ninness in development of this manuscript. Correspondence concerning this work should be directed to H.A. Chris Ninness, PhD, Associate Professor and Director of School & Behavioral Psychology, Department of Human Services, PO Box 13019 SFA Station, Stephen F. Austin State University, Nacogdoches, TX, 75962. (E-mail: **cninness@titan.sfasu.edu**). The current School & Behavioral Psychology web address is http://titan.sfasu.edu/~F_ninnessca/INDEX.HTM

Prologue to Analogues

This book begins where it ends. At both points, we put forth the proposition that there are now practical and scientific methods of teaching people to enhance their own behavior. We submit that at this stage of our scientific development, we have an efficient and practical technology of behavior change. This technology incorporates functional assessment, treatment, and follow-up evaluation, and we hold ourselves accountable for our results. Most importantly, our technology offers all people (and particularly students) an effective means for achieving their own potential.

We have written much of this book around our current behavioral psychology research and practice as it applies to school age children. We address many issues that are experimental in nature and many more that are based on applied research. Much of the work throughout this book was conducted in our own laboratories and in school districts where we have conducted functional assessments, developed intervention systems, collected empirical data, and published our results in peer reviewed professional journals. Large sections of this book follow the applied research of our colleagues in school psychology and behavior analysis throughout the academic/professional community.

A growing proportion of the current research in behavior analysis has begun to focus on people who demonstrate fairly sophisticated verbal skills during computer-interactive behavior and how behavior changes in various social and academic contexts. This has required that we take a closer look at the language process as well as some of our most cherished notions in behavior analysis. For the most part, we have found that our fundamental principles are correct--as far as they go. But up until the past few years, they have not gone far enough. The analysis of verbal behavior has introduced another level of complexity, and as Richard Malott has written, "Life no longer looks that simple to us." (Malott, Malott, Trojan 2000, p.366). We are now at a stage in our technological evolution where we are well positioned to incorporate additional concepts that address language processes. Many of these concepts may be understood as analogues to the early analysis of the contingencies of reinforcement.

For the most part, this is not a book about "how to" conduct behavioral or school psychology. Rather, it is our attempt to examine and extend the experimental analysis of human behavior as it pertains to the growing literature in computer-interaction, functional assessment, behavior analysis, and school psychology. Our book is divided into just six chapters. The first chapter describes some of our oldest and most fundamental theories of learning. We begin by delineating the particulars of autonomic learning; however, we characterize these fundamental processes within the broader context of natural selection. In this framework, we provide an account of why classical conditioning affords special survival value and why it may also interfere with some cultural/behavioral processes. Many of these classical conditioning theories (and studies) are old, but they have weathered the test of time and still have much to tell us about *learning* at its most primitive level. Chapter 1 also introduces the reader to Herbie--a somewhat disturbed child. In part, his problem behavior is under the influence of an unfortunate history of classical conditioning. Throughout the book, Herbie goes through a series of academic and social changes. Many of these changes are closely tied to the learning processes we describe in the following chapters.

Chapter 2 describes learning without language. It addresses the type of learning that most textbooks call operant. This chapter describes the basics of operant learning and adds a little more perspective to the evolution of particular learning processes in our species. Herbie falls into deeper academic distress in this chapter, and much of his difficulty is derived from an inauspicious operant history. Because his learning history is not unique (and in many ways it is typical of disturbed children), we give it a continuing narrative within a broader discussion of human evolution and the expanding technology of the experimental analysis of human behavior.

Chapter 3 brings our analysis of human behavior into contact with the more recent experimental and applied research. We delve into issues regarding verbal instruction, superstitious behavior, types of rule-governed behavior, stimulus equivalence, computer-interactive behavior, paradigms regarding analogues to direct-acting contingencies, and human behavior under the influence of particular schedules of reinforcement. As our technology addresses verbal processes, we consider how humans adapt under the influence of language. Of course, language processes only get Herbie into more serious trouble.

Chapter 4 continues the discussion of basic human computer-interactive research. Several of the concepts and studies in this chapter may appear rather abstract in the sense that they may seem far removed from real classroom issues and events. But, computer simulations gave us a chance to more thoroughly examine student verbal interactions on a safe and concentrated platform. In fact, many of the studies in this chapter explicate (or retrospectively clarify) the procedures that we describe in Chapters 5 and 6. For example, using a computer-interactive model we demonstrate that arranging consequences in particular ways makes these consequences much more compelling than they are under normal circumstances. These reinforcement strategies have a way of making people much more "interested" in getting things they might normally take for granted. In addition, Chapter 4 describes powerful procedures for changing peoples' verbal interpretations of "how things work." That is, this chapter gives special insights into behavioral techniques for *shaping* belief systems. Although the concepts in this chapter are demonstrated in experimental settings, their implications for applied settings are discussed. Their value becomes increasingly obvious in the following two chapters.

In Chapter 5 we direct the reader's attention to the current controversy and confusion surrounding functional assessment, describing the legal, bureaucratic, and psychological complications involving this newly mandated law. We provide a description of a software system that makes this new form of federally mandated assessment easy to perform and useful in developing behavior intervention plans for students with particular types of behavior problems. We provide a CD and operating manual that allows the reader to conduct functional assessments in real time, calculate associated probabilities of outcomes, and develop behavior intervention plans based on these outcomes.

In Chapter 6, we expand on some of our most recently completed applied research that may serve as models for implementation of functional assessment and self-assessment procedures by school psychologists and behavior specialists. The interventions are based on information derived from the types of functional assessment procedures described in the previous chapters, and they are recently enhanced by way of our software package. This chapter details a strategy for applying functional assessment and self-assessment procedures to reduce destructive and aggressive behaviors. We believe that these results are a good first step toward building more powerful behavior change programs that have a special emphasis on teaching self-control. Also, these procedures are aimed at improving the *generalization* of newly learned academic and social skills, and they address a wide range of growing problems in our schools and in our culture.

another level of complexity, and as Richard Malott has written, "Life no longer looks that simple to us." (Malott, Malott, Trojan 2000, p.366). We are now at a stage in our technological evolution where we are well positioned to incorporate additional concepts that address language processes. Many of these concepts may be understood as analogues to the early analysis of the contingencies of reinforcement.

For the most part, this is not a book about "how to" conduct behavioral or school psychology. Rather, it is our attempt to examine and extend the experimental analysis of human behavior as it pertains to the growing literature in computer-interaction, functional assessment, behavior analysis, and school psychology. Our book is divided into just six chapters. The first chapter describes some of our oldest and most fundamental theories of learning. We begin by delineating the particulars of autonomic learning; however, we characterize these fundamental processes within the broader context of natural selection. In this framework, we provide an account of why classical conditioning affords special survival value and why it may also interfere with some cultural/behavioral processes. Many of these classical conditioning theories (and studies) are old, but they have weathered the test of time and still have much to tell us about *learning* at its most primitive level. Chapter 1 also introduces the reader to Herbie--a somewhat disturbed child. In part, his problem behavior is under the influence of an unfortunate history of classical conditioning. Throughout the book, Herbie goes through a series of academic and social changes. Many of these changes are closely tied to the learning processes we describe in the following chapters.

Chapter 2 describes learning without language. It addresses the type of learning that most textbooks call operant. This chapter describes the basics of operant learning and adds a little more perspective to the evolution of particular learning processes in our species. Herbie falls into deeper academic distress in this chapter, and much of his difficulty is derived from an inauspicious operant history. Because his learning history is not unique (and in many ways it is typical of disturbed children), we give it a continuing narrative within a broader discussion of human evolution and the expanding technology of the experimental analysis of human behavior.

Chapter 3 brings our analysis of human behavior into contact with the more recent experimental and applied research. We delve into issues regarding verbal instruction, superstitious behavior, types of rule-governed behavior, stimulus equivalence, computer-interactive behavior, paradigms regarding analogues to direct-acting contingencies, and human behavior under the influence of particular schedules of reinforcement. As our technology addresses verbal processes, we consider how humans adapt under the influence of language. Of course, language processes only get Herbie into more serious trouble.

Chapter 4 continues the discussion of basic human computer-interactive research. Several of the concepts and studies in this chapter may appear rather abstract in the sense that they may seem far removed from real classroom issues and events. But, computer simulations gave us a chance to more thoroughly examine student verbal interactions on a safe and concentrated platform. In fact, many of the studies in this chapter explicate (or retrospectively clarify) the procedures that we describe in Chapters 5 and 6. For example, using a computer-interactive model we demonstrate that arranging consequences in particular ways makes these consequences much more compelling than they are under normal circumstances. These reinforcement strategies have a way of making people much more "interested" in getting things they might normally take for granted. In addition, Chapter 4 describes powerful procedures for changing peoples' verbal interpretations of "how things work." That is, this chapter gives special insights into behavioral techniques for *shaping* belief systems. Although the concepts in this chapter are demonstrated in experimental settings, their implications for applied settings are discussed. Their value becomes increasingly obvious in the following two chapters.

In Chapter 5 we direct the reader's attention to the current controversy and confusion surrounding functional assessment, describing the legal, bureaucratic, and psychological complications involving this newly mandated law. We provide a description of a software system that makes this new form of federally mandated assessment easy to perform and useful in developing behavior intervention plans for students with particular types of behavior problems. We provide a CD and operating manual that allows the reader to conduct functional assessments in real time, calculate associated probabilities of outcomes, and develop behavior intervention plans based on these outcomes.

In Chapter 6, we expand on some of our most recently completed applied research that may serve as models for implementation of functional assessment and self-assessment procedures by school psychologists and behavior specialists. The interventions are based on information derived from the types of functional assessment procedures described in the previous chapters, and they are recently enhanced by way of our software package. This chapter details a strategy for applying functional assessment and self-assessment procedures to reduce destructive and aggressive behaviors. We believe that these results are a good first step toward building more powerful behavior change programs that have a special emphasis on teaching self-control. Also, these procedures are aimed at improving the *generalization* of newly learned academic and social skills, and they address a wide range of growing problems in our schools and in our culture.

A WORD ABOUT SOFTWARE

The text is supplemented with *FOCAL* Point CD. (This includes an easy-to-use operating directions within Chapter 5.) *FOCAL* Point is a working acronym for Functional Observation of Classrooms And Learners. This software provides the reader with the necessary tools to conduct and calculate outcomes for functional assessment procedures on notebook computers. Functional assessments have a unique characteristic separating them from traditional psychological assessments--an emphasis on accountability. Functional assessments are mandated and conducted with an eye toward locating the variables that interact with the student's maladaptive behavior. Once these variables are identified, the success of intervention is based on the student demonstrating improved performance under the same (and more general) conditions. Thus, functional assessments serve as a guide for developing efficient behavior plans, and they provide criteria for demonstrating effective treatment outcomes.

Using Windows 95 or newer operating systems, *FOCAL* Point functional assessment software is designed for making direct observations of the target behaviors in natural settings. The assessment strategies in this software package take behavior assessment well past the traditional technique of simply taking baseline on diversified and undefined behavior problems. They provide the observer with information as to "when" "why" and "where" baseline data is occurring. Rather than using retrospective teacher logs, office records, Lykert scales, or personality profiles, this software provides the school psychologist, diagnostician, counselor, or behavior specialist with a direct observation format that tracks problem behaviors as they occur across real time. And, it allows the observer to select the observation procedure that is best suited to operationally define and reliably identify particular types of problem behaviors in the contexts in which they are most likely to be exhibited. Our software package allows trained observers to generate functional assessment outcomes accurately and efficiently. Following data collection, *FOCAL* Point outcomes are easily transferred and graphed within Excel or Lotus spreadsheets. Details on performing these operations with Excel are provided within Chapter 5 of this text. Lotus graphing procedures can be accomplished in much the same manner.

A large portion of this book is devoted to providing a current foundation in the experimental and applied analysis of human behavior. It is not until we have completed four chapters of theoretical background that we delve into the dynamics and application of applied functional assessments. Subsequently, we provide a description of behavior intervention strategies that are developed on the basis of functional assessment procedures.

Most of the software for the research in this book was written by the first author. Developing such software is much more fruitful than it was even a few years ago. Modern programming languages have allowed our research possibilities in human computer-interaction to expand exponentially. Programming languages are not what they were even a few years ago. As we move into the new millennium, the specific programming languages are becoming less consequential; however, the graphical interfaces to applications are becoming essential. Programming languages today, such as Visual C++, Visual Basic, Visual J++, and to some limited extent even QBASIC, are very distinct from the previous generation of simple text-based tools that wrote commands line by line. Modern programming languages allow the researcher to generate complete applications that quickly interact with every aspect of an operating systems. For the behavioral researcher/programmer this provides the critical instrument for exploring much of the complexity of human verbal and nonverbal learning in a controlled, safe, and very replicable set of conditions.

Seven of our principal studies described in this book were conducted in computer-interactive environments. These studies have only recently been published or are now *in press*. Additionally, outcomes from other studies incorporating computer-interactive formats are given extensive discussion. We believe that computer simulations of real problems provide controlled settings to explore new treatment protocols that would have been unimaginable a generation ago. When our results prove useful in a computer-interactive context, we are much better positioned to examine our protocols in more natural and chaotic settings.

psychStats

For those researchers who would like to run a wide range of statistics, we suggest visiting our experimental web site at www.lcsdg.com/psychStats. The procedures on www.lcsdg.com/psychStats run a wide range of tests for analyzing small group data on line. Procedures on psychStats require no downloading, and results are immediately available.

Among other traditional experimental and quasi experimental statistics, our web site runs a series of nonparametric procedures called randomization tests that are particularly useful when analyzing data derived from extremely small numbers of subjects (fewer than 15 data points). Unlike standard, normal curve statistics, these randomization tests entail no assumptions regarding how data are collected. Roughly stated, randomization tests are a series of nonparametric procedures that provide a test statistic to be repeatedly computed for all possible permutations of any given data set. The size of the sample is completely irrelevant to the internal validity of the test statistic; however, as with other statistical procedures, external validity may be gauged by addressing the logical probability that other populations share the relevant characteristics of the sample (see Edgington, 1995, for a review and discussion). Additionally, psychStats runs correlations, multiple correlations, regression analysis, and many other standard statistical strategies.

Chapter 1

AUTONOMIC LEARNING

INTRODUCTION

Following what must have been a very loud bang, our solar system emerged approximately 15 billion years ago. The earth reached its present size and location about 4.6 billion years ago. Our planet cascaded and cooled for several hundred million years as the oceans formed. The primordial seas ripened in a few hundred million years as the earth prepared the genesis of life in the form of bacteria and cyanophytes (blue-green algae), somewhere around 3.5 billion years ago. Although these tiny creatures were essentially incapable of *learning*, they proved quite proficient at very slowly passing "information" to subsequent generations in the form of genetic mutations and adaptations. However, since organisms at this stage of evolution propagated asexually, each individual had only one genitor, and there was no consolidation of diverse gene mutations as when two unique members of a species combine (Kurten, 1993). Indeed, it was the drive for sexual union that provided the necessary genetic material for species expansion. The dawn of conjugating oxygen-breathing organisms broke roughly 1.5 billion years ago when sexual merger allowed evolution to really pick up the pace.

The earliest multicellular animals surfaced roughly 800 million years ago, and just 400 million years later, plants loomed on the land masses (Lewin, 1984). This formatted the landscape for insects and amphibians which arrived about 400 million years ago as the forests began to grow. This was followed by the arrival of the dinosaurs and the earliest mammals roughly 200 million years prior to the advent of the computer age. As flowering plants germinated, primal birds launched against the ancient sky 100 million years before the first guided missile. There is considerable speculation regarding the sudden demise of the dinosaurs some 65 million years ago. Climatic changes were no doubt involved in what has been called the Cretaceous extinction period (Lewin, 1984), but there is growing evidence that asteroidal impact may have made a substantial contribution to their demise.

Primates were evolutionary embryos at this time, but their progeny were, nevertheless, among the mammals to survive. These animals were very good at *learning*. In fact, the first primates established themselves as a very successful modification of the mammalian line. Eaton, Shostak, and Konner (1988) provide some very interesting details regarding their progress. Generation after generation, they flowed like a living river over Africa, Asia, and America. But when these continents began to drift, so did our earliest ancestors. With the shifting of the land masses, somewhere around 45 million years ago, primates in Asia and Africa and those in North and South America went their separate ways. Subsequently (about 12 million years later), Asia and Africa provided accommodations for the original great apes as they became increasingly diversified. Eaton et al. (1988) point out that the earliest gibbons flourished in the African jungles about 15 million years. These were followed by orangutans and gorillas, 13 million and 9 million years ago, respectively. For the following 2 million years, the mutual predecessor of apes and humans proliferated throughout Africa, but primates with erect carriage would not stroll this planet on two feet for another 3 million years, about 3.5 million years before the advent of compulsory education.

Our current genetic endowment emerged 90,000 years ago, and even though our physiology is the same now as it was then, our interaction and relationship with the earth have been drastically transformed. Consider that 100,000 generations of humans have been hunters and gatherers; through 500 lifetimes we have been agriculturists; only ten of our generations have lived in the Industrial Age with widely accessible education; and only three have been exposed to the world of computers (Eaton et al., 1988).

Our dilemma is that our genetic endowment has not had time to evolve in conjunction with our technology. As our polar icecaps melt, we are forced to recognize industries' impact on the global environment. Indeed, whereas hundreds of thousands of years are necessary for significant genetic adaptations to occur within a species, technology and industry "upgrade" our species' environment almost daily. Our genetic structure, however, is essentially the same now as it was 90,000 years ago when our ancestors spent most of their time hunting and foraging for food. Now, when environmental conditions abruptly deviate from those in which a species has evolved over a period of some 3.5 billion years, a certain amount of social/environmental stress should not be surprising. The ever-growing popularity of pharmaceutical alternatives to stress attests to the difficulty our species is having adapting to the current wave of technological and social "progress." Another obvious example of such stress presents itself in our schools, where a growing number of our children have difficulty learning to adapt to the constraints of an intensely structured social and academic environment.

Fear and Loathing in the First Grade

Each student read aloud for the other members of the first grade class as they followed along the page using their index fingers to keep their places. Most students, it seemed to Herbie, read amazingly well. He secretly marvelled, "How do they do it?" Students were now reading their respective sentences, (some whole paragraphs) one at a time, each taking his or her turn, moving across the front row toward Herbie. He felt the too familiar churning sensation deep in the pit of his stomach. The sensation grew ever more intense as the students' reading progressed across the front row in his inevitable direction. Now, they were reading only three students away. His mouth felt dry, and he noticed his palms were sweating. Now, they were only two students away, and the aching in his stomach was moving up his parched throat. Now, the smart little girl, who sat right next to him, was reading eloquently, and Mrs. Monday was smiling a cold smile. Herbie was not smiling; he was squirming. His bladder felt as if it would burst any second. Now, it was his turn to read and Mrs. Monday and the girl who was sitting next to Herbie and the whole class were watching him--intensely--suspiciously--curiously.

He began his appointed sentence. It was the wrong sentence! Herbie's finger had "momentarily" lost its place. Mrs. Monday recommended that he place his index finger on the proper word and begin reading, again! His finger shook as he tried to blend the letters of the correct word into some meaningful vocalization. But his voice quivered, and presently, his knees began to shake. Mrs. Monday patiently pronounced the first word for Herbie and told him, very politely, to go on to the next word. Herbie's face was burning red, and he noticed that not only were his knees shaking, but now his teeth were also chattering. Mrs. Monday crisply called the second word for Herbie and told him to go on to the next word. Herbie went on to what he hoped would be the correct pronunciation of the third word--and he almost made it. But before he could quite finish getting it through his chattering teeth, Mrs. Monday interrupted and told the next person behind Herbie to begin reading. So it goes.

As the other eloquent first grade reading voices in the second row gradually worked their way back across the other side of classroom,

Herbie's pulse began to slow down. His heart was no longer pounding so loudly inside his small aching chest. His face gradually stopped burning, his teeth quit chattering, and his knees slowly became still. The little girl who sat next to Herbie looked at him sympathetically.

Variations on this distressing scenario were revisited almost daily throughout the long duration of Herbie's first grade year at Greenfield Elementary. Although Mrs. Monday never lifted a finger in his direction, by the end of his first year in public school, young Herbert was quite incapable of even speaking (much less reading) to groups of two or more people. At this point it was probably quite reasonable to diagnose Herbie as having a chronic phobia.

Phobia: An unreasonable and exaggerated fear of an object or event which, "in reality," is incapable of inflicting (or very unlikely to inflict) any "real" form of pain or suffering upon the individual who has the phobia. Phobias are notorious for *generalizing*!

Stimulus Generalization is the tendency for behaviors which are learned under a specific set of conditions to be exhibited under conditions which are similar to those in which the behavior was initially learned. Herbie's phobia continued, and in some ways grew and generalized all over the place.

Note: Several researchers have suggested that humans may be "phobia biased" (genetically predisposed) to selectively fear certain objects, e.g. snakes (Tomarken, Mineka, & Cook; 1989). Others have noticed fears can become attached to a multitude of diverse objects and events such as dentist drills, tests, public speaking, and even authority figures (Ost & Hugdahl, 1985).

Have you ever been afraid? It's something we learn. Herbie learned to be afraid, to make his knees shake, to make his teeth chatter, to make his stomach ache, and to produce a large lump in his dry throat. On several occasions, he came very close to learning how to wet his pants. What's more, he learned to perform these and other seemingly bizarre behaviors on cue.

THE FIGHT OR FLIGHT SYNDROME

Our ancestors survived on the savannah (among other exacting locations) precisely because physiological mutations were naturally selected and passed to the next generation. Those mutations increased our species' probability of successfully addressing life-threatening situations (immediately, intensely, and efficiently).

In our primal human context, conflict scenarios often required prompt escape from, or intense combat with, fierce predators or competing clans (fight or flight). In order for humans to survive as individuals, and as a species, it was necessary that they be optimally prepared to address various confrontations post haste. Those individuals who quite luckily acquired physical/emotional characteristics which selectively elicited increased levels of strength, speed, and agility at the moment of critical need were more likely to survive and pass those attributes on to their progeny.

Maximizing our ability to run or fight is accomplished by a series of visceral and vascular changes that occur so quickly within our bodies that we need not even give these behaviors direct consideration. In fact, these mutations that survived in our ancestors' physiology were naturally selected precisely because they did not require deliberation. Our ancestors, their mutations, and their primitive defense mechanisms are still very much alive in us.

For the most part, however, modern environmental sources of stress usually do not necessitate these intense bodily fight or flight reactions in order to ensure survival, and in a sense, many of our emotional reactions are anachronisms within our current social conventions. Usually, it is not imperative or even advantageous for us to tremble, sweat profusely, or void our bowels when faced with a social stressor. Yet, our physiology is largely incapable of distinguishing social threats (or anxiety provoking circumstances) from physical threats. Presently, when we are faced with provocative social circumstances, we may find ourselves occasionally producing spontaneous bodily secretions and reactions which prepare us to fight or flee predators successfully but which only exacerbate our social dilemma.

Again, our culture, technology, and social conventions have evolved at a faster pace than our physical/emotional defense mechanisms. Ironically, one of the most obvious characteristics of the so-called "fight or flight" syndrome is that it so often seems to help us produce responses quite incompatible with those needed to adapt to the stressful conditions typically encountered in our complex, technologically oriented, "civilized" culture. Certainly this was true in Herbie's civilized first grade reading class. To some extent, we all are victims and survivors of our ancestors' primeval confrontations with a hostile environment.

**Classical Conditioning in the Sympathetic Branch of the
Autonomic Nervous System of a First Grader in Pittsburgh.**

The type of learning described above prepares us both to confront
feared objects or events under some conditions and to address the
maintenance of normal body functioning under others. This kind of learning
does not require decision making or deliberation. It occurs spontaneously
and automatically. Thus, it is often called Autonomic or Classical
Conditioning. It is the kind of learning which is sometimes referred to as
involuntary--involuntary in the sense that what our bodies do, when
operating under its influence, is not what we specifically want them to do. It
just seems to happen to us. In many ways, some of these behaviors seem to
be out of our control. Behaviors that are learned by way of Classical
Conditioning are primarily relegated by the autonomic nervous system.

THE AUTONOMIC NERVOUS SYSTEM

The autonomic nervous system is a highly specialized division of the
peripheral nervous system. It is partitioned into two subdivisions referred to
as the sympathetic and the parasympathetic systems. Almost all of our
visceral (internal) organs receive innervation from both the sympathetic and
the parasympathetic branches; however, these mutually associated nerve
fibers have antagonistic functions. For example, one's heart rate is increased
under the influence of the sympathetic impulses but slowed under
parasympathetic impulses. Digestive enzymes are secreted into the stomach
under the influence of parasympathetic impulses but inhibited by
sympathetic impulses. The pupils of our eyes are constricted by
parasympathetic activity, while they dilate during sympathetic arousal.

When Herbie was trying to sound out various words in *Fun with Dick
and Jane*, and his anxiety was in full flush, the sympathetic branch of his
autonomic nervous system was exerting primary control over his body's
visceral functions. Increases in neural transmitter substances called
adrenaline and noradrenaline throughout his sympathetic pathways
compelled his mouth to become dry, his palms to sweat, his digestive
secretions to abort, his blood vessels to constrict, his heart to race, his
skeletal muscles to tremble, and his sphincters to contract. All these arousal
activities were performed involuntarily and in unison, in a collective effort to
prepare Herbie to fight or flee; however, they actually interfered with his
limited ability to concentrate on reading. When Mrs. Monday suggested that
the next student begin reading, Herbie's autonomic nervous system changed
its area of primary impulse. Gradually, as the reading moved away from his

direction, his parasympathetic impulses regained control, and he stopped sweating, flushing, shaking, and chattering. He was no closer to reading fluently, but he certainly felt better.

Interestingly, these extremely divergent behaviors demonstrated first by the sympathetic branch and then the parasympathetic branch of Herbie's autonomic nervous system were operating under the influence of environmental events. These environmental events had become associated with various states of arousal, and gradually, these environmental events came to produce these states of arousal.

Listen, here's part of what probably happened to Herbie. States of sympathetic arousal, i.e., shaking, sweating, flushing, etc., were initially triggered when he was physically punished for misbehaving at home. Various forms of physical punishment (environmental events which directly cause pain) are a form of unconditioned stimuli (UCS). They are unconditioned, because such directly aversive physical events do not require any conditioning (learning) in order to produce their inevitable effects, namely the sympathetic arousal (unconditioned responses) (UCR). So far we have:

UCS ⎯⎯⎯⎯⎯⎯⎯▶ UCR
Physical punishment   Sympathetic arousal

This is an unlearned physical mechanism, but it is positively pregnant with possibilities for new associations. Neutral stimuli (those which initially produce no responses) can become associated (paired in time and space) with unconditioned stimuli (UCS). With repeated associations, these neutral stimuli become conditioned stimuli (CS), and they usually are sufficient to produce a conditioned response (CR).

In Herbie's early home environment, we can assume that particularly harsh or "cold" words and tones of voice (CS) were consistently predictive of forthcoming physical pain (UCS). These words (CS) then took on the arousing properties of the actual painful events and produced the same responses (CR) as the actual painful events (UCS). This is the process of association within classical conditioning. Within the context of Herbie's home, we have:

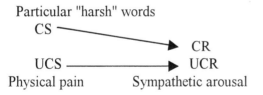

Particular "harsh" words
CS
CR
UCS ⎯⎯⎯⎯⎯⎯⎯▶ UCR
Physical pain   Sympathetic arousal

Later, when Herbie was in his first grade classroom, while he was making a rather feeble attempt to read, Mrs. Monday apparently employed some of the same chilling words, inflections, or just facial expressions as those used by Herbie's parents when they were angry with him. (In all fairness to Mrs. Monday, Herbie was probably predisposed to receive an inordinate amount of these CS's as he really was an extremely poor reader.) As previously mentioned, the tendency for behaviors which are learned under a specific set of conditions to be exhibited under conditions which are similar to those in which the behavior was initially learned is a phenomenon we call stimulus generalization. Within the context of Mrs. Monday's first grade class, we now have generalization and physical pain is no longer necessary in order to produce sympathetic arousal

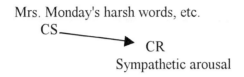

Mrs. Monday's harsh words, etc.
CS
CR
Sympathetic arousal

It is important to understand that Herbie had a few well-chosen words for himself under these conditions. As soon as he heard his fellow students reading in the first row, he would inevitably begin his own internal dialogue, "Oh God, here it comes," and so on. (We now know that a person's own fear-inducing, internal dialogue plays a very powerful role in the formation and continuation of most phobias. There will be more on this point later in the book.) Herbie told himself some very terrifying things about what was going to happen to him as soon as he began to read. And, sure enough, Herbie's conversation with himself helped produce those very terrifying things--a sort of self-fulfilling prophecy. Herbie's horrifying words that he used on himself and Mrs. Monday's rather intimidating words and tone of voice were just loaded with classically conditioned associations.

This kind of classical conditioning and generalization of classical conditioning served an obvious evolutionary function on the savannah. It provided a means whereby diversified environmental events (and words), which were correlated with painful stimuli, could become predictive of those painful stimuli. Under these conditions, our ancestors were optimally prepared for "fight or flight." Today, this kind of visceral conditioning may be less advantageous, especially within the confines of the current public school system.

Do not despair, this is only one version of classical conditioning as it might be depicted within the context of the sympathetic branch of the autonomic nervous system. It is important to realize that the same type of learning can take place within the parasympathetic branch of the autonomic nervous system. People can learn to relax, constrict their pupils, and even salivate. That which is learned within the autonomic nervous system can be unlearned within that same system--mostly.

Parasympathetic Classical Conditioning

As previously indicated, parasympathetic pathways within the autonomic nervous system perform activities which are antagonistic (opposed) to those in the sympathetic pathways. Under normal, non-stressful conditions, our bodies maintain visceral conditions compatible with ongoing essential metabolic functions. Ideally, our blood pressure, pulse, perspiration, digestive processes, and respiration are stabilized at the optimal levels necessary to sustain healthy body maintenance (homeostasis). Under these conditions, we may feel relaxed and comfortable. One might say that parasympathetic activities are the reciprocal (reverse) of sympathetic.

In the early part of this century, a Russian physiologist, Ivan Pavlov, quite accidentally discovered that the parasympathetic activity of salivation could be conditioned in laboratory animals. Part of his initial investigations involved the pre-digestive processes in dogs. In his experimental arrangements, dogs had fistulas inserted into their salivary ducts in order to measure the amount of salivary secretion which occurred during food ingestion. But, as often happens in science, fate intervened. Quite to his amazement, Pavlov noticed that his dogs quickly began to salivate even before their food (meat powder) was presented. Various sounds produced by the kennel keepers which were associated with forthcoming food presentation began to elicit the salivation in the same way that the actual presentation of food had initially. Through serendipity (a happy coincidence), Pavlov discovered parasympathetic classical conditioning. He began to experiment with bells, metronomes, and all sorts of novel neutral stimuli. Pavlov determined that virtually any neutral stimulus (CS) which reliably preceded food would soon elicit the same amount of salivation (CR), just as the presentation of real food (UCS) (Pavlov, 1927). Pavlov was the first to organize this process into a paradigm (model) which could be investigated and replicated by other scientists. His original classical conditioning paradigm looked like this:

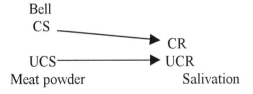

Pavlov eventually determined that neutral stimuli which preceded the UCS by about .5 seconds were most likely to become strong CS's. His early research in parasympathetic arousal laid the foundations for much of the empirical (observable) research in human behavior. In fact, today many textbooks describe classical conditioning as Pavlovian conditioning. The terms are now somewhat synonymous.

Another Big Bang: Enter John B. Watson.

In the 1920's, a brilliant (if slightly eccentric) psychologist named John B. Watson, at The Johns Hopkins University, became totally enamoured with the work of Ivan Pavlov. Since psychology up to this point in time had not proven itself to be a particular useful discipline, and Pavlov's investigations had demonstrated empirical and replicable outcomes, Watson began to study a multitude of variations on classical conditioning with human-oriented applications. His most famous (possibly infamous) inquiry involved the treatment of, you guessed it, "phobia." No, Herbie was not the subject for this particular piece of renowned research. An eleven-month-old boy named Albert participated in Watson and Rayner's (1920) study of the conditions under which benign and neutral stimuli (potential CS's) may quickly take on the fear inducing properties of truly painful (aversive) objects or events (UCS).

Watson searched for and found a truly benign object to represent Albert's CS. He determined that a white, fluffy bunny (sometimes a white rat) was ideally suited. Certainly, Little Albert (as he came to be known) would have no natural fear of a cute, fluffy bunny. Children usually love white, fluffy bunnies--children who have not spent too much time with John B. Watson!

Following Pavlov's lead on the classical conditioning paradigm, Watson arranged the following sequence of notorious events. The cute, white, fluffy bunny (or rat) was quite casually presented to Albert, and about .5 seconds later, a loud *banging* of a 120-centimeter-long steel bar and hammer occurred just behind Little Albert's young, smiling head. Albert didn't smile much longer. Probably, Albert's eyes dilated, his palms sweated, and his blood pressure and heart rate accelerated; he definitely produced a very conspicuous and overt "startle response." He also started to cry! A few of these paired associations produced a complete change in Little Albert's sympathetic impulses upon the presentation of the white rabbit (even without the banging hammer and steel bar).

The pairing of the rabbit and the aversive noise was performed for a total of five trials after which it was noted that the presentation of the rabbit alone was sufficient to make Albert cry. Albert had been conditioned, classically! Albert's paradigm looked a lot like Herbie's:

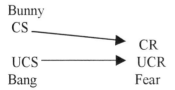

Bunny
CS

CR

UCS   UCR
Bang   Fear

Albert had "learned" his phobia--in a psychological laboratory no less. This classically conditioned fear of the white rabbit was likewise manifested when he was presented objects which only resembled the rabbit: white fur coats, fluffy white piles of cotton, and so on. The experimenters were surprised as to how widely this induced fear generalized.

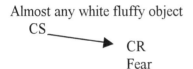

Almost any white fluffy object
CS

CR
Fear

Although this classic study produced a flood of replications and related investigations on classical conditioning, and likewise brought about some very useful psychological procedures which eliminate phobias, this was probably of small consolation to Albert. It is often cited that Little Albert was removed from Watson's laboratory before he could be counter-conditioned. Perhaps, somewhere out there, on the plains of middle America, roams a modern man who would prefer to maintain a safe distance from white bunnies, and perhaps, white fluffy objects in "general." So it goes.

Psychology from the Standpoint of the First Behaviorist

Dr. Watson published his research on Little Albert as well as other important findings and extrapolations of his findings. In so doing, he created quite a stir throughout the scientific community. Scientists and psychologists, during the 1920's, were astounded by the ways in which the direct application of principles derived from a laboratory in Russia could be astutely applied to human beings. Dr. Watson went on to found a particular school of psychology which quickly became exceedingly popular in the United States. He called this new school of psychology, "Behaviorism," and he claimed that the primary business of all psychologists should be the exclusive study of overt (external) behavior. He suggested that "thinking" was nothing more than covertly talking to one's self, and that most of what we call thinking actually takes place in the minute muscle potentials emitted within our larynxes. These could and should be measured in order to understand the thinking process itself (Watson, 1919; Max, 1934). No longer should men of science ponder the unseen and unseeable workings of the human "mind."   According to Watson, such phenomena were only speculative and could not be verified by empirical (observable) data. Naturally, this annoyed a very large number of psychologists and philosophers who were convinced that their minds could do things which no one could directly observe. Even before it got off the ground, Behaviorism was becoming quite controversial in some quarters. Incidentally, this is probably a good place to point out that the Behaviorism of John B. Watson's day bears very little resemblance to the principles and procedures used in Behavior Analysis as it is practiced today.

EXTRAPOLATION IN PSYCHOLOGY

You will probably notice, if you study psychology very long, that psychologists (and perhaps academicians in general) have a magnificent capacity for expanding and extrapolating their findings. Often, these extrapolations are somewhat beyond the bounds of their empirical data. Watson extrapolated his findings further to put forth the proposition that *all* human behavior is learned and that absolutely no human behavior was innate (genetically programmed). He suggested that he could turn any child into virtually any kind of adult you could imagine. Watson said,

> Give me a dozen healthy infants, well-formed, and my own specialized world to bring them up in, and I'll guarantee to take any one at random and train him to become any type of specialist I might select--doctor, lawyer, artist, merchant chief and yes, even beggarman and thief, regardless of his talents, penchants, tendencies, abilities, vocations and race of his ancestors ... and so on (Watson, 1919, p. 103).

Assertions like these had some especially strong implications for psychologists. This sort of thing had been pontificated before (e.g., Locke, 1950), but never with such profound conviction and compelling empirical data to seemingly substantiate the argument.

Well, behavioral psychology was really cooking now. For a time Watson enjoyed an especially large following in the educational community.

America became fascinated by the possibilities of molding its children into any and all forms of happy, productive, and successful adults. Remember, however, that Watson was basing his theorizing on data derived primarily from the responses initiated within the autonomic nervous system. In the 1920's, it was not entirely clear to everyone that the human nervous system was largely delineated into divisions of labor. It would remain for future behavioral psychologists to demonstrate that more sophisticated principles were necessary to account for the wide range of complex human behavior under the control of the central nervous system (the brain and spinal cord).

Replication

In behavior analysis and school psychology, as in all academic disciplines that attempt to derive factual information from experimental research, it is critical that new findings be subjected to further inquiry before they are accepted as being correct. To address this issue, a procedure called replication has become widely accepted throughout the scientific community. Replication is essentially the process of attempting to duplicate the same experimental procedures as employed during the initial experiment to see if the same findings can be obtained. Naturally, the more often different scientists determine the same outcomes when using the same methods, the more confidence we can have in the findings of the initial research.

Very often psychologists use two types of replication: direct and systematic (Sidman, 1960). *Direct replication* is simply the process of making a concerted effort to "reperform," as consistently as possible, exactly what was done in the initial study. If the outcome is the same, then our confidence in the *internal validity* of the research, the extent to which the results are exclusively a function of the treatment and nothing else, is increased. *Systematic replication* is a little more complicated. This procedure requires that we make small changes in the form in which the initial research was conducted. Systematic replication is a method for testing the limits or *external validity* of our experimental procedures. Here, we systematically alter what we have done in the initial experiment. This allows us to see how strong our treatment is when it is applied in ways not exactly the same as those originally used. It allows us to obtain more details as to the wide-ranging effects of our treatments. You might think of this as a way for psychologists to control some of their extrapolations before they really get ahead of themselves and their data.

Watson's initial findings have indeed been replicated many times in various ways, using diverse species and multiple forms of CS's, UCS's, and

UCR's. Outcomes, in so far as they address behavior within the confines of the autonomic nervous system, have been fairly consistent.

Mary Cover Jones's Systematic Replication

One very important replication of Watson's research was conducted by Mary Cover Jones. Dr. Jones pretty much picked up where Watson had left off with the study of induced phobias; however, she performed a systematic replication. Since Little Albert was no longer available for further scientific inquiry, Jones found a few other participants who essentially received the same independent variable that Albert had received. That's right, the banging of bars and other diversified UCS's continued to be paired with various neutral stimuli which quickly became CS's and produced their inevitable CR's. But Jones took her research one step further by way of systematic replication. She performed what has come to be known as counterconditioning.

Counterconditioning: The elimination of an unwarranted fear (phobia), by gradually and sequentially associating the feared object or event with calming conditions. This procedure classically conditions states of relative relaxation (parasympathetic responding) with circumstances (CS's) that previously elicited anxiety. This procedure results in the gradual elimination of many phobias. The paradigm follows the same pattern as previously illustrated but the emphasis is on parasympathetic associations:

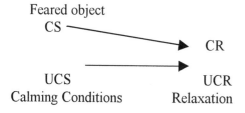

Feared object
CS ———————→ CR

UCS ———————→ UCR
Calming Conditions   Relaxation

By the process of associating a calming, relaxing condition as an unconditioned stimulus, and slowly reintroducing the feared object as a conditioned stimulus, a new association may be learned. Through this systematic replication of the work of Watson and Pavlov, Mary Jones was able to show, rather elegantly, that phobias could be learned and unlearned, systematically (Ullmann, 1969).

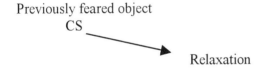

Previously feared object
CS

Relaxation

SCHOOL PSYCHOLOGY AND BEHAVIOR ANALYSIS

School psychology is often seen as the applied branch of educational psychology. School psychologists spend much of their time using instruments, principles, and procedures which may have been developed (at least in part) by educational psychologists. School psychologists are trained in the assessment and treatment of children with learning disabilities, mental retardation, autism, developmental disabilities, and emotional or behavioral disorders. They also spend much of their time developing systems to preclude or curtail the effects of these handicapping conditions.

With the advent of the National Association of School Psychologists (NASP) as a national certifying and accrediting body, school psychology has become a growing and distinctive professional discipline in its own right. Most urban school districts and many rural school districts retain school psychologists who are trained in the assessment and treatment of the various developmental and behavioral disorders.

Behavior analysis crosses a wide range of academic disciplines, including behavioral psychology, behavior modification, behavior management, contingency management, applied learning theory, behavioral engineering, and in some cases, cognitive behavior therapy. It embodies a range of principles and procedures that have been developed over the last thirty years in the scientific, pragmatic, and empirical investigation of behavior. The term *applied behavior analysis*, however, is frequently understood to carry a special emphasis on the evaluation of data derived from a functional analysis of human behavior under various environmental changes.

Behavior analysis originated in the laboratory with the study of basic behavioral processes. Much of this early research was performed with nonhuman organisms and was restricted to the formulation of basic scientific principles. This experimental analysis of behavior continues; but, along with it has emerged research on the application of behavioral principles for the purpose of solving socially important behavioral problems.

Presently, the disciplines of school psychology and behavior analysis have merged in the educational arena. Particularly in the areas of learning disabilities and behavior disorders, behavior analysis and school psychology have consolidated into an overlapping and unified area of academic and professional specialization. At this point in time, the disciplines of school psychology and behavior analysis have more in common than in contrast. Usually, graduate students who are trained as school psychologists are also trained in the principles and procedures of behavior analysis. Richard Malott has coined the term *Behavioral School Psychology* to represent the blending of these two overlapping disciplines (Malott, Whaley, & Malott, 1997). From our perspective *Behavioral School Psychology* suggests a particular emphasis on the development and application of the experimental analysis of human behavior within the school-age population. Thus, this field represents a merging of basic and applied research in the effort to understand the complexity of human learning.

Down and Out in Denton and Dallas

Dr. Larry Pritchard was living in Denton but working each day for the Dallas School District, some 35 miles away, as a school psychologist and behavior analyst during his year of post-doctoral residency. His residency was under the supervision and direction of Dr. Maria Manning, the Supervising School Psychologist, for the duration of his final academic year. Larry felt as if he had been in school, or in some kind of practicum, or internship, or residency, or something academic since childhood. And, as a matter of fact, he had. After completion of his undergraduate degree, he had completed four more years of class work, then one more year as a pre-doctoral intern in the public schools, and finally, a year as a post-doctoral resident in the psychological services division of the public schools. This protracted education, with all of its pre-doctoring and post-doctoring, had cost him a lot of money, and money was something that he was going to be paying back to the federal government for a very long time.

Larry was thinking that he was near the end of his fiscal rope, and he was feeling a little sorry for himself. After all he had been through, after all his time and effort, he only had a facsimile of an office in the rear of the high-school (actually it was more like a corner with a partition). Just when he was precariously tilting back in his hard wooden chair and starting to put his boots on his desk as a gesture of financial frustration and quiet indignation, Nelda Hudson walked into his "office"--without knocking. Her abrupt entrance disrupted what was left of his professional and physical equilibrium, and he nearly fell straight back off his chair. Luckily, clumsily, Larry caught himself just before his chair and he made the hazardous backward descent. She mused that his awkward attempt to regain balance looked as embarrassing as it did foolish.

She was a tall, muscular, blonde senior with a slightly anxious expression on her thin lips. Her lips quivered with her first words.

"You've got one of them with you, don't you?" she alleged.

"One what?" said Larry trying to regain his physical and professional composure.

"One of those nasty, stinking, yellow weeds!"

"Young lady, we're not allowed to have <u>any</u> kind of weeds, stinking or otherwise, in this building. And why are you rushing into my office without even knocking on my door?"

"What door? You don't have a door, that's just a partition," she pointed out insubordinately.

"Never mind that, I'm getting a door. What can I do for you?"

"Mrs. Swartz, my biology teacher, says I have a phobia, so she sent me to see you."

"A phobia regarding what?"

"Sunflowers," she said, with just a little self-consciousness.

"What?"

It was true. Nelda Hudson, star of the track team, honor student, and secretary of the student council, was really terrified (petrified) of sunflowers--of all things. If she were driving and saw them by the side of the road, she changed lanes immediately, irrespective of traffic conditions. When they were in season and blooming near her home or school, she had serious difficulty sneaking past them to get inside. Truth is always stranger than fiction and infinitely more complicated, or so it seemed to Nelda. Why did she have this stupid fear, and how could this clumsy psychologist be of any help?

Larry knew it didn't make any sense. It didn't seem possible, and it didn't seem reasonable to be afraid of sunflowers. But sometimes, that's how these things worked. Larry knew that phobias aren't based on logic. They are at least partially based on associations and impulses in the sympathetic branch of the autonomic nervous system. That's not a place where much of our human logic resides.

IN SUMMARY

So far, we have confronted the foundation of phobia and a small evolutionary chronology of its neurological significance and treatment history. We have discussed the roles of the sympathetic and parasympathetic branches of the autonomic nervous system. We've looked at some of the early history of psychology's attempt to understand phobia and at some of the ways in which psychologists have attempted to maintain order in their research. In addition, we have seen a few of the professional and academic areas addressed by school psychologists.

The emphasis in this first chapter has been on anxiety and phobia, and this may be an unusual place to begin a discussion of school and behavioral psychology and computer interactive functional assessment. But apprehension is not that uncommon in education. Many children, and even a few teachers and administrators, are more than a little apprehensive. Although most of them don't demonstrate the chattering of teeth, the shaking of limbs, or a particular horror of flowers, many of them feel constant consternation and tension. These behaviors are, as previously described, autonomic reactions which many of us have learned all too easily. It seems that our inherited physiology has over-prepared us to be extremely sensitive to physical as well as social forms of pressure. These emotional behaviors are also the product of more complex types of learning, which we will discuss in subsequent chapters.

We have met a few people in the public schools who are having (or creating) difficulties. We will meet others as the book progresses. Herbie is more than a little nervous about reading in public. Mrs. Monday is "seemingly" oblivious to her students' obvious anxiety. Larry Pritchard, subsequent to twenty-some years of education, is disgusted and wondering if it is worth all the aggravation. And Nelda Hudson, strange as it may seem, is horrified by the prospect of confronting a sunflower. While these problems may seem a little peculiar, they are certainly not trivial, particularly from the perspective of the parties involved.

In a sense, every problem of every student and every teacher is a little peculiar and a little typical of our society and our educational system. To be a student or teacher in today's technologically advanced and socially diverse society is to inherit a wealth of potential and perplexity. We are a people who have been bequeathed with an enormous and unwieldy educational edifice, an extraordinary and primitive neurological structure, and a compassionate but seriously confused culture.

We are full of good intentions and ambitions, but many of our best resources are not well directed or utilized. Those of you who want to become teachers, counselors, psychologists, etc. would like to make a difference. But perhaps, you, too, are a little apprehensive. Perhaps, you have good reason! The public schools are in a state of chaos, particularly in our inner cities. Almost daily, the headlines recount the educational hazards: falling national achievement scores, falling academic standards, lowering of teacher morale, administrative corruption, and students shooting other students and teachers. Drugs are illegally dispensed, and violence is irrationally dispersed.

Teachers are variously described as underpaid, unappreciated, overworked, and apprehensive.

Possibly, the problems of Herbie, Nelda, Larry, and Mrs. Monday may appear trivial by comparison. But the solutions to their problems may be part of the source of solutions to other, more complex, individual and cultural challenges.

Chapter 2

LUCY IN THE SKY
Learning Without Language

INTRODUCTION

In 1974, when the lyrics to "Lucy in the Sky with Diamonds" still filled our planet's airwaves, the most complete skeleton of the earliest hominid was exhumed in Ethiopia. With a stroke of irony, the small female skeleton was dubbed "Lucy" (Johanson & Edey, 1981). Her fragmented remains represented only 40 percent of her original person. Yet, Lucy and her cohorts, *Australopithecus afarensis*, are unquestionably part of the human lineage. Until Lucy's remains were unearthed, paleontologists had no reliable way of confirming bipedal locomotion among hominids prior to about two million years ago. Lucy's bones, particularly her pelvis, legs, and feet, demonstrate that she walked and ran the earth with a stride no different from that of our own--more than three million years ago (Eaton et al., 1988).

When Herbie met Lucy

Herbie sits in a hard wooden chair on the third floor of his grandmother's grocery store. His bones, particularly his pelvis, legs, and feet, are getting stiff. The room is slightly damp, dark, and chilly, and he is erratically and ineffectually attempting to solve problems from his second grade math homework assignment. He loathes school and he detests homework. But every night he goes through the superficial motions. At his grandmother's insistence, he retires to his attic/bedroom, begrudgingly opens his books, and surreptitiously turns on his radio. Melodious vibrations fill the attic as the lyrics from "Lucy in the Sky with Diamonds" (a Beatles masterpiece) spill across the cold night air.

Is there some kind of message here? One thing is clear, Herbie's attention span and general academic proclivity are getting worse. By now, Herbie is not only extremely fearful of reading aloud (and speaking) in public, he is completely distressed with every aspect of education. His present vexation with schoolwork, eye strain, plus the cold, hard, wooden chair in which he is planted, combine to make him feel physically and emotionally uncomfortable. Without "conscious awareness," Herbie begins tilting back in his chair and stretches his feet on the desk before him. While doing so he closes his eyes, takes a deep breath and immediately feels more relaxed. He is dimly aware of the fact that he is somewhat further removed from life's primary source of aggravation--textbooks! For just a moment, he envisions a primal image of running free in the forest with his earliest ancestors--free of social conventions and academic irritations. Once again, Herbie is avoiding his homework, and in some very primitive way it feels good!

Looking at young Herbert with his feet propped up on his desk, his books open and his "eyes wide shut," one might be tempted to conclude that, at the very least, he appears to have a poor "academic attitude." Interestingly, Herbie, his physiology, and his poor academic attitude, are a product of a very pervasive process called *selection*.

NATURAL SELECTION AND SELECTION BY CONSEQUENCES

The prehistoric conditions in which various species evolved were erratic and perilous. Environments that may have been secure one moment were menacing in the next. Individuals whose physiology and behavior were capable of adapting to dramatic and sudden changes were more likely to survive than those who remained physiologically and behaviorally rigid. In this context, physiological mechanisms evolved that provided a means whereby some species (and individuals) adapted better than others.

The Physiological Context

As commonly understood, cells that are specifically designed for reproductive purposes (sex cells) contain only 23 pairs of chromosomes, half the number found in other human cells. During impregnation, these halves combine and establish the entire coding of the genetic material from both parents. This process provides constant variation in the characteristics in the offspring. Thus, one form in which genetic variations occur is by the process of merging sex cells of the parents to form new characteristics within the progeny.

But a less commonly understood form of individual and species variation occurs as a function of mutation. Mutation is a sudden aberration in chromosome structure that is inconsistent with the genetic information provided by the parent chromosomes. Most mutations are spontaneous and unpredictable (Conner, Ferguson-Smith, 1987). Sometimes, the changes that occur within any given individual cellular anomaly are relatively innocuous; however, over the course of many generations, such mutations may become structurally or functionally significant. During each generation, individuals emerge with uniquely and randomly mutated characteristics that may prove beneficial, lethal, or equivocal to themselves and their descendants. Those hapless individuals who unfortunately inherited (or mutationally acquired) structural characteristics that operated to their detriment had an increased probability of personal and familial extinction. They and their characteristics were not selected. Conversely, physiological attributes that increased vitality, and provided various means of overcoming predation, increased the individual's chances of living long enough to procreate and pass its genetic endowment to its offspring. For example, during the early part of the industrial revolution in London (during 1840's), the majority of moths were of a prominent white coloration. This salient feature of their appearance made them contrast conspicuously against the increasingly industrialized and murky environment in which they flew; it also made them more susceptible to predation. Specifically, various species of birds could identify the white colored moths against the dark sooty and increasingly polluted background atmosphere. Over the course of about 80 years, particular individual mutant moths emerged with a darker pigmentation that made them less conspicuous to their predators. These camouflaged individuals had an increased longevity and increased probability of procreation as did their offspring. Thus, the majority of moth species currently surviving in this area (as well as other industrialized areas) manifest a dark-sooty complexion (Mulinksy, 1989).

Physiological attributes that increase the species' probabilities of continuing to thrive in a given environment are said to be selected by the contingencies of survival. This continuing process of genetic variation in physical structure and function, resulting in survival or extinction, is the ubiquitous mechanism of natural selection. Genetic variations in structure and function that occur within a species during its evolution are often referred to as being products of phylogeny. In the words of Morgan (1998):

> The constructive process, selection, is the fact that these varying genotypes are differentially reproduced. Those individual organisms who best meet the demands of the local ecology are more likely to reach an age of reproductive maturity, thus passing their genes on to successive generations. It is in this sense that environmental pressures are said to "select" the most adaptive or fit genotypes. It is important to remember, however, that "fitness" is a term defined by local condition, not a singular, optimal criterion. Thus, "selection theory" alludes generally to the process by which certain variations, genotypically defined in the case of biological evolution, become selected for in a population over time. It is the combined

operation of genetic variation and natural selection that is celebrated by scientists and non-scientists alike. (p 441).

Natural selection is a dynamic process, as powerful in our modern context as it was in the primitive one. However, in terms of addressing immediate hazards (predators, drought, pestilence, extreme temperature variation, food deprivation, and so on), natural selection is an exceedingly slow process, even in single celled and relatively short-lived organisms. Adaptations, which can be initiated more quickly than those selected only during consecutive generations, are especially helpful to the particular organism and its species in adjusting to the unrelenting environmental instability.

The Behavioral Context

At some important evolutionary juncture, organisms mutated a pivotal attribute that permitted them to perform immediate adaptations to various changes in their surroundings. Specifically, in the presence of particular environmental conditions, or cues, many organisms developed the capacity to have their behavior modified by the environmental consequences that immediately followed specific behaviors. For example, some organisms probably mutated the ability to perform minor movement away from sources of irritation and toward sources of sustenance. These successful behavioral adaptations were then more likely to occur under similar conditions in the future of those particular organisms. Thus, some organisms acquired the facility to have new and specific *behaviors* immediately selected by their consequences and to perform these behaviors under similar conditions in the future (Catania, 1993; Skinner, 1938). These organisms inherited the capacity to learn.

This capacity to perform immediate physical relocation (or other valuable responses), as a function of environmental consequences, dramatically improved the individual's possibilities for survival. This was an adaptation that empowered the particular organism with an instantaneous advantage over other species--an accelerated form of natural selection that occurred within the lifetime of the individual. Henceforth, organisms inheriting this capacity to have new behaviors selected by their consequences were able to produce immediate adaptive responses to their continuously changing circumstances. Behavioral changes that occur during the lifetime of an individual (learned behaviors) but are not passed on to succeeding generations are referred to as being products of ontogeny.

As an analogous process to natural selection, behavioral selection by consequences was a critical step toward individual and species progression.

For example, when a food deprived organism performed any behavior that acted on the environment and resulted in the acquisition of food, that behavior was selected by its consequences. Having been selected, that behavior became more likely to occur again under similar antecedent conditions (environmental cues) in the future of that particular organism. In fact, the new behavior demonstrated an increase in frequency under all conditions that were similar to the one in which the favorable consequence originally occurred. This was a process called generalization. The more similar the conditions, the more likely it was that the new behavior would be repeated. On the other hand, behaviors that were inconsistent with acquisition of food under these conditions were extinguished (eliminated from the individual's repertoire).

In this example, the act of acquiring food can be understood as a behavior that operates on the environment and results in a favorable consequence (reinforcement). Reinforcement with food selects a particular behavior and makes it more probable on subsequent similar occasions. This type of behavior that operates on the environment and is selected by its consequences has come to be known as *operant*. Operant behavior, unlike classically conditioned behavior, occurs primarily within the realm of the central nervous system (the brain and spinal column). Sometimes, operant behavior is colloquially referred to as "voluntary behavior."

Note: Psychologists frequently refer to environmental cues that precede particular operant behaviors as *discriminative stimuli*. This is to suggest that individuals learn to discriminate (distinguish) particular stimuli which are present in the environment because responding in the presence of these discriminative stimuli has previously led to reinforcement. In the following pages, we will use the words antecedent conditions, discriminative stimuli, and environmental cues interchangeably.

Operant behavior is defined as behavior that acts on the environment to change the environment. In the presence of particular environmental *cues* (or discriminative stimuli), behaviors are emitted which produce consequences. When in the presence of similar environmental cues, these consequences increase the likelihood of certain behaviors. Operant behavior includes such everyday activities as bicycle riding and walking to school. It includes doing homework and talking to your friends; however, it is most important to understand that we may, or may not, be aware of many of our "habitual" operant behaviors.

A FEW BASIC DEFINITIONS

For a few pages, we will supply a little jargon. Understanding these definitions will make the concepts that follow much easier to grasp. Although many of these terms are in fairly common usage, we have found that furnishing very specific definitions gives many people an added "sensitivity" to the nomenclature.

Reinforcers and Punishers

If a certain immediate consequence increases the frequency of an operant behavior, we say that the consequence acts as a reinforcer. Inversely, if an immediate consequence acts to decrease the frequency of that behavior, we call it a punisher. Note: No mention is made regarding whether the consequence is pleasant, enjoyable, or even rewarding. Nor is there reference to painful or unpleasant sensations or qualities. The empirical fact that the behavior increases or decreases speaks for itself. Here are a few examples of the various types of reinforcers. All of these categories of reinforcement have one thing in common. They all increase the probability of behavior.

Positive Reinforcement: Any immediate stimulus presentation which increases the probability of a behavior. For example: Someone, relatively important to you, nods his/her head and smiles at you as you look in his/her direction. For most people, this is a reinforcing event. It may increase the chances of you looking in his/her direction in the future.

Reinforcement may be seen in the classroom as a teacher makes eye-contact, nods her head, and smiles at a student who has just spelled a word correctly. Although subtle in form, smiling, heading-nodding, and eye-contact are usually strong and pervasive sources of positive reinforcement.

Negative Reinforcement: Any immediate stimulus removal which increases the likelihood of making a particular response in the future. Important to note is the fact that negative reinforcers always increase the probability of behaviors upon which they are contingent (dependent). For example, if we find ourselves inadvertently touching something that is painful (maybe an electric fence), we may quickly withdraw our hands. The withdrawing of our hands is the behavior that has been reinforced by escaping the aversive (painful) stimulus. This form of negative reinforcement is called escape. Hand withdrawing will be more likely to occur in the presence of similar discriminative stimuli in the future. In fact, withdrawing one's hand will be more likely to occur in the future under all similar conditions--even in those in which fences are touched but shock does not occur.

Later as you inadvertently approach a wire fence, you may find that you withdraw from it long before actually touching it (even before you instruct yourself to do so). This form of negative reinforcement is called **avoidance.** In fact, you and your hand may be very reluctant to touch a wide range of fences for quite a long time (generalization).

In a school setting, a teacher may raise his voice and scold a student as she is caught drifting off-task. As the student begins working, the teacher terminates his reprimand. In this common, but usually inadvisable, procedure of reprimanding, the teacher has initially created an aversive situation from which the student escapes by performing a particular behavior (getting to work). Subsequently, the student's initiating her academic activity results in the teacher withdrawing the aversive scolding and the student's behavior is negatively reinforced in the process. Although, somewhat imprudent as a general strategy for increasing on-task behavior, it is clear that a student's on-task behavior is, at least temporarily, increased as a function of this form of negative reinforcement.

Negative reinforcement occurs under two conditions: escape and avoidance. Escape requires that the individual actually make contact with the aversive stimulation; subsequently, an escape maneuver allows the person to be relieved. Avoidance only requires that the individual respond to a discriminative stimulus (cue) indicating potential aversion. If the individual performs an avoidance maneuver in the presence of the discriminative stimulus, he/she does not need to actually make direct contact with the aversive event in order to be negatively reinforced. The behavior is reinforced by the active avoidance of contact with this stimulus.

Avoidance behavior occurs because in the past it has had the effect of precluding onset of a stimulus event. Sometimes, the behavior is limited to specific situations. A student might perform on-task behaviors in the presence of a particular teacher if such work prevents scolding that would otherwise occur.

As an aside, let us point out there is another element involved in both of these examples--punishment. **Punishment**, simply put, is an immediate stimulus presentation which decreases the probability of a behavior upon which it is contingent. In the previous example, your hand was initially exposed to shock (punishment contingent on touching the fence) and subsequently, escape and relief was obtained by withdrawing your hand quickly (negative reinforcement in the form of escape). In the second example, the student was initially exposed to scolding (a form of punishment contingent on off-task behavior), and subsequently, escape (negative reinforcement) was accomplished by the student's initiating some academic activity. Although there is an obvious element of verbal behavior in this all too common scenario, it is quite likely that neither the teacher nor the student could adequately describe the direct-acting negative reinforcement contingencies involved. In both cases, however, some behavior (actively avoiding fences and initiating on-task behavior) has been increased as a function of negative reinforcement.

Continuing with reinforcers, it is important to note that there are also primary and secondary reinforcers. **Primary reinforcer/s** are stimulus events produced by behavior that ensure survival, either of the individual or of a species. Some primary reinforcers are food, water, warmth, and sexual stimulation. In a school setting, popcorn, pizza, and trips to the water fountain and the lavatory may serve as primary reinforcers. **Secondary reinforcers** are stimulus events that have acquired reinforcing value because of their association with primary reinforcement. As a function of this association, secondary reinforcers also increase the probability of behavior producing them. Typical secondary reinforcers include money, tokens, and most important in the acquisition of social behavior, praise and acknowledgement from others. Particularly in school, praise and attention may be sources of secondary reinforcement. Of course, tokens and grades (if used properly) may serve as secondary reinforcers as well.

Activity based reinforcers are physical movements which have reinforcing value in their own right. Such activities may have either primary or secondary reinforcing properties. Primary reinforcing activities might include simply moving one's arms and legs following a period of relative immobility, stretching, and even the "acts" of chewing and swallowing various substances (independent of their nutritional content or taste).

Secondary reinforcing activities include all of the things we have learned to enjoy "doing." Playing basketball and *chess*, running computers and marathons, jumping hedges and *kings* are activities which, in most cases, we may not have found entertaining on our first attempt. Many of us will never learn to enjoy marathons. Others insist that they find them quite "invigorating!" Irrespective of which particular activities we claim to enjoy, it is clear that none of these activities were reinforcing before they were learned.

A Few More Basic Principles

In general, it may be said that almost all reinforcers lose their effectiveness as reinforcers after the individual has had an extended period of exposure to the particular reinforcing object, event, or activity. **Satiation** is a decrease in reinforcer effectiveness following over-exposure to a particular substance or event. Satiation occurs when we have had too much of a "good thing." Partaking of large quantities of food, drink, or even sexual stimulation reduces the probability of behavior that will produce those kinds of stimulation. Primary reinforcers are especially likely to produce satiation, but sometimes secondary reinforcers temporarily lose their value. The decreased rate of behavior that produces the reinforcer will eventually result in deprivation, and the cycle will be repeated.

What happens when a previously reinforced behavior no longer results in any form of reinforcement being provided? Usually, the immediate answer to this common question is, "the behavior is *extinguished* (eliminated)." (Note: The person is not extinguished--his or her behavior is!)

Procedurally, **extinction** occurs when behavior that is no longer reinforced simply "dies out" and is eventually eliminated from a person's repertoire. When Little Billy continually and excessively raises his hand in class, and Mrs. Wall continually ignores Billy's attempt to gain her attention by this method, eventually, his hand raising, at least in the presence of Mrs. Wall, is extinguished. However, a more rigorous and accurate answer regarding what happens during the extinction of Billy's hand raising is: it depends. It depends on how strenuous the behavioral requirements are (the more strenuous the behavioral requirements, the faster the extinction). It also depends on how the reinforcers are scheduled (delivered in terms of time and number of required responses).

While extinction suggests that the behavior of interest eventually terminates following a period of "no reinforcement," the rate at which this reduction in responding occurs is extremely variable. Behaviors are more **resistant to extinction** (more likely to continue even when reinforcement ceases) if reinforcement has been scheduled intermittently (erratically). In fact, the more intermittent the schedule of reinforcement, the more likely the individual is to persist in responding once reinforcement has been terminated.

For example, if Mrs. Wall calls on Billy very intermittently on occasions when his hand is raised, we would expect that he would be more likely to persist in hand raising, even in the event that she suddenly decides to quit calling on him. His hand raising behavior would be more resistant to extinction because the reinforcement (being called upon by Mrs. Wall) has been provided intermittently. A great deal of variation in resistance to extinction can be understood by examining the schedule or reinforcement that the individual has previously been provided. We will give this matter of intermittent reinforcement more attention shortly, but for now, it is important to understand that extinction (the cessation of responding when reinforcement is stopped) does not occur at the same rate for all individuals. It will depend on their previous reinforcement history.

Furthermore, it is important to understand that Billy's excessive hand raising behavior may even intensify during the early moments directly after that it has been placed on extinction by Mrs. Wall. Behavior that is placed on extinction usually increases in frequency during the time immediately following the initiation of the extinction procedure. This temporary increase in behavior is referred to as an **extinction burst**. It is not uncommon for teachers and parents to get the impression that extinction procedures are ineffective precisely because the problem behavior usually escalates in frequency directly after being placed on extinction; however, if the extinction procedure is adequately maintained over a sufficient period of time, the problem behavior will decrease and eventually cease entirely. Remember, however, this may take a longer period of time than is deemed acceptable by some teachers or parents.

Shaping: The Emergence of New Behavior

In the same way natural selection operates to choose particular physical characteristics of a species by providing survival value, the environment also selects particular behaviors of an individual by providing reinforcing consequences. Usually, these reinforcing consequences have survival value for the individual and make these behaviors more likely to occur at a greater frequency.

So, perhaps, it is not hard to see how particular responses are selected by their consequences and how these particular behaviors become more likely to occur in the future of that individual. But, what about behaviors that the individual has never performed before? If an individual has never performed a particular behavior, how can that behavior be selected by its consequences?

This is a question that strikes at the heart of all learning theory, and it is a particularly puzzling question when we are analyzing behavior that is not related to verbal instructions. That is, if people or lower organisms are not told how to perform new behaviors, how can they come to behave in new and different ways? The explanation goes back to the concept of *selection by consequences*. The environment may be arranged in such a way so as to select (reinforce) particular behavioral units *differentially*. To select behavior differentially means that particular response variations are reinforced, while others are ignored (extinguished). This process is called shaping. In shaping, we have the blending of two procedures, extinction and differential reinforcement. This is a powerful behavioral change technique.

In an experimental arrangement, a rat may learn to press a lever--something it has never done before. When first it looks at the lever, we might provide our initial reinforcing consequence--perhaps a small portion of food or water is mechanically dropped into the experimental space. Next, we will increase our criterion. Only if the rat approaches the lever will we give the reinforcer. If it moves away, we would do nothing, waiting for the rat to look at the lever and move in its direction before providing the consequence. We will reinforce next if, and only if, some behavior occurs that is getting the rat closer to the target behavior (bar pressing). At each step the criterion for reinforcement will change so that the next consequence is contingent on a closer approximation to the target behavior (bar pressing).

In discussing differential selection of moment-to-moment responding, Morgan (1998) is justifiably fascinated by Calvin 's (1987) account of the underlying functions of brain activity as a "Darwin Machine":

> And, for at least a century, it has been known that even the highest-known biological function, human thought, involves random generation of many alternatives and is only shaped up into something of quality by a series of selections. Like elegant eyes and ears produced by biological randomness, the Darwin Machines' final product (whether sentence of scenario, algorithm or allegory) no longer appears random because of so many millisecond-long generations of selection shaping up alternative sequences off line. (p. 34).

In the procedure of differential reinforcement, a particular behavioral unit produces a reinforcing consequence, and other behavioral units that might occur instead do not produce the consequence. The behavior that produces the consequence is strengthened and the other behavior extinguished. In the procedure of shaping, the behavior that produces the consequence keeps changing because the consequence is delivered only if later behavior more closely approximates the target behavior.

Shaping is the differential reinforcement of successive approximations of a target behavior. Behavior gradually changes as the criterion for reinforcement shifts in the direction of a new and different type of behavior, while unacceptable or previously reinforced behavior is ignored (extinguished).

Furthermore, in the true sense of the term, shaping is only in progress when the individual who is being shaped has no "awareness" of the fact that his/her behavior is being influenced by a combination of extinction of some responses and differential reinforcement of others.

Note: Individuals who have their behavior changed under the influence of verbal instructions are not being "shaped." Their behavior is operating under the influence of instructions or directions, and this is an entirely different type of behavioral phenomena--one which we will discuss in greater detail in the next chapter.

Whaley and Malott (1968, 1997) were the first to provide an illuminating and entertaining example of shaping as it may be correctly (if deviously) applied to human behavior. Notice in their example that although the person's behavior comes under the influence of differential reinforcement, the person has no active awareness of this process at it occurs.

The Peculiar Professor

According to popular legend, a professor used to stand on the right side of the classroom while he lectured, rarely moving to the left side. Students on the left side had to strain to hear. And students on the right side grew tired of the professor's breathing down their necks for the whole class period.

One student recorded the professor's bias. He spent 46 minutes lecturing from the right side of the classroom, 3 minutes from the podium in the middle of the room, and only 1 minute from the left side, while he wrote on the left section of the blackboard.

The students got together one evening before class and agreed on the following: They would reinforce lecturing only from the left side of the room. They wouldn't reinforce lecturing from any other place. They had no trouble selecting a potential reinforcer. As with all professors throughout the universe of universities, nothing was more reinforcing than the smiling face of a student hanging on his every word. So whenever he lectured from the left side of the room, 35 faces would smile and look at him. But when he moved from that spot to the right side of the room, all students would suddenly look down at their desks.

At the next class, the students started percolating their pernicious plot. The professor began to lecture from his favorite right corner, and all eyes looked away. As soon as he filled the right-hand half of the blackboard with definitions and diagrams, he started on the left-hand half. And when he turned from the blackboard to the class, 35 smiling faces were looking at him. He stayed there for 5 minutes. When he moved to the other side, his attentive audience immediately fell away. During the next several minutes he moved from one side of the room to the other. Then he stopped at the far left spot and lectured there for the last 20 minutes of the class. After class, the students checked their records. The professor had spent a total of 28 minutes on the "smiley" side of the room, not his measly 1 minute of the day before.   ELEMENTARY PRINCIPLES OF BEHAVIOR 4/E by Malott/Malott/Trojan, © 1971. Reprinted by permission of Prentice-Hall, Inc., Upper Saddle River, NJ.

The above example of shaping human behavior has become the source of psychological lore. Other than demonstrating how devious college students are capable of being, it illustrates some very critical but popularly misunderstood features of shaping. The shaping procedure does not rely on any form of verbal instruction in order to be implemented. In the above example, no verbal instructions were provided to the professor by the students. Indeed, if an individual is learning new behavior under the influence of verbal instructions, we are not justified in describing such new behavior as having been shaped.

Much of our moment-by-moment behavior operates under the influence of discriminative stimuli (cues) and the immediate naturally occurring consequences of our behavior. Sometimes, these discriminative stimuli, behaviors, and their consequences are rather "subtle", and we are not aware of their occurrence. Yet, in various elusive ways, our behaviors are often reinforced, punished, or extinguished, and we may have no words to describe these experiences. In a sense, it might be said that we are "unaware" of *some* of the "voluntary" or operant behaviors which we perform *very routinely*. Sometimes, this type of behavior is colloquially referred to as being "habitual."

In other cases, motor activities (those requiring gross and fine coordination) may start out with the help of verbal instructions, but later the verbal aspect of the behavior drops out. Some of our more complex motor activities initially are performed under the influence of directions from other people or under the influence of our own dialogue with ourselves (thinking). Gradually, we are weaned from the verbal assistance used to facilitate many of these activities, and these behaviors may no longer be performed with the help of external or internal dialogue.

Motor activities such as riding a bicycle or driving a car usually require considerable verbal instruction during the initial stages of learning. We are told how to hold the handlebars and how to engage the clutch while changing gears. Later, we may tell ourselves the same instructions others have given us as we practice the new behaviors. Hopefully, as we talk to ourselves about what we are doing correctly and incorrectly, we concurrently make the necessary physical adjustments.

Over the course of many rehearsals, we eventually learn to let the clutch out more slowly as we accelerate. The car makes the transition into first gear with more positive momentum and less hesitation (or termination!). Under the influence of changes in particular driving cues (road changes, green lights), we immediately produce correct behaviors (steering, accelerating) that hopefully result in favorable consequences. With sufficient practice, these responses no longer necessitate verbal instructions from ourselves or others. We have been directly and immediately reinforced by a series of naturally occurring consequences; our improved driving behavior has been selected (it is more likely to occur under similar conditions in the future).

Over the course of several bicycle riding attempts, we may gradually learn to shift our body weight ever so slightly in response to the subtle cues of slight gravitational pull. As we peddle, the bicycle moves forward with more positive momentum and without wobbling. Our more well balanced bicycle riding behavior has been reinforced by the naturally occurring consequence of moving forward (not to mention avoiding the negative effects of crashing), and it is more likely to occur in the future under similar circumstances. Our lives are filled with diversified and subtle discriminative stimuli, "unconscious" behaviors, and elusive reinforcers. With practice, we may gradually quit talking to ourselves about many of our well learned motor behaviors--even as we are still learning to perform them with more and more skill. In doing so, we come under the influence of the immediate effects of the environment we encounter while steering our bicycles and cars, and the various consequences associated with successfully navigating through traffic. Thus, some rather complex behaviors, which originally operated under the influence of verbal control, may gradually come under the more subtle but direct control of the environment. Again, such behavior is selected by its consequences.

Most people find that once they have successfully learned how to ride a bicycle, or how to drive a standard transmission vehicle, they will be able to perform these behaviors automatically (without talking to themselves about it) even after many years without practice. Sometimes, traditional psychologists refer to this type of seemingly spontaneous recall of nonverbal behaviors as procedural memory.

Direct-Acting Contingencies

A contingency is a relationship that exists between a behavior and its ensuing consequence/s. If a particular reinforcing consequence depends on the performance of a specific behavior, we could say that reinforcement is contingent (dependent) on the occurrence of that behavior. A given contingency may entail instantaneous reinforcement (as in a student's receiving a smile or a pat on the back upon completion of an assignment) or extremely delayed reinforcement (as in the case of receiving money for obtaining an excellent report card upon completion of six weeks of school work). However, a contingency is direct-acting only when it results in behavior which is maintained by the immediate consequences that follow. Thus, only the former example of instantaneous reinforcement can be accurately described as entailing a **direct-acting contingency**.

A direct-acting contingency may be described as a process whereby behavioral units emerge through selection by consequences and are maintained as long as the consequences support them. The individual does not need to and often does not verbally describe the details of what he/she is doing or why he/she does it. The behavior that emerges as a function of direct-acting contingencies is often called **contingency-shaped**. This term is often used to convey the notion that behavior is shaped and maintained by contingencies into which the behavior enters.

In the Presence of Particular Discriminative Stimuli.

When looking at behavior that is *not* operating under the immediate influence of verbal instructions (from one's self or others), there are, nevertheless, important sources of direct influence. Under the influence of certain discriminative stimuli, particular behaviors are more likely to occur than they are under other conditions.

Discriminative stimuli are environmental cues that precede particular behaviors. These preceding environmental conditions act as "cues for responding" and evoke certain types of responding because responding in their presence has previously led to reinforcement. As we have seen, many human behaviors operate under the influence of discriminative stimuli and are not prompted by our internal dialogue with ourselves (or the external instructions from others). These behaviors do not occur erratically or without cause. Rather, various discriminative stimuli in the natural environment set the occasion for particular types of responding.

In the presence of particular discriminative stimuli, certain behaviors consistently (or at least intermittently) lead to reinforcement. Under the influence of other stimuli, these behaviors do not result in reinforcement. Thus, the behaviors that are selected by reinforcers gradually come to occur *only* in the context in which particular discriminative stimuli are present. This phenomenon, in which discriminative stimuli set the occasion for particular behaviors because these behaviors have been reinforced only when they occur in their presence, is referred to as **discriminative stimulus control** (or simply **stimulus control**).

Discriminative Stimulus Control

The general name for the selective control over responding that is acquired by particular discriminative stimuli (cues) is discriminative stimulus control. Such control is a function of a specific reinforcement history. If reinforcement is provided *only* when a particular response occurs in the presence of a particular discriminative stimulus, then these occasions will reliably evoke that behavior in the future. As long as reinforcement occasionally occurs and motivational conditions are present (e.g., deprivation), the stimulus- control relationship remains quite constant.

Students who consistently sit up straight and pay attention in the presence of one teacher but who slouch and stare out the window in the presence of a second teacher are demonstrating the influence of discriminative stimulus control. We could say that the students have learned to discriminate the conditions under which sitting up straight and paying attention result in important consequences. Although this effect (paying attention) may be accompanied by the students' internal verbal description of the particular consequences associated with being attentive in the presence of each teacher, it is certainly not necessary to demonstrate the effect. Lower organisms are notorious for being attentive and following directives only in the presence of specific trainers. We have noticed that good teachers serve as conspicuous discriminative stimuli and strong sources of social reinforcement for important behaviors learned by their students.

Learning to Discriminate Speech Sounds

A person who operates under discriminative stimulus control has learned to discriminate the conditions under which particular responses result in reinforcement. We might say that when a person has learned a new and useful behavior and the individual has learned when and how to perform a particular response, a discrimination has been learned. Learning a discrimination may be as simple and nonverbal as learning to duck your head when approaching a low doorway or as complex as learning particular speech patterns.

If, for example, a person has extreme difficulty differentiating the sound of "s" from the sound of similar sounding letters like "z" or "c" we can refer to this as an inability to discriminate the sound of "s" from other similar sounds. Likewise, we can say that the person is not under the discriminative stimulus control of the sound of "s." There are many children who have extreme difficulty making this discrimination in the first years of elementary school. This deficit usually shows up in the form of both problems in articulation and discrimination of the sound "s." In an experiment by Holland and Matthews (1963), students showing this type of deficit listened to tape recorded sounds that only approximated "s" and to the perfect enunciation of the sound of "s." They pressed a button and were reinforced whenever they were able to discriminate the sound of "s" from the other sounds.

At the beginning of training, the sounds to be discriminated were obviously different. As the students' discriminations improved with training, the difference among the sounds was reduced. Students progressed through a precisely formulated sequence, moving from conspicuous discriminations to subtle discriminations, with practically no errors. Follow-up assessments demonstrated that not only had the children learned to discriminate the sound of "s" from similar sounding letters but that almost all of the students demonstrated a corresponding and immediate improved articulation of the sound as well. This experiment seems to suggest that the auditory discrimination of the precise speech sound is necessary (or at least very helpful) for students to replicate the correct pronunciation of that sound.

Establishing Operations

There is another very important variable relating to the conditions under which certain types of behaviors are more likely to occur. An understanding of this variable is needed in order to adequately appreciate learning *without* language. That variable references the conditions under which individuals are "*in the mood*" to receive particular kinds of reinforcers. This refers to both primary (e.g., food or water) or secondary (e.g., playing softball or computer games) reinforcers. We all know that there are times when we are more likely to enjoy various foods or activities than others. We are, perhaps, more likely to be in the mood for ice-cream on a sultry, muggy day in August after being deprived of any food for a few hours than we would subsequent to completing a large meal and dessert on Thanksgiving. The sweltering day in August and the deprivation of food operate together to establish a physical condition that makes us more "appreciative" of ice-cream.

The same may be said for various activities. Given that we have a history of enjoying softball, we are probably more likely to relish the prospect of playing softball on a crisp, sunny day if we have slept well during the previous night, have not played softball just recently, and are not in a present state of physical exhaustion. These conditions may optimize or establish our mood for such an activity.

Even more obvious, perhaps, is the reinforcing value of food or water after we have been deprived of either for an extended period of time. In fact, it is generally the case that almost all items or activities that are potentially reinforcing only become reinforcing under certain conditions. These conditions that optimize our appreciation for various objects or events are called **establishing operations**.

Establishing operations may be either intentionally performed upon individuals (as when teachers or parents withhold access to reinforcers), or they happen naturally (as in the simple passage of time during which we have had no opportunity to eat). Establishing operations alter the effectiveness of various reinforcing items and activities. As a result, the reinforcers that are subsequently provided are "more reinforcing" than they would be otherwise. Behaviors that are reinforced subsequent to an establishing operation are said to be increased in strength. This means they are *much more* likely to occur in the future under similar conditions. An establishing operation is anything that alters the reinforcing effectiveness of something else and anything that increases the strength of the behavior that has been reinforced by that thing (Michael, 1982).

For example, food deprivation increases the reinforcing effectiveness of food. Food deprivation also increases the strength of any behavior that has been reinforced by food. Activity deprivation (such as being confined for an extended period of time, perhaps while taking a very long examination) increases the reinforcing effectiveness of many activities. It also increases the strength of the behavior that has been reinforced by the activity. Certain drugs may also be interpreted as producing effects that correspond to establishing operations. If a particular substance or medication alters the reinforcing effectiveness of an activity (makes that activity more reinforcing than it would be otherwise) then that substance or medication has acted as an establishing operation.

Some people have noticed that they have particular difficulty attending to their work unless they have first had a cup of coffee, or sometimes two. For these people, the caffeine content of coffee acts as a central nervous system stimulant which provides them the temporary energy needed to attend to a given task. The caffeine has put the individual in the mood to study, write, or listen attentively to a lecture. It has been suggested that other central nervous system stimulants, like methylphenidate (Ritalin), may perform similar functions relative to children who have been diagnosed with Attention-Deficit/Hyperactivity Disorder. Zametkin et al. (1990) have demonstrated that some individuals with this diagnosis demonstrate lower than expected glucose metabolism levels (energy levels) in critical areas of the brain associated with "paying attention." Under the influence of methylphenidate, these areas of the brain showed increased metabolic function, and many students describe the activity of studying as a more reinforcing activity than it was in the absence of this medication. We are not advocating the wholesale ingestion of caffeine, or other stimulants, as a general means of motivating students to develop better study habits. However, it is interesting to note that some common substances and medications may "put people in the mood" in which particular activities are more reinforcing than they would be otherwise. In this way these substances might be said to be "mimicking" naturally occurring establishing operations (Belfiore, Lee, Vargas, & Skinner, 1997).

The Three-Term Contingency

When describing the environmental and behavioral features of selection by consequences, we addressed three primary terms: 1) the discriminative stimulus - symbolized as S^D, 2) the response (or behavioral unit) - symbolized as R, and 3) and the consequence of a reinforcing stimulus - symbolized as S^{R+}. (Note: The S represents stimulus. The superscript R in the consequence represents reinforcement.) When the subscript R is followed by the superscript + this indicates that the reinforcing consequence is positive. As we will see later, reinforcing consequences might also be negative and symbolized as -. Sometimes, the consequence is reinforcing, sometimes punishing, or sometimes nothing. Moreover, there are many other possibilities when we look at the various schedules of reinforcement which are well documented, but for now these terms will suffice.

This total phenomenon is usually described as the three-term contingency or the operant paradigm, and it is the basic building block for many types--but certainly not all--*learned* behaviors. Diagramming the three-term contingency (S^D, R, and S^{R+}) provides a working model that illustrates and predicts the flow of occurrence during the learning and performance of many operant behaviors. Most particularly, it predicts well for behavior for which we have no words and for which we are, thus, "*unaware*" of the controlling variables.

$$S^D \longrightarrow R \longrightarrow S^{R+}$$

Discriminative   Response   Stimulus Reinforcer (Positive)
Stimulus

In the following chapters, we will look at some current research that entails language development. This research suggests that when humans begin to develop verbal skills, new types of relationships emerge which entail more complex paradigms. For now we will focus on the types of learning that occur without the use of language.

Learning without Language in the Laboratory

Having furnished an overview of the way in which *learning without language* may take place in natural settings, let's look at how this phenomenon may be illustrated under more rigorous laboratory conditions. In order for learning without language to be demonstrated by adult humans in some empirical and systematic way, we must provide an experimental setting in which the participants learn a unique, identifiable and recordable behavior. Again, this new behavior must be one that is not accompanied by a verbal description of the activity. That is, the research subjects must not be aware of the target behavior that is being observed and recorded by the experimenter.

Psychologists began investigating this question with some degree of technological sophistication in the early 1960's. Perhaps, one of the most well known studies was conducted by Hefferline and Keenan (1963). They developed a method of recording an operant behavior so small that subjects were unaware of the fact that they were producing it. Using an electromyograph (an instrument that measures minute muscle potentials), they were able to record thumb contractions which were so small that subjects were unable to describe these movements when they performed them.

In the experimental arrangement, subjects were seated comfortably in a sound attenuated room with various "dummy" electrodes strategically located in various diversionary positions. After taking a baseline measure, or an established measure from which to make comparisons, of each subject's thumb muscle twitches for 10 minutes, subjects were then told that they could earn 5 cents each time they incremented a nearby counter stationed directly in front of them. They were not, however, told how this might be accomplished. In order for the subjects to increment the counter, it was necessary that they produce very exacting minute muscle potentials in their thumbs (e.g., just between 25 and 30 microvolts.) Participants went about the business of earning a substantial number of nickels during six consecutive 10 minute training sessions. Subjects quickly demonstrated an obvious operant ability to control their minute thumb muscle movements, but very few ever guessed that they had done so by way of the activity emanating from their thumbs. Subsequently, this new (but covert) operant behavior was extinguished in each subject; that is, emitting these very small and precise thumb movements no longer resulted in reinforcement, and this behavior no longer occurred. And still, subjects were unable to identify any of the variables for which their very distinct but minuscule behavior was a function.

Among other things, this early study demonstrates how infinitesimally small an operant behavior can be and still come under the influence of selection by consequences. More importantly, it was one of the first studies to demonstrate empirically that human behavior may come under operant control in the absence of any verbal recognition by the subject. We will come back to this study in more detail in the next chapter.

Learning without Language in a Natural Context

When Herbie (remember Herbie?) was attempting to do his homework and "inadvertently" and "unintentionally" leaned back in his chair and put his feet up on the desk, he immediately felt more relaxed. Many people perform similar rituals that may be incompatible with staying on-task. If drifting off-task and putting one's feet on the desk results in an immediate sense of comfort and relaxation, the individual may find that he or she often places his/her feet in that position without much (if any) internal verbal description of the event--provided there are no obvious social sanctions to the contrary. In this context, the consequences of "feeling comfortable and relaxed" act as a form of direct-acting reinforcement that is likely to sustain that activity under similar circumstances in the future.

Now, we are not suggesting that Herbie could not specifically describe this behavior if he were called upon to do so. Rather, it is simply the case that many of us, like Herbie, quit working and elevate our feet rather spontaneously under some conditions (and not under others), and that this behavior need not be accompanied by any internal verbal description of the episode.

In order to predict and influence this behavior, we need to know something about the person's history of reinforcement in his or her environmental context. Looking at Herbie's behavior as interacting with the immediate environment, we could point to some of the variables for which his off-task behavior is a function. These variables include establishing operations, discriminative stimuli, specific types of motor behaviors, and physically relaxing (and thus reinforcing) consequences.

First of all, Herbie's third floor attic/bedroom is a secluded location where there are no social sanctions regarding the placement of feet (or anything else for that matter). The poor lighting, the hard upright wooden chair in which he is seated, and the academic assignment at which he is squinting strenuously now function to make Herbie's eyelids feel heavy, his back ache, and his head hurt. Together, these conditions operate to establish his general state of physical discomfort. He is definitely in the mood for some kind of cerebral/postural repositioning. A conspicuous establishing operation is in progress. Now, in the past, when he has experienced this form of general discomfort and has been sitting in the presence of his desk and various homework assignments (and the absence of his grandmother), he has often leaned back in his chair to elevate his feet. Under the influence of an establishing operation (stiff back, eye strain, and academic irritation), as well under as the discriminative stimuli (presence of the desk and homework), it is highly probable, given Herbie's previous history in these circumstances, that a particular response is forthcoming. Here we have performed something called a **functional analysis** of Herbie's off-task. That is, we have identified some of the variables for which his problem behavior is a function. (We will have much more to say about various types of functional analyses in the coming chapters.)

After about five minutes of eye strain, back ache, and general inability to solve any of the math problems, Herbie slowly rocks back in his chair and places both of his feet flatly on the desk before him. This behavior brings about an immediate and gratifying sense of spinal, optical, and cerebral relaxation and relief, and no words have been used in the process. In fact, the only words to which Herbie is attending during this small behavioral episode are emanating from the radio.

Herbie does not take his math book with him on his reclining respite. His math book lies agape but ignored as he drifts into a soft state of reverie. The background music fills the air of Herbie's attic and the auditory canals of Herbie's cranium. A sense of relief and relaxation saturate his body. Herbie's behavior has been selected by the immediate consequences of leaning back in his chair and elevating his feet.

The probability of Herbie maintaining this position is presently increased. As well, the probability of him performing this same behavior under the influence of similar establishing operations and discriminative stimuli in the future is increased (symbolized as $P \uparrow$). His three-term contingency may look something like this:

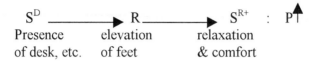

$$S^D \longrightarrow R \longrightarrow S^{R+} \ : \ P \uparrow$$

Presence   elevation   relaxation
of desk, etc.   of feet   & comfort

Notice that we have described Herbie's consequence as being one of obtaining positive reinforcement (S^{R+}). Why are rest and relaxation, subsequent to escape from eye strain, back ache, and academic tension, forms of positive reinforcement and not negative reinforcement? The answer is simply that this is only one way to describe and predict this episode. It's just that we normally define "relaxation" as something we "get to do" or "have," i.e. we are looking forward to obtaining rest, or we are in a state of relaxation.

Many people might point out, quite correctly, that it is equally accurate in this particular behavioral episode to suggest that the relief obtained by tilting back in one's chair and reducing the general feeling of discomfort is a form of negative reinforcement--namely escape (Malott et al. 1997). And, they would be correct in so doing. From this functional analysis, our three-term contingency will look like this:

$$S^D \longrightarrow R \longrightarrow S^{R-} \ : \ P \uparrow$$

Presence   elevation   relief
of desk   of feet   from pain

Describing the reinforcer as positive or negative does not change the fact that the probability of this behavior occurring in the future is increased. As a matter of fact, most positive reinforcers only become reinforcing after an individual is in the mood to receive them. We are not always in the mood to relax any more than we are always in the mood to eat. Remember, being "in the mood" is a function of an establishing operation.

This may sound more complex and tedious than merely describing Herbie's poor study habits in the traditional way: "When Herbie is tired, he often leans back in his chair and stops working." But this traditional description puts the problem inside of Herbie and does not direct our attention to the principles and procedures that may improve his study behavior. The traditional way of describing a problem tells us what the *individual does*, not how or why he or she interacts with the environment. The traditional way of describing behavior problems may diagnose Herbie with a learning disability or even a behavior disorder, but it does not tell us nearly enough about the variables that interact with Herbie in the context in which he behaves.

In Herbie's case, it is not so much that he plans on drifting into a state or relaxation and reverie as soon as he opens his books at his desk. Quite to the contrary, he would very much prefer to complete his homework and avoid the unpleasantness associated with giving his teacher another lame excuse on the following day. His off-task behavior is not based on a "conscious decision" to avoid his academic task. His maladaptive study behaviors are at least partially related to his personal history with direct-acting contingencies. We need to understand this part of his maladaptive behavior as well as that part which is related to learning with language.

Looking at Herbie's off-task behavior as a function of a direct-acting contingency provides a pragmatic and *functional analysis* of some of the variables responsible for his present "inability" to attend to his homework. While this elevating of feet, relaxing, and so on, may appear incidental, it is also becoming habitual for Herbie (and many other students). Very often, students, when instructed to do their homework in the absence of direct supervision, are inclined to perform a number of competing behaviors that are more enjoyable and relaxing than their assignments. Such behavior may be spontaneous and unplanned, and often, students may not "recognize" that they are drifting off their academic tasks until someone draws their attention to it. Occasionally, of course, such behavior may entail premeditation on the part of the student as he/she actively avoids or escapes his or her homework.

Backward Chaining

Another behavioral phenomenon that operates independently of language is that of backward chaining. **Chaining** is the behavioral procedure whereby particular discriminative stimuli (S^D) become connected to particular responses (R) in such a way as to provide extremely long sequences or "chains" of behavior to be performed. As is also the case with schedules of reinforcement, this behavior does not depend on language. The individual who learns a long sequence of behaviors based on chaining has learned these behaviors under the control of direct-acting contingencies. Rule-governed behavior (instructional control) is not part of this process. Expanding our basic three-term contingency, chaining is simply an extended series of stimulus   response sequences in which discriminative stimuli act as cues to initiate the next response in the chain of behavior.

There are many people in our culture who have very limited verbal capabilities. They are usually unable to follow complex verbal directions. In some cases, these people are identified as mentally retarded. For these individuals, even the basic acts of brushing teeth or putting on trousers may constitute a very difficult and extremely time-consuming maneuver. The development of procedures such as backward chaining provides us with the tools necessary to teach nonverbal or semiverbal individuals to develop important, but otherwise exceedingly difficult, self-help skills.

What We Have Here is a Failure to Communicate

Sally was a fourteen year old high school student at North High. She had been identified as moderately mentally retarded since about the age of three. Although she generally appeared to be a happy and gentle person, there were occasions during which she became extremely obstinate and stubborn. Most noticeably, she was likely to become tenacious when asked by her teacher, Mr. Wells, to practice any of the basic vocational skills taught in her classroom.

The class was designed to teach students like Sally to master vocational skills that could be applied in other settings. Among other vocational skills, Mr. Wells was interested in helping Sally to learn to systematically separate and place various eating utensils within particular color coded slots of specially designed trays. This was a skill which would potentially allow Sally to join her classmates for a short time each day in organizing silverware at a local hotel and restaurant.

Mr. Wells was polite but persistent in his verbal instruction to Sally. Over and over again, he would instruct her: "Sally, pick up the spoon like this and place it in the green slot with the big circle at the top." "Do it like this Sally!" and so on. But, Sally would have no part of it. When Mr. Wells gave his specific instructions and pointed at the spoons, Sally would only grimace and walk away. Mr. Wells would chase after her and dutifully bring her back and begin again, but to no avail. Evidently, Sally was really not very interested in organizing spoons or other eating utensils in the classroom or anywhere else. However, North High School had access to a school psychologist who was in the process of completing his post-doctoral internship in Dallas. This particular school psychologist had developed a special interest in helping disabled children learn to follow complex directions. So, as one of his final acts as a school psychology intern, Larry Pritchard was asked to help Mr. Wells devise a plan for Sally.

After listening to Mr. Wells explain Sally's inability to "understand" his directions, as well as her general reluctance to participate in any form of vocational training, and after observing Mr. Wells demonstrate another of his failed attempts to instruct Sally in the proper technique of utensil sorting, it seemed to Larry Pritchard that there was, indeed, a "failure to communicate." Although Sally did have the ability to speak a very few words, and although she had learned to follow one and two step directions, this sorting and arranging of diversified eating utensils represented a completely new and extremely complex task for Sally--one that she neither understood nor wished to understand or perform.

Nevertheless, "understanding," in the way that most of us think of it, was really not the point. What was important was the development of a strategy which would allow Sally to connect all of the minute behaviors required in the sorting of silverware into a sequence of smooth and continuous actions. Moreover, it was necessary to find some way to "motivate" Sally to perform this succession of behaviors without the use of verbal instructions.

Backward chaining seemed like a reasonable intervention. But what could be used to reinforce this new behavior? With a little inquiry, it soon became clear that Sally had a real affinity for ice cream. She could never get enough! And so, access to a spoonful of ice cream was made contingent on the very last behavior in the silverware sorting chain. Larry placed a fork in Sally's hand and gently guided her hand to the proper position where he helped her release it into the color coded slot. This is called *prompting*, and sometimes, such physical assistance is used to initiate a new behavior in a chain. A prompt is usually faded (gradually removed) from the training procedure as quickly as possible.

As soon as Sally let the fork drop into the correct location, she was given her favorite treat as well as lavish praise from Mr. Wells and Larry. Over a series of about ten of these trials, Larry's prompt was faded out, and Sally was required to place the fork in the proper slot, independent of any assistance, in order to receive her ice cream. Thus, the last link in the silverware sorting chain was trained first.

When developing a new behavioral chain, this last link is always the most important, and it is always trained first. All subsequent learning segments must be connected to this link in order to maintain the flow of behavior. After this response is learned, the remaining elements of the chain can be connected. In Sally's circumstance, the next response to be trained was that of picking up the fork from the table on which it rested. Once the fork was actually in her hand, Sally would "know" exactly what to do with it in order to get her ice cream.

This new response was trained in essentially the same manner as the previous response. Larry gently guided Sally's hand over to the location on the table on which the fork rested. He then prompted her through the process of picking up the fork. With the fork in her hand, Sally had access to a discriminative stimulus. That is, this fork holding position had been associated previously with moving the fork to the color coded slot in the tray. The simple act of holding the fork functioned as an S^D for the next response of placing it within the proper slot.

Once this new response was learned, it too, quickly came under the influence of a particular discriminative stimulus. When Sally saw the fork resting on the table (S^D) she picked in up in her hand (R). Holding the fork (S^D) she immediately placed it in the color coded slot (R) for which action she immediately received a bite of ice cream and praise from her teacher (S^{R+}). Now, Sally's repertoire contained a new behavior chain consisting of two basic responses. They were linked by two discriminative stimuli and two responses, and they were maintained by a positively, reinforcing consequence. Adding a third element to the chain was easy. Sally was moved away from the table and then prompted to move in that direction. Upon approaching the table she came within reach of the fork sitting on the table and progressed through the behavior chain. Sally's chain looked like this:

S^D (table with utensils)
R   (move toward table)
S^D (fork on table)
R   (pick up fork)
S^D (fork in hand)
R   (place fork in slot)
S^{R+} (ice cream and praise)

In total, the learning of this new skill required approximately 45 minutes. Moreover, once fork sorting was mastered, Sally quickly learned to achieve the same results with spoons and other eating utensils. Sally became so good at sorting utensils that she required only intermittent praise and very occasional access to ice cream in order to sustain this behavior. Additionally, Mr. Wells had learned a strategy for teaching Sally and several of her classmates to perform complex behaviors. In fact, he found that many complex skills could be taught even when his students were incapable of "understanding" complex verbal rules.

IN SUMMARY

In summary, when speaking of the type of human behavior that is selected by its immediate consequences and that does not require the support of internal or external dialogue, there are at least two distinct possibilities. In the first, our behavior is learned under the control of discriminative stimuli and the immediate consequences of our behavior. Often, we may not be "verbally conscious" of these cues, behaviors, or consequences. These may include such mundane movements as nail biting, beard tugging, knuckle popping, foot shaking, propping our feet up on a desk, and so on. These behaviors have consequences, but they often occur "below the level of our awareness."

A second category of behavior maintained by immediate consequences includes more complex behavioral units. Complex behaviors such as bicycle riding initially require some verbal instruction in order to be performed successfully when they are initiated. However, with a little practice they may no longer entail verbal support in order to be performed effectively. For most of us, these behaviors may quickly come under the influence of the environment (i.e., discriminative stimuli in the environment and the naturally occurring consequences of the new behavior). In both cases, we describe the form of eventual behavior (operating under the influence of discriminative stimuli for particular kinds of responding and immediate consequences) as being a function of direct-acting contingencies.

This chapter has covered a lot of territory. After noticing no substantial improvement in Herbie's academic disposition, we dropped back 4.5 billion years to gather some background information on Herbie's ancestors. We described some of the parallel features of natural selection and the way in which specific behaviors are selected by their immediate consequences. We characterized learning through selection by consequences as very often being a nonverbal process which accounts for many of our simple and complex motor behaviors. We have noted, however, that verbal behavior may interact with the effects of immediate consequences to enhance the acquisition of new skills.

This chapter also detailed the principles of reinforcement, punishment, extinction, satiation and an overview of learning without language. Basic principles relating to direct-acting contingencies, such as discriminative stimulus control, establishing operations, and the relations involved in the three-term contingency, were discussed. Hopefully, it is becoming apparent that much of what we do throughout our daily lives is influenced by events for which we have little or no verbal awareness. This does not mean that we are acting erratically or without purpose. It is only to suggest that our behavior interacts with our environmental contexts at several complex levels concurrently. The more we understand these interactions, the more we will be able to predict and beneficially influence ourselves and our students.

However, much of what humans do in their social environment is not adequately predicted from a three-term contingency. Human behavior is complicated by the extent to which we talk to ourselves about the relationship between the behavior we perform and the consequences of those behaviors. Most of us spend a considerable amount of time and energy just anticipating our actions and their potential consequences. We may perform these deliberations efficiently, and they may facilitate our academic and social progress. We may anticipate our behaviors and their consequences poorly, and this will inevitably deter our progress. This matter of anticipating and deliberating and deciding and developing new ideas is an especially challenging area of investigation in behavioral and school psychology. It is to the foundations of verbal and social variables in human learning that we now turn.

Chapter 3

THE EVOLUTION OF LANGUAGE AND RULE-GOVERNED BEHAVIOR

THE EVOLUTION OF WORDS AND RULES

Language is a form of behavior, the most significant feature of which is *instructional control.* Most of the behavior performed by children after they develop the rudiments of verbal behavior is maintained (at least in part) by language. Obviously, this does not mean that children spontaneously follow the verbal instructions given by their parents and teachers. It only means that as children gain verbal skills, their behavior quickly comes under the influence of a large number of competing verbal sources -- including their own verbal behavior. One of the most fascinating features of instructional control is the fact that verbal stimuli may override the effects of natural (direct-acting) contingencies (Catania, 1992).

Human verbal utterances probably began as attempts to replicate naturally occurring sounds in the environment. Primal vocalizations likely bore a distinct similarity to the objects or events they represented. During our slow progression from preverbal hominids to *Homo sapiens,* vocal behavior expanded phylogenically and ontogenically. Over the millennia, primitive "calls" became increasingly differentiated and afforded a means for humans to give rudimentary vocal cues to one another (Catania, 1994). At some critical juncture, the use of particular vocalizations became *arbitrarily applicable* (Hayes & Hayes, 1989). That is, particular utterances, which bore no explicit similarity to a given object or event, became associated with specific aspects of the environment. Thus, *words* were used to "represent" aspects of the environment and took on the "meaning" of various objects or events in the environment (Sidman & Tailby, 1982). This process enabled verbal descriptions to be reproduced and passed among individuals in a group. Now, more complex instructions (or rules) could be conveyed among group members, and directions could be followed even when the speaker was not on location to provide specific cues. Moreover, this form of verbal behavior, language, could be preserved and maintained within a culture (Glenn, 1995) as well as in the individual repertoires of its members. As cultural rules emerged it became inevitable that children would often be instructed to follow *rules* that they neither understood nor wished to obey.

Take Your Hands Out of Your Pockets

At the beginning of his third year of formal education, Herbie transferred to Catholic school where he began to find out much more about rules. It was always cold at Saint Rosalia's. The girls wore navy blue jumpers, white blouses, and beanies. The boys wore dark dress pants, white shirts, and blue bow ties. Herbie's first teacher at Saint Rosalia's was Sister Servula (a.k.a., *The Ice Nun*). She was tall, a pale and expressionless figure inside her blue and white habit. Grade school legend, lore, and *superstition* had it that Sister Servula could actually see what was going on behind her by glancing at the reflection in her glasses. Everyone believed it! With her third grade class came supplementary Latin lessons, diagrams of complex sentences, enigmatic verb conjugation, intricate mathematical operations, and the instilling of a reverence for authority. Sister Servula had "rules." She permitted no disruption and tolerated no insubordination. Students who drifted off-task or got into any mischief in her class were advised immediately that they were "fresh articles" and had their sideburns stretched forthwith. On cold winter days at Saint Rosalia's, the boys were regularly admonished, "Take your hands out of your pockets, I know what you're doing!" Herbie did not understand this particular rule at all, and he really couldn't imagine what Sister Servula thought they were doing. He wondered, "Am I missing something here?"

Rule-governed Behavior and Believing

What does it mean to say we *believe* the truth of a given statement or rule? Defining a belief in a rule is especially problematic since such behavior is internal and covert. Nevertheless, some have asserted that the difference between human and infrahuman behavior is primarily a function of the human capacity to generate and follow rules (e.g., Lowe, Beasty, & Bentall, 1983). Conversely, it has been submitted that internal verbalizations are merely secondary manifestations of direct-acting contingencies and symbolize nothing more than subordinate effects (e.g., Baron, Perone, & Galizio, 1991). By whatever level of importance we assign *internal rules* or *beliefs*, it is now commonly accepted that internal verbal behavior plays an important role in overt human behavior.

While many interpretations have been proposed, one functional definition of *believing a rule* might be performing in accordance with that rule. As a practical matter, we often make the tacit assumption that a person who behaves in accordance with the dictates of a particular rule, in the absence of any other compelling forces in the environment, *believes* in the accuracy of that rule. Under such circumstances, such a person's behavior may be characterized as **rule-governed**.

As a type of verbal behavior, *rule-governed behavior* is evoked by a statement describing the relations between particular behaviors and their consequences. If such behavior is reinforced, rules may become an influential part of the environment that affects the person's on-going behavior. Moreover, when behavior is governed by a rule, a person need not directly undergo the environmental repercussions specified in the rule in order to learn.

Clearly, many people can quote an impressive array of rules regarding correct, productive, and beneficial behavior, but their actual behavior may not be significantly influenced by these words. In order for behavior to be rule-governed, the rules that one recites must evoke responding consistent with those rules. There are two features that need to be stressed respecting the functions of rule-governed behavior: (1) the rule describes contingencies of reinforcement that serve in the natural environment -- "Smoking cigarettes will damage your health" -- or in the social environment -- "If you speak out in class, you will be sent to detention after school." The rule specifies the target behavior, along with its antecedents and consequences; and (2) the rule operates as a discriminative stimulus for the behavior that it describes and will maintain that function if the consequences appear to be forthcoming as advertised. Here, the rule clarifies ambiguous natural contingencies and affords a clear discriminative stimulus. Once a person has learned to behave under the influence of a rule, the rule comes to maintain behavior that would rarely emerge without it (Ninness, Glenn, & Ellis, 1993). For example, an individual who is informed that smoking dramatically influences the probability of developing lung cancer or emphysema may actually quit. This may occur despite the fact that the person has never encountered any direct and serious negative physical effects while smoking. Thus, rule-governed behavior would seem to be a very fast and advantageous method of learning and performing; however, even a casual observation of the generalized effects of such rules should reduce our confidence in the unequivocal control rules exert over *all* behavior.

In the Absence of Supervision

Herbie was still academically avoidant, and he often went to extremes to discover activities that were more entertaining than conjugating verbs in Latin. This always required avoiding the perilous proximity of Sister Servula. The boys' lavatory at Saint Rosalia's was located deep in the bowels of the basement below the library where no nun would dare enter. There, pulpy paper towels became spongy dodge balls, and the plumbing pipes above the toilet stalls were magically transformed into overhead gym bars. There, Herbie discovered that he could break the rules and swing like a chimp from the pipes above the toilets. For the amusement of his peers, he gave a Tarzan yell as he tapped his feet on the toilet plunger each time he swung back and forth--occasionally daring to beat his chest with one hand. Following recess, when the students were specifically instructed to use the lavatory and then go directly to class, the toilets were kept in a state of constant swirling agitation as Herbie and his fellow third-grade fugitives gleefully took turns pushing the plunger with their feet as they swung back and forth like little laughing apes. Breaking all the rules, they called themselves the "flushing furies," and each convulsion of a commode brought echoes of delirium resounding through the cement ceilings and steel septic tanks of Saint Rosalia's.

RULE-GOVERNED BEHAVIOR AND THE PREMACK PRINCIPLE

What will it take to get some people to follow simple directions? Are there any underlying principles we can use to improve rule-following behavior? Maybe so, but there is also a great deal of misunderstanding in this area. More and more, we see that a human subject's description of how and when reinforcement is delivered may be more relevant to his or her performance than how and when the environment actually dispenses reinforcement. As Hayes, Zettle, and Rosenfarb (1989) stress, even when it appears that the behavior of human subjects is conspicuously under the control of immediate consequences, other forces may be at work. To the extent that subjects may be able to describe the relationship between their behavior and related antecedent and consequent conditions, they may be concurrently operating under the influence of socially mediated or self-generated rules. For example, it is popularly believed that the Premack principle underlies an effective set of procedures for improving student behavior. Since this principle has served as a guiding light for many school psychologists and educators, it may be worth some special examination.

The **Premack principle** was originally developed in the laboratory using nonverbal organisms to generate a model of "motivation" as it pertains to the acquisition of reinforcement. The Premack principle states that any high-probability behavior can be used to reinforce any low probability behavior (Premack, 1965). In his early research, Premack arranged direct-acting contingencies so that water-deprived rats could perform the operant response of wheel-running to obtain access to the drinking of water. In this circumstance, the opportunity to engage in drinking was a high-probability behavior, and the opportunity to engage in wheel-running was a low-probability behavior. First, Premack demonstrated that drinking could act to reinforce wheel-running and then Premack reversed the contingencies. After wheel-running had increased in frequency, the rats were deprived of the opportunity to engage in wheel-running (in fact all physical movements were restricted), but they were provided constant access to water. Premack demonstrated that, under the later conditions, rats would drink three to five times as much water in order to gain access to an opportunity to run on the wheel. Thus, either wheel-running or drinking may be at high or low probability, depending on their respective levels of deprivation. Moreover, depending on current states of deprivation, either behavior may function as a reinforcer for the other.

Procedures derived from these findings have been applied rather cavalierly to many human contexts; however, something of an analogue (Malott, Whaley, & Malott, 1993) may be operating in the application of such a paradigm to human affairs. That is, while the Premack principle seems to predict human behavior in a way that is similar to that of nonverbal organisms, there are more complex verbal factors that need to be considered when predicting and influencing human behavior. For example, Homme (1974) has translated the Premack principle into what he calls Grandma's Law. "First you finish your dinner and then you get your dessert." This description certainly seems more consistent with procedures based on complex instructions (rule-governed behavior) than behavior operating exclusively under the control of natural, *direct-acting contingencies*.

Educators first became enamored with the Premack principle during the 1960's and 70's, and since then, many behavior management programs have been developed around this format. This strategy usually entails the development of *verbal rules* regarding behavioral contracting procedures, or classroom contingency management programs. For example, elementary students may be put on notice: "If you complete 20 arithmetic problems correctly, you may have five minutes of free time after lunch." Under the terms of such a verbal contract, math calculations must be monitored and verified for accuracy by the teacher before any recreational activity is forthcoming. Such behavioral contracting procedures have a strong track record for improving student behavior (See Ninness & Glenn, 1988 for a discussion); however, interpreting this procedure in terms of the Premack principle as a paradigm for contractually improving math performance may be problematic because there are no direct-acting consequences associated with the improved math behavior. It is important to remember that stimulus control established via direct-acting reinforcement cannot operate effectively across extended time periods (Wasserman & Neunaber, 1986). The time between the completion of arithmetic (low-probability responses) and the eventual access to free time (high probability responses) is far too great for us to assume that a three-term contingency could be maintaining this complex behavior. Nevertheless, the Premack principle is often extolled as an effective behavioral strategy for promoting improved classroom behavior--even when it is presented and maintained primarily in the form of a contractual agreement (e.g., Slavin, 1994).

TYPES OF RULE-FOLLOWING BEHAVIOR

Hayes, Zettle, et al. (1989) describe a particular type of rule-following governed by the "apparent correspondence" between the rule and the way the environment appears to be organized as **tracking**. A person who "believes" a particular verbal statement to be true may perform in accordance with, or track, the particulars of that rule even in the absence of guidance or supervision. In any given circumstance tracking may or may not work to a person's advantage, but it is most likely to be demonstrated by individuals who have a certain history. According to Hayes, Zettle, et al., tracking is influenced by the listener's history of making contact with the consequences of following directions, the *similarity* between the rule and other rules in the person's repertoire, and the gravity of the consequences for violating or following the rule.

Tracking stands in contrast to **pliance** which has been defined as a type of rule-following that is contingent on the correspondence between the rule and the *socially mediated* consequences provided during *supervision* of the relevant behavior. A person who performs in accordance with a rule due to pliance may or may not believe in the merits of the rule per se. More important is the person's belief in the forthcoming consequences for violating or following the rule (Hayes, Zettle, et al., 1989). Individuals who follow rules in the form of pliance do so primarily because they anticipate consequences (negative or positive) will be provided by someone who is aware of their behavior as well as the rules for what they should be doing. Note that both in the case of tracking and pliance, our conclusion that a particular person "believes" a rule is predicated on their performance in compliance or opposition to the rule. A student who follows rules only under the influence of social mediation (supervision) is performing according to pliance. We have noticed that, in the absence of conspicuous supervision, student behavior may come under the control of competing variables.

RULE-GOVERNED BEHAVIOR AND SCHEDULES OF REINFORCEMENT

Schedules of reinforcement are defined as patterns of reinforcement delivery classified on the basis of time or number of responses between programmed deliveries. Note: sometimes, the term *programmed contingencies* is used synonymously with *schedules of reinforcement*. Basically, schedules of reinforcement recycle a given set of contingencies; that is, the same criteria for accessing reinforcement are in effect during consecutive cycles of the same contingency. To cite a common example, fixed interval (FI) schedules have been demonstrated to produce somewhat similar patterns of responding across many different species. FI schedules require a specific amount of time to elapse before a response results in reinforcement. A FI 3-min would require that 3 minutes pass before reinforcement is delivered for the first response that occurs *following* that 3-min interval. This schedule often produces a particular pattern of responding in nonverbal organisms and preverbal children. Nonverbal organisms usually produce a positively accelerating pattern of responding up to the point at which they receive reinforcement. Following reinforcement, the pattern of responding slows down momentarily and then gradually accelerates toward the time at which reinforcement is delivered again (Ferster & Skinner, 1957). This pattern of relatively slow behavior subsequent to reinforcement, followed by a positively accelerating rate in responding, has come to be called a *fixed interval scallop* and has been documented in various ways among a wide variety of species (Whaley & Malott, 1968). It is important to point out, however, that there has been some conspicuous incongruity in what various researchers have been willing to classify as "good examples" of FI scallops (see Hyten & Madden, 1993 for a discussion).

Organisms (or people) who perform at a rate and pattern of responding normally associated with a given schedule are said to be performing in a manner which is *"schedule-appropriate," "schedule-sensitive,"* or *"schedule-typical."* Operating in a schedule-sensitive manner, the organism's behavior is exclusively controlled by the way in which the direct consequences follow particular behaviors. The behavior is exclusively a *function* of direct-acting contingencies. The pattern of behavior demonstrates a *functional relationship* to the pattern of reinforcement delivery. It is not necessary (or advisable) for us to postulate any mechanism inside the organism that controls this pattern of responding (e.g., a fixed-interval scallop).

Early Research Findings

As in the case of the Premack principle, early research findings regarding this and other schedules were obtained in laboratories using infrahumans (rats, pigeons, monkeys, etc.). With few exceptions (Breland & Breland, 1961), the rates of responding associated with particular schedules of reinforcement proved to be amazingly ubiquitous across diversified species. Initially, it appeared that all manner of organisms (including verbal humans) were endowed with particular rates and patterns of responding under the control of various schedules. By the late 1950's, many psychologists proposed that we might predict and control a wide range of human behaviors by carefully examining various schedules of reinforcement (e.g. Azrin, 1958; Long, Hammack, May, & Cambell, 1958).

By the 1970's, it was proposed that the positively accelerating pattern of new legislation enacted near the end of each congressional session might be a function of a FI schedule of reinforcement (Weisberg & Waldrop, 1972). There has been a more or less continuous progression of efforts to provide other real life and/or laboratory examples wherein schedules of reinforcement may have a subtle but pervasive influence on human behavior (see Lattal & Neef, 1996 for a discussion). It has even been suggested that such aberrant phenomenon as "date rape" might be attributed to the effects of intermittent schedules of reinforcement unwittingly generated by female companions (Marx & Gross, 1995).

Nevertheless, laboratory research into the ways in which humans perform under the influence of schedules of reinforcement has fired some strong uncertainty regarding the all pervasive continuity between animal and human behavior (e.g., Kaufman, Baron, & Kopp, 1966). For example, as early as 1967 Lippman and Meyer found that human subjects seemed to generate patterns of responding consistent with their verbal interpretation of the contingencies rather than the actual scheduled contingencies. Most subjects who were led to believe that reinforcement was based on interval schedules evidenced accelerated behavior near the end of the interval; those who believed that a specific number of responses were required for each reinforcement demonstrated a brief pause after reinforcement followed by a constant high rate of responding. Interestingly however, all subjects, in all conditions, were performing under the same type of schedule, FI 20-s.

A particularly enlightening series of studies conducted by Lowe and colleagues (Bentall & Lowe, 1987; Bentall, Lowe & Beasty, 1985; Lowe,

1979; Lowe, Beasty & Bentall, 1983) suggested that schedules of reinforcement did, in fact, influence some human behavior in the manner as that exhibited by infrahumans. However, this consistency was seen, almost exclusively, in humans who were preverbal or nonverbal. For example, during the first year of life, human infants showed patterns of scalloping that corresponded to those of nonhumans under the influence of FI schedules. But as older children were tested under the same schedules, such conspicuous consistencies in patterns of responding were no longer discernible.

Human Fixed-Interval Responding

A study by Harzem, Lowe, and Bagshaw (1978) illustrated that human subjects who exhibited long FI scallops while on FI schedules described their experimental conditions as requiring temporal regularity in order to obtain reinforcement. Other subjects performing under the same schedule of reinforcement, but who "believed" that reinforcement was contingent on the number of actual responses performed, rather than on the amount of time elapsing, did not manifest patterns of responding resembling a FI schedule of reinforcement. Here again, it was the rule that described the contingencies, rather than the actual programmed contingencies that appeared to drive the rate at which the human subjects performed.

To aid in clarifying exactly what constitutes a scallop, Hyten and Madden (1993) proposed an interval-by-interval classification system indexed by patterns into the following categories:

1. Scallop - Postreinforcement pause followed by a gradual acceleration in responding to a terminal rate at the end of the interval
2. Break-run - Postreinforcement pause followed by an abrupt transition to a terminal rate at the end of the interval
3. Terminal Minimum - Extended pausing until the very end of the interval when only a few responses occur
4. Constant Rate (Low, Moderate, High) - A constant response rate throughout the interval
5. Other Discernible - Any identifiable and repeated pattern not fitting into the above categories. The research should define the characteristics of any pattern in this category, labeling or naming each distinct pattern
6. Unclassifiable - Erratic response patterns with a form not repeated in several intervals (p. 492)

Fixed-Interval Responding During Human Computer-Interactive Problem Solving

Following Hyten & Madden's classification system, we decided to test these response patterns during a series of computer-interactive experiments (Ninness, Ozenne, McCuller, Rumph, & Ninness, in press). Five fifth- and sixth-grade students participated in our first experiment. We conducted all experimental sessions during the school day in a partitioned classroom on one of two Toshiba notebook computers. The experimental conditions investigated the students' patterns of responding during FI 30-s schedules of reinforcement. The students responded to multiplication problems by typing answers, which were calculated by the computer program and recorded on disk. The computer displayed the message, "TRY WORKING A FEW PROBLEMS. TYPE 'U' IF YOU UNDERSTAND." Then student/s could engage in interactive problem solving as the message, "WORK PROBLEM TO CONTINUE. TYPE 'E' TO END THE PROGRAM," appeared. If the student answered the problem, a new problem appeared with the same message above it. During the session, monetary reinforcement appeared on the computer screen according to a FI 30-s schedule. At the end of the experiment, we questioned students regarding what they believed to be the "best way to earn the most money while performing problems at the computer?"

Figure 3.1 illustrates eight representative 30-s intervals for each subject beginning at the tenth min of each session. As you can see, subject 2 was the only one of five students to demonstrate a performance approximating a scallop or pause-respond pattern in the majority of her FI 30-s intervals. Moreover, her post-session verbal description of the scheduled contingencies, which was consistent with the manner in which she performed, suggested that she believed that the passage of time was a relevant variable associated with the delivery of monetary reinforcement (cf. Lippman & Meyer, 1967). The remaining four subjects in Experiment 1 showed high rates of continuous responding throughout the majority of the intervals in their respective sessions. Unlike subject 2, post session commentaries by these students suggested that they "believed" reinforcement to be a function of the number of correct answers to computer-posted problems.

We conducted Experiment 2 to contrast the effects of FI 30-s reinforcement when students were pre-exposed to a *socially-mediated* (Hayes, Zettle, et al., 1989) accurate rule describing the best way to gain monetary reinforcement while working problems at the computer. Subject 2 provided this rule when we placed her words on the computer screen just before the session began. One male and one female student from the same class were exposed to the same experimental conditions as Experiment 1 subjects. Before beginning the session, they were allowed to read the description of contingencies developed by Subject 2, Experiment 1 which stated, "ONE STUDENT SAYS SHE MADE HER MONEY BY WAITING FOR A WHILE AFTER EVERY NICKEL AND THEN WORKING 5 TO 7 PROBLEMS. TYPE 'U' IF YOU UNDERSTAND."

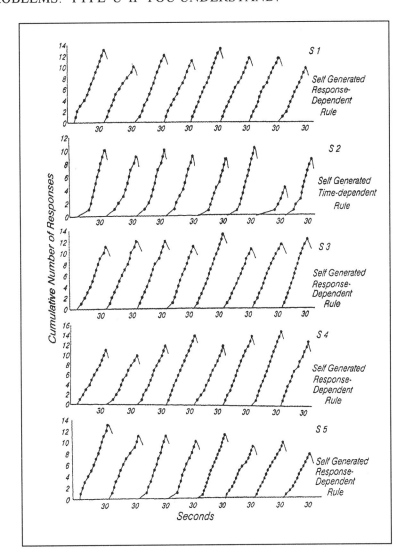

Figure 3.1. [Cumulative number of responses for five subjects provided FI 3-s reinforcement. Graphs illustrate response patterns generated after the first 10-min of the session. Subject 5's data begins on the eighth min, as adapted from Ninness, Ozenne, McCuller, Rumph, and Ninness, 2000, p.393]

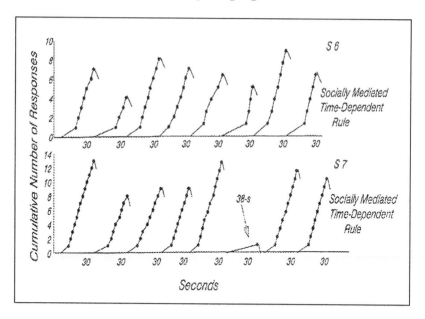

Figure 3.2. [Cumulative number of responses for 2 subjects provided FI 3-s reinforcement following exposure to a computer-posted rule. Graphs illustrate response patterns generated after the first 10-min of the session, as adapted from Ninness, Ozenne, McCuller, Rumph, and Ninness, 2000, p. 396]

Figure 3.2 illustrates that both Subjects 6 and 7 produced responding classified as *pause-respond*. And, both students described the programmed contingencies as requiring a certain amount of time to pass prior to responding and gaining reinforcement. Interestingly, both students described the rule they were given prior to the session as being very useful.

Because previous research (e.g., Lowe *et al.*, 1983; Hayes, Dixon, Caslake, Beckwith, & Shurr, 1997) suggested that many human and infrahuman subjects require prolonged sessions for scalloping to emerge in their response patterns during FI reinforcement we decided to conduct Experiment 3. The two subjects in Experiment 3 participated in five consecutive 18-min sessions (one per day) that each replicated the preparations from Experiment 1. The subjects were *not* given any specific rules regarding the programmed contingencies prior to beginning, and they were not asked to describe any of the experimental contingencies until the completion of the final session.

As seen in Figure 3.3, Subject 8 generated *unclassifiable* responding in that the data depict wildly variable patterns, and Subject 9 produced responding classified as *constant high rate*. Both subjects' verbal descriptions of programmed consequences were identified as response-dependent. *Implications* - Humans, with the development of language skills, display a growing sensitivity to social contingencies that support rule-following (Catania, 1993). This may not be a result of becoming less sensitive to scheduled reinforcement. Instead, it may be due to humans becoming more sensitive to socially mediated contingencies (cf. Cerutti, 1991) communicated in the form of rules (Hayes, Zettle, et al., 1989; Hayes, Brownstein, Zettle, Rosenfarb, & Korn, 1986).

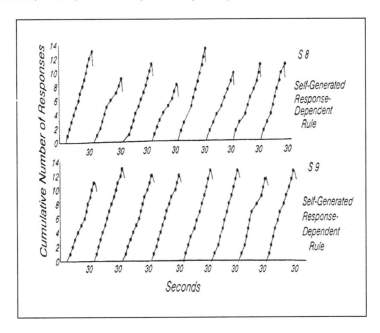

Figure 3.3. [Cumulative number of responses for 2 subjects provided FI 3-s reinforcement. Graphs illustrate response patterns generated in the fifth of five sessions after the first 10-min of that session, as adapted from Ninness, Ozenne, McCuller, Rumph, and Ninness, 2000, p. 398]

It is not entirely clear as to *why* and *how* Subject 2 (Experiment 1) produced a relatively accurate description of the programmed contingencies. However, this student has a quite advanced background in computer-interactive technology. Prior research (e.g., Catania, Shimoff, & Matthews, 1989) has shown that technology training previous to programmed contingencies optimally prepares a subject to respond more efficiently. We note, however, that more research is needed to identify the variables pertaining to the subject's acquisition of accurate rules.

Schedule-like Responding

The above study suggests that verbal humans may produce something called schedule-like responding. That is, a person who comes to "understand" (is able to correctly identify) the response requirements of a given schedule may perform at a rate and pattern of responding consistent with that of a lower organism exposed to the same scheduled contingencies. For example, a third-grade student may be told that after 3-min of performing math problems, she will receive a particular reinforcer (perhaps points or stickers). Note that the student is "told" the conditions under which reinforcement will be forthcoming. Here is where the complication arises. While this may sound comparable to the above FI schedule requirements, there are some very distinct differences. Upon hearing the description of how and when reinforcement may be delivered, such a student may immediately begin to demonstrate "some" of the characteristics associated with the FI schedule.

Even before the points or stickers are dispensed, the child may perform various math problems rather quickly, particularly as the end of the 3-min interval approaches. Following reinforcement delivery, the student may slow her math performance momentarily before resuming a gradually accelerating rate of calculating. This rate and pattern of responding appears somewhat similar to that of an infrahuman performing on a FI schedule of reinforcement. Such outcomes have been well documented, both anecdotally and in the literature (e.g., Holland, 1958; cf. Rosenfarb, Newland, Brannon & Howey, 1992). However, these effects are somewhat deceptive. Notice that in the above example, the student began to demonstrate the required behavior even before the promised reinforcers were actually delivered. How can a schedule of reinforcement produce its effects before it has been initiated? The answer is simple. *It cannot!* A student who demonstrates responding reminiscent of a particular schedule of reinforcement upon being "told" how and when reinforcement will be delivered is not behaving under the exclusive control of that schedule. The behavior of such a student is very likely to be driven by the verbal rules established by the teacher, together with rules generated by the student herself. Such a student might be performing math calculations at a rate similar to those typically seen in FI responding by a nonverbal organism, but there are great differences in the sources of control of such responding. As Malott, Whaley, & Malott (1993) point out:

These cases of delayed reinforcers and promises of delayed reinforcers involve more than the simple procedure of reinforcement. We're talking about rule control. The behavior occurs not just because of the contingency but because someone has stated the rule. The stater of the rule might be the person doing the behaving, or it might be someone who has stated the rule to that person (p. 345).

Analogues to Direct-Acting Contingencies

The above description refers both to the effects of a *promise of forthcoming reinforcement* as well as to the effects *of delayed reinforcement*. Malott et al. describe behavior generated and maintained by instructions or rules but which appears similar to behavior operating under the control of direct-acting contingencies as a rule-governed analogue (analog). They distinguish between these two classes of behavior by asking the question:

> Could the contingencies have controlled the behavior of a nonverbal animal? If they could have, then we may be dealing with a direct-acting contingency--simple reinforcement. If not, then we must be dealing with an indirect-acting contingency--a rule-governed analog to reinforcement (p. 361).

It is very unlikely that the lever pressing of a rat (much less its math performance) could be generated by the promise of reinforcement. Rats (and all manner of lower organisms) require direct contact with real schedules of reinforcement over an extended period of time before specific patterns of responding associated with the schedule emerge. For a rat, a promise just won't cut it--irrespective of the level of sincerity rendered by the experimenter.

"Then," you may well ask, "what difference does it make, since both direct-acting contingencies (by way of schedules) and rule-governed analogues to schedules produce similar patterns of behavior?" The answer again is simple but critical to the understanding of human behavior. If humans can produce schedule-like behavior by simply being furnished with descriptions of contingencies (rules), then they may change those patterns of responding just as quickly as the rules change. Such abrupt behavioral transitions are not seen in lower organisms. Only verbal humans are endowed with the capacity to exhibit rates and patterns of responding based on verbal descriptions of contingencies rather than making direct contact with actual contingencies. In humans, the patterns of behavior, as well as the specific types of behaviors performed, often change as quickly as the sources and details of instructional control.

MASKING SUBJECTS

Perhaps, scheduled contingencies are impacting humans at a level at which words do not come into play. One point of inquiry has pursued the question of whether human subjects who have their verbal behavior masked might come under the influence of the programmed contingencies in a way that more closely resembles that of nonhumans. In general, masking procedures usually entail an attempt to keep human subjects distracted and naive during an experiment in order to reduce their ability to "focus" on relevant experimental variables. Generally, masking procedures preclude or interfere with the subjects' ability to generate accurate descriptions of what they are doing--as they are doing it.

For example, the Hefferline and Keenan (1963) study, previously described in Chapter 2, revealed that operant behavior in the form of minuscule thumb twitches, which occurred below the subjects' level of awareness, could be controlled by systematic application of direct-acting contingencies. In light of our present discussion, this study is worth revisiting.

Using an electromyograph (an instrument that measures minute muscle potentials), Hefferline and Keenan were able to record thumb contractions so small that subjects were unable to describe their movements when they produced them. In the experimental arrangement, subjects were seated comfortably in a sound attenuated room with various "dummy" electrodes strategically located in various positions all over their bodies. Following a 10-min baseline, subjects were told that they could earn five cents each time they incremented a nearby counter stationed directly in front of them. They were not, however, told how this might be accomplished. In fact, in order to increment the counter, it was necessary that the subjects produce very exacting minute muscle potentials in their thumbs just between 25 and 30 microvolts. Amazingly, participants quickly went about the business of earning a substantial number of nickels during six consecutive 10 minute training sessions. Subjects demonstrated an obvious operant ability to control their minuscule thumb muscle movements, but very few ever guessed that they had done so by way of a low level activity emanating from their thumbs. Subsequently, this new (but "unconscious") behavior was placed on extinction, and the newly learned diminutive behavior disappeared. Again, subjects were unable to identify their changing behavior or any of its controlling variables. This was one of the first studies to demonstrate unequivocally that human behavior can come under the control of direct-acting contingencies even when the experimental arrangements preclude the subjects' ability to understand or describe any of the relevant variables.

The Greenspoon Effect

The above study begs the question as to whether similar strategies might influence human language. That is, if certain well-defined muscle movements in our thumbs can be subtly controlled by direct-acting contingencies, can the same be true of our verbal behavior? In an early, and now classic experiment, Greenspoon (1955) confirmed that adult human verbal behavior may, indeed, come under the control of direct-acting contingencies.

College students were asked to say words at random, while particular words (plural nouns or all parts of speech except plural nouns) were targeted for reinforcement or punishment. For the first 25-min of each session, reinforcement consisted of the experimenter simply vocalizing 'mmm-hmmm' (reinforcement) or 'huh-uh' (punishment) after these selected parts of speech. In the second 25-min of each session, the experimenter did not respond to any of the subjects' vocalizations. At the end of each session, subjects were asked to try to identify the experimental contingencies. Most subjects could not do so; those few subjects (only 10 of 75) who could discern the purpose of the experimenter's 'mmm-hmmm' (or 'huh-uh') were eliminated from the experimental analysis. Results from different groups established quite conclusively that differential reinforcement with 'mmm-hmmm' elevated the frequency of plural nouns, and conversely, 'huh-uh' could be used to selectively diminish the same behavior. Interestingly, while the frequency of the precise class of words elevated dramatically during contingent reinforcement, there was little tendency for subjects to repeat the same words over and over. Once again, this outcome points to the importance of *operant class* as a functional and highly malleable unit of behavior, particularly when human subjects have "no idea" that their behavior is the target of some intervention.

Subtle Psychotherapeutics

Elusive verbal reinforcers also may be operating in therapeutic contexts. For example, psychologists and counselors who provide subtle ongoing interpersonal feedback to clients (perhaps in the form of 'mmm mmm' or 'uh huh') during therapy may be shaping the client's verbal behavior. This may be happening even when the therapist has no explicit intentions of responding differentially to the client's commentary.

Truax (1966) examined the possibility that such subtle shaping procedures might play a role in therapist-patient interactions during what has come to be known as "non-directive" (Rogerian) therapy. One of the primary theses of non-directive therapy is *unconditional positive regard*. That is, the therapist provides an environment which is verbally supportive and non-judgemental irrespective of the client's commentary. But is this really what goes on?

Using tape recordings from a successful case conducted by Carl Rogers himself, Truax confirmed that during psychotherapy, Rogers tended to respond differentially (favorably) to client comments that were suggestive of the client's growing "insight," improved style of expression, and improved personal judgments (discriminations). Recordings revealed that following the client's high expression of "feelings," the therapist was more likely to demonstrate therapeutic "warmth," "empathy," and utter low level intonations such as, 'mmm mmm.' Accordingly, increased rates and complexity of the client's self-expressive statements ensued. This will not come as a surprise to behavior analysts. To the extent that any form of therapy includes differential reinforcement of particular classes of verbal behavior, we would anticipate that such verbalizations should become more elaborate and occur at a higher rate. This type of control may be even more likely to occur when it is not an "identified" part of the psychotherapeutic process. In this case, neither the client nor the therapist was aware of the dynamic.

So there is a substantial body of evidence suggesting that "under some conditions" keeping human subjects from being able to verbally attend to (or identify) aspects of the immediate environment may increase the likelihood of them coming under the control of direct-acting contingencies. This is a very important concept because it provides a way for us to understand how human behavior may be systematically influenced without the individual's "knowing" that this influence is taking place.

It is important to point out, however, that simply creating diversions during the course of an experiment may not be sufficient to produce this effect. Usually, it is not enough to merely *distract* subjects. They must remain completely naive regarding all reinforcement contingencies. To the extent that subjects even may "speculate" about the distribution of ongoing reinforcement, their behavior pattern may be changed by that speculation. Just as soon as subjects begin talking to themselves about what they are doing, and how, when, and why they are doing it, their behavior begins to conform to their own self-generated "expectations." They are then more likely to act in accordance with their own verbal descriptions of how the environment operates. Such verbal descriptions (rules) may or may not be accurate, but they are almost always instrumental in changing behavior.

An Important but Unsuccessful Attempt at Masking

A study by Flora, Pavlik, and Pittenger (1990) makes this point abundantly clear. They found that when subjects were reinforced for bar pressing according to variable ratio (VR) and Fixed-Interval (FI) schedules while simultaneously solving anagrams (the masking task,) these subjects *did not* demonstrate responding reminiscent of FI schedules. For that matter, masked subjects did not even respond differentially to the VR and FI schedules. Patterns of responding for both schedules appeared almost identical.

Masked subjects were even less sensitive to the scheduled contingencies than control subjects who were *not* provided this masking task. In fact, during extinction "masked" subjects were so *insensitive* to the scheduled contingencies that they continued to perform bar pressing while solving anagrams for 20 minutes after all reinforcement had terminated.

This is a paradoxical outcome indeed. When subjects were asked why they persisted in bar pressing in the total of absence of any reinforcement, they provided such comments to the researchers as "I trusted you." Thus, despite the distracting influence of deciphering anagrams while bar pressing, the masked subjects were "concerned" about the way in which bar pressing led to reinforcement. The anagram activity may have served as a distraction, but it proved to be a totally inadequate masking procedure for keeping subjects exclusively under the control of scheduled contingencies.

A crucial finding in this experiment was that control subjects, who were not required to solve anagrams while bar pressing, came under the immediate and conspicuous influence of extinction procedures almost as soon as it went into effect. Unlike the masked subjects, when the program stopped providing reinforcement, control subjects stopped performing. By that standard, the "unmasked" control subjects appeared more schedule sensitive than subjects who were masked. Flora et al. suggest that control subjects were probably better able to verbalize the experimental contingencies (generate accurate rules) and thus stop responding when reinforcement was terminated.

Fallacious Rules

Very often, fallacious rules may override the effects of natural or programmed contingencies. For example, elementary school students seem particularly ingenious when it comes to inventing their own rules. In fact, many children appear to be endowed with a special capacity to "invent their own reality." Historically, the approach of summer vacation has inspired generations of students to develop imaginative but questionable new rules-- particularly in locations that are inaccessible to teacher supervision.

Miracle at Saint Rosalia's

On the last day of his third grade year, during the final period, Fast Freddie "double-dared" Herbie to do it one last time. Herbie was washing his hands when the verbal gauntlet was cast down. Young Herbert was just a little superstitious, and he believed that refusing to take a double-dare would bring bad luck. Leaping from the floor, he clutched the plumbing pipe with his wet hands. To his own amazement, he was able to swing forward, push the plunger with his foot, perform a half twist, and swing back in the direction of his audience before letting go. The toilet roared and swirled as Herbie opened his arms made a perfect two-point landing right in front of the flushing furies. For a moment all was still, then he beheld the unthinkable. At eye level were a pair of folded, shrouded arms and a white habit behind a large crucifix.

Herbie saw his short life pass before him. In the next second, he was seized by the sideburns and smartly escorted up the stairwell and down the long corridor. "You're a fresh article, you are!" Sister Servula declared. Herbie wasn't feeling very fresh. His sideburns were scorching, and his little heart was pounding.

She was still maneuvering him by the sideburns when a miracle took place in the halls of Saint Rosalia's. Over the intercom, Mother Felicitous announced that the school year had now come to a close. "See you in September," she announced cheerfully to all, "See you in September." The public address system echoed her divine message throughout the building. "See you in September." It resounded off the church walls next door and reverberated back through the school library, lavatories, and classrooms.

Instantly, there swelled a wave of primitive exhilaration gushing through the cramped corridor. Before Herbie realized what was happening, he was immersed in the cascading crowd of ecstatic students, and Sister Servula was left holding a few strands of sideburn between her thumb and forefinger. As in a trance, he watched himself drifting down the hall and out the double doors of the school. Before him, the summer sun radiated in the open sky. Herbie looked up and smiled, "Thank you, Jesus." and he was gone.

IN SUMMARY

This chapter has focused on the experimental analysis of human verbal behavior. We have addressed issues on instruction, rule-following, superstition, stimulus equivalence, paradigms regarding analogues to direct-acting contingencies, and human behavior under the influence of particular schedules of reinforcement. As our technology focuses more and more on verbal processes, we are better positioned to consider how human language interacts with various reinforcement procedures in computer-interactive environments.

Chapter 4

AN EXPERIMENTAL ANALYSIS OF RULE-GOVERNED BEHAVIOR AND HUMAN-COMPUTER INTERACTIONS

INTRODUCTION

This chapter brings our analysis of rule-governed behavior into contact with some of the basic research that includes computer-interactive simulations of real world conditions. Several of these studies may appear rather abstract in the sense that they may seem far removed from natural classroom issues and events. But, computer simulations give us a chance to more thoroughly examine student rule-governed behavior on a platform that is free of extraneous variables. In fact, many of the studies in this chapter explicate (or retrospectively clarify) the procedures that we employ in natural environments (described in Chapters 5 and 6). As we move through some of our basic research on such issues as the contingencies of superstition, analogues to higher-order schedules of reinforcement, and computer-interactive procedures for *augmenting* the effectiveness of self-assessment, note that these same strategies will re-emerge in the coming chapters when we focus on assessment and treatment of behavior problems in natural school settings.

The Ice Nun Cometh

That night, as Herbie tried to fall asleep, he felt a slight burning sensation right next to his ear where some of his sideburns had been removed. It occurred to him that the long white fingers of Sister Servula might still reach out and seize him. He squirmed restlessly ruminating over what might happen next year when he would be forced to confront a seriously disconcerted Sister Servula. Finally, he began to drift into a soft summer dream when he suddenly sensed that he was not alone. There in the dark, a tall, shadowy silhouette stood before him, her shrouded arms folded--staring. As his eyes met hers, she loomed over him, reaching for his sideburns, and then--astonishingly--faded into a mist with a whisper, "You're a fresh article, you are. I will see 'you' in September--Sir!"

Now Herbie's imagination was getting way out of control! How did these spooky thoughts ever get started? Herbie was beginning to find out that mysticism and *superstition* may take many forms. The more he tried to make his phantoms and superstitious thoughts go away the more intense they became. Eventually, it occurred to him that he needed a completely new way of looking at things. He needed a totally new set of rules and beliefs. And, as he lay there wondering where he might find such things, he gradually fell into a fitful dream in which Sister Servula was giving his whole class an intense lecture on the "critical differences between *belief* and *superstition*." Sister Servula had considerable insight into such matters. And, at least in his dreams, Herbie listened very carefully to the following lecture.

SUPERSTITIONS

Superstitions in allegories and fables often forecast ominous connections between meaningless events. Walking beneath ladders or breaking mirrors portend assorted misfortunes; forgetting to knock on wood may nullify a positive prediction; and so on. While almost everyone recognizes that there is no logical relationship between such implausible and inauspicious events, people often feel compelled to act as though there just might be some kind of enigmatic underlying logic. Often, people who accidentally break mirrors or who have black cats cross their path begin to ruminate over the possible consequences. Eventually, "something" unfortunate is bound to happen. When it does, they attribute the misfortune to fate and this closes the loop of the self-fulfilling prophesy. But, for humans, superstitions also may be fortuitous. Falling stars and wishing wells provide those special opportunities for making dreams come true. Often, when wishes comes true (and sometimes they do) attributions are given to the heavens or the wells.

Malott, Whaley, and Malott (1997) pointed out that humans appear to be at particularly high risk for developing superstitions in contexts that establish increased probabilities for accidental or coincidental consequences.

For example, due to the game's intrinsic potential for generating coincidental reinforcement, baseball players have become notorious for developing a wide range of superstitious beliefs and behaviors--particularly while in the batter's box. A player who "gets a hit" for reasons that are not completely clear at the moment it occurs may "attribute" his performance to some irrelevant feature of the environment or to some irrelevant feature of his own behavior (e.g., number of practice swings). By doing so, he generates a superstitious rule (Malott et al., 1993).

From a behavioral perspective, a rule may be described as "superstitious" if it describes contingencies that are not in effect. A person behaves "superstitiously" if he or she performs as though the rule is accurate when it is not. Thus, a given rule might be correct in one circumstance and superstitious in the next. As with all rule-governed behavior, superstitious rules function as discriminative stimuli, or contingency-specifying stimuli (Schlinger & Blakely, 1987), for the behavior described and may continue to operate that way as long as the advertised negative or positive consequences are not immediately and conspicuously disconfirmed. Once a person has learned to respond under the stimulus control of a superstitious rule, the superstition comes to control behavior that would seldom be maintained without it; that is, the rule-governed compliance may override the effects of scheduled contingencies (cf. Catania, Matthews, & Shimoff, 1982).

Superstitions Among the Animals

Early laboratory research demonstrated that superstitious behavior is not the exclusive domain of humans. Skinner (1948) was the first to demonstrate that laboratory pigeons maintained stereotypical and ritualistic behavior under the influence of response-independent schedules (those that provide consequences independent of responding) of reinforcement. Staddon and Simmelhag (1971) replicated Skinner's work and argued that such behaviors were related primarily to terminal responses in the anticipation of food rather than superstitious behaviors. In turn, Timberlake and Lucas (1985) replicated Staddon and Simmelhag only to determine that such behaviors were species-specific patterns of responding associated with patterns of feeding. So it goes. Irrespective of theoretical interpretations of the phenomena, the fact remains that fixed-time (FT) schedules of reinforcement often generate stereotypical patterns of responding in a variety of organisms. (Davis & Hubbard, 1972).

In a fixed-time, response-independent, schedule (e.g., every 15 seconds), reinforcement depends on the passage of time and is provided entirely irrespective of what the organism happens to be doing at the moment reinforcement is delivered. For example, in an experimental space, a bird may just happen to be turning when a pellet of food is dispensed from the food magazine. The turning behavior is adventitiously reinforced but, nevertheless, selected by its consequences. The experimenter has had no particular designs on shaping the bird's turning behavior. Still, particular behaviors are selected by their immediate consequences. Once turning is reinforced, the probability of future turning behavior is increased. If the bird continues to turn following the previous reinforcement and it is once again reinforced while doing so, the rate of turning may really begin to accelerate. Note that the reinforcement is *not* provided according to any *behavioral contingency*--only a *time-based contingency*. The bird's turning behavior is absolutely irrelevant to the acquisition of reinforcement. Nonetheless, it is common laboratory lore that birds caught in such a "behavioral trap" may be found spinning like little "whirling dervishes" after a few hours of such time-contingent reinforcement (Whaley & Malott, 1971).

Superstitious Preschoolers

Wagner and Morris (1987) conducted a systematic replication of Skinner's famous "Superstition" experiment (described above) using preschool children rather than pigeons as subjects. However, their methodology attempted to copy the primary features of Skinner's experimental space with special emphasis being placed on maintaining all of the elements of a free-operant environment. Subjects were permitted to do whatever they wanted while in the experimental setting.

Taped sessions were conducted according to ABA design. During baseline, children demonstrated *no* form of consistent responding, superstitious or otherwise. In the following response-independent condition, when children received *marbles* (later exchangeable for toys) according to either a FT 15 s or a FT 30 s schedule, 7 of the 12 children exhibited a clear and "specifiable dominant response" pattern (e.g., touching a clown on the nose) reminiscent of superstitious behaviors. Interestingly, these superstitious behaviors extinguished quickly during a return to baseline condition.

Left out of this study was any discussion of the role played by verbal mediation. What, if anything, did the students believe about the relationship between their behavior and getting the marbles? It would have been particularly interesting to know whether any of the children had self-generated *fallacious rules* during the response-independent reinforcement condition. Rules such as these may play a prominent part, even among preschoolers, in the emergence of superstitious behaviors.

Verbally Mediated Superstitions

Current research suggests that there appears to be something of an analogous relationship in the way that superstition operates in verbal and nonverbal organisms. We might say that superstitious behavior in humans is a verbal analogue to superstitious behavior performed by nonverbal organisms. In animals, superstitious behaviors are a direct function of the relationship among environmental events--specifically, response-independent (or noncontingent) reinforcement. *Analogously,* superstition in human behavior is usually driven by the individual's inaccurate verbal description of behavioral and environmental events. But the real questions are: Under what conditions do people tend to develop their own superstitious rules that erroneously guide their behavior, and under what conditions do they behave superstitiously because they believe the fallacious rules proffered by others?

We usually determine that a person is behaving "superstitiously" when we see that their pattern of responding follows some illogical rule rather than the way consequences are actually provided in the real world. Humans appear most likely to behave superstitiously when inaccurate rule are given by a "believable source" and when the rules are expressed in such a way that the consequences for violating them do not "seem" to lead to conspicuous disconfirmation (Galizio, 1979). That is, when you follow the illogical rule it seems right, and you have no direct way of knowing when it is not. The baseball player who always wears the same of pair socks because it seems to bring him good luck will get a certain number of hits in any given game. The player has a verbal logic describing how the socks are associated with hits. Probably, the hits would have happened with or without the socks, but if he continues to wear the lucky socks he will never be confronted with this knowledge.

From an experimental perspective, the strength of a superstitious behavior is identified by examining the rate and duration of a behavior and the extent to which the actual consequences are irrelevant to that behavior. In other words, how obvious is it that the certain consequences are happening with or without the rule-following and how much irrelevant behavior is being performed? If a person persists in performing in accordance with an illogical rule at a very high rate, we are inclined to say they are behaving very superstitiously.

Superstition in Higher Education

A study conducted by Ono (1994) provides an excellent perspective into the complexity of superstitious behavior in adult humans by way of verbal mediation. In this study college students were assigned to experimental or control groups and asked to generate rules regarding the best way to earn points when pulling a lever in an experimental setting. This device was programmed to provide points according to a particular schedule of reinforcement called differential reinforcement of high (DRH) rate responding which required 5 responses per 15 seconds. If the subject performed at least 5 responses or more in 15 seconds a reinforcement lamp illuminated, and the subject earned a point.

Control subjects worked in isolation and were asked to write their self-formulated rules regarding the best way to earn the most points as they pulled the lever. Note: the schedule of reinforcement was not described to these control subjects; rather control subjects had to determine the best pattern of responding from their own experience in pulling the lever.

The experimental subjects were each provided a partner with whom they exchanged information while taking turns at the experimental apparatus. After completing each experimental session, experimental subjects formulated rules regarding how to best perform on the apparatus. They wrote these rules on the bulletin board seemingly for the benefit of their partner with whom they were taking turns. Ostensibly, the confederate did the same. This required the confederate to communicate with the real subject by way of writing rules on a bulletin board which the subject would read upon entering each experimental session.

The experiment was designed so that *it would appear that* experimental subjects would "benefit" from their own experience, as well as the experience of their partner. While the real subjects enthusiastically pulled the lever on the apparatus and attempted to generate and write accurate rules accordingly, the confederate subjects provided the real subjects with *fallacious rules*. In various phases of the experiment, the confederates recommended pulling much faster than necessary--more psychological knavery.

While this may seem like a wicked way to treat unsuspecting and cooperative research participants, it also provides a clever method of obtaining inside information regarding how individuals behave in accordance with their own self-generated rules and how they may be affected by other people's fallacious rules. Working by themselves, control subjects had absolutely no difficulty determining the most advantageous rate of responding throughout the entire experiment. Furthermore, they were quickly able to describe the rules they had generated for bar pulling while operating under the DRH schedule. The experimental subjects, on the other hand, were not so efficient. Even in the absence of any form of supervision, they tended to adapt their response rates to the rules posted on the bulletin board by their conniving confederate partners.

In the initial phases of the experiment, many of the experimental subjects pulled the lever four to five times faster than necessary when following incorrect rules. Yet, even then, most of the subjects' performances did not correspond exactly with the prescriptions provided by their partners. More often the subjects appeared to be operating according to a combination of their own self-generated rules while concurrently adhering to some of the rules provided by the confederates. That is, the subjects' performances were conspicuously influenced, but not exclusively controlled, by the confederates' recommendations. However, by the end of the experiment, the fact that they had received questionable advice from their partners was not entirely lost on most of the subjects. When, in the final phase of the experiment, they were again advised to pull the lever very quickly in order to earn the most points, six of the eight subjects did not follow this recommended strategy at all. Perhaps, by this stage, most of the experimental subjects were becoming a little skeptical about the advantages of complying with their partners' suggestions.

One of the most interesting facets of this experiment is the fact that even though subjects were not always performing in accordance with social rules provided by their partners, their responding always corresponded with the rules *they* expressed. That is, subjects always performed in a manner which was roughly consistent with that which they had described on the bulletin board.

Superstitions College Students During Random Reinforcement

Are there other conditions in which students are likely to generate their own special superstitious rules? It would seem so. Bruner and Revusky (1961) found that college students tended to develop idiosyncratic and superstitious rules regarding reinforcement schedules when operating four separate telegraph keys. They found that subjects quickly developed the false belief that at least one key was critical to setting up the schedule of reinforcement on one of the other keys. Although subjects' inaccurate descriptions of the criteria for reinforcement differed, they all had two things in common. They all developed illogical and superstitious rules regarding the experimental contingencies, and they all insisted on following their rules as though they were perfectly correct.

In a somewhat similar vein, Vyse (1991) examined written statements provided by uninstructed subjects subsequent to key-pressing their way through a computer-generated maze. Stereotyped responding emerged when point acquisition was placed on a random-ratio (RR) 2 schedule. On a RR 2 approximately two responses are needed in order to obtain reinforcement. Thus, on any given bar press, your chances of getting reinforced are about fifty-fifty. In this experimental preparation, subjects who showed very inefficient but highly repetitive bar-pressing styles while on this schedule produced written commentaries that "accounted" for their superstitious performances; their attempts to explain why they behaved as they did represent classic examples of self-generated superstitious rules. In a replication (Heltzer & Vyse, 1994), college students again were asked to deduce the contingency by which points were delivered after key-pressing their way through a computer-generated maze. Subjects who performed under the influence of RR schedules were more likely to produce superstitious rules than those who operated under FR 2 or continuous reinforcement. They suggested that haphazard consequences associated with random ratio schedules are most likely to occasion superstitious rule formation.

Students Superstitiously Avoiding Random Tones

In another illustration of how we can come under the influence of fallacious rules in a chaotic environment, Cerutti (1991) had subjects attempt to avoid time-based, response-independent tones by pressing panels during mixed random-time (RT) and FT schedules. During RT schedules the tones came on erratically and completely independent of the subjects' panel pressing behavior, but during FT schedules, these tones always came on after a specific amount of time had elapsed. Either way, there was really nothing the subjects could do to avoid the inevitable random or fixed-time tones. Cerutti found that shaping the subjects' guesses (regarding how they might most "efficiently" press the panels to avoid the tones) was most effective during RT schedules. Shaping guesses was not nearly as powerful a process during the more predictable FT tones. A follow-up study by Cerutti (1994) supported the theory that shaping subjects' inaccurate interpretations of cause and effect was most easily accomplished when consequences were randomly delivered. Following these outcomes, Cerutti forwarded the notion that random distribution of events *across time* increased human vulnerability to fallacious rules and illogical behaviors (cf. Ninness & Ninness, 1998). Cerutti (1991) suggests that, "Perhaps a defining feature of human superstitions is that they are predicated on variably scheduled events; there may be few superstitions based on events that occur with regularity" (p. 63).

Superstitions During Lean and Random Schedules

Newman, Buffington, and Hemmes (1995) examined the effects of rule-following under the influence of increasingly "thin" schedules. They exposed subjects to CRF, FR 2, and FR 3 schedules while the accuracy of instructions provided by the experimenter was sequentially altered. Note that a CRF schedule references continuous reinforcement; that is, reinforcement occurs after every completed response. FR schedules require a specific number of responses—in this case either two or three responses are needed.

The experiment entailed having college students follow or violate instructions to remove pegs from either the left or right side of a game board in order to earn points toward a raffle. The students were advised previous to the experiment that sometimes the experimenter's instructions would not be accurate and that they were to act accordingly. Accuracy of instructions varied between 0 and 100% during various phases of the experiment.

Subjects exposed to CRF schedules either flagrantly violated or obediently complied with experimenter instructions; however, subjects operating under FR 2 and FR 3 schedules were much more likely to follow instructions irrespective of the correctness. Newman et al. suggest that the leaner FR 2 and FR 3 schedules may have compromised the subject's ability to discriminate accurate from inaccurate instructions given by the experimenter. Because reinforcement also functions as a form of "feedback" during leaner schedules, subjects on these schedules were unable to generate accurate rules regarding the advantages of either following or defying the experimenter's instructions. From this perspective, one's probability of "unwittingly" following fallacious rules is more likely when the scheduled contingencies are more "lean" as compared to more "random."

Shifting Schedules

In a unique analysis of time-based, adventitious contingencies, Hackenberg and Joker (1994) contrasted the effects of schedule and instructional control on humans' choices between FT and progressive-time (PT) schedules. (During PT schedules, reinforcement is dispensed at the end of gradually increasing time periods; however, nothing the subject does has any direct bearing on when the reinforcer is delivered.) Initially, the instructions accurately described the scheduled contingencies, and under these conditions, subjects' choice patterns provided the greatest amount of monetary reinforcement. Although instructions remained constant, optimal choice patterns gradually shifted across conditions through changes in the PT schedule. Instructional control was maintained for several conditions, but eventually diminished as responding came under schedule control. On the basis of verbal reports gathered at 15-min intervals during the course of the experiment, Hackenberg and Joker suggested that for at least some subjects, responding may be attributable to gradually changing accurate or fallacious self-instructions during the programmed contingencies.

Fallacious Rule-Following and Extinction

Rosenfarb, Newland, Brannon, and Howey (1992) asked three groups of college students to formulate rules, follow rules, or try to avoid developing any form of rules during their experiment. Both groups of students that had rules learned to perform most efficiently; however, during extinction, students who had generated or who had been furnished rules were more likely to persist in responding than those who had been told to specifically avoid developing any form of rules. Rosenfarb et al. note that both self-generated and socially generated rules appear to promote the acquisition of schedule-appropriate behavior, but these rules may impede subjects' ability to recognize the fact that their behavior is on extinction. It is important to point out, however, that subjects in this study *were not given* a specific opportunity to formulate rules during the extinction phase of the experiment as they had during the acquisition phase.

SUPERSTITIONS DURING COMPUTER-INTERACTIVE MATH

Following leads from the above research, we (Ninness & Ninness, 1998) attempted to see how superstitious behavior might emerge during computer interactive academic behavior. Experimental conditions were designed to examine sixth grade students' responsiveness to both superstitious and accurate rules while students worked basic math problems on the computer. Students solved problems by typing answers on the keyboard and reinforcement consisted of a brief (.5-s) flashing message on the computer screen indicating the earning of five cents.

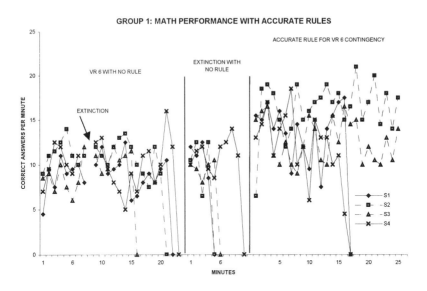

Figure 4.1. [Frequency and duration of correct math problems per minute for subjects in Group 1, as adapted from Ninness and Ninness, 1998, p.52]

The most critical part of the study came in the third condition when students in the two experimental groups saw a rule posted on the computer screen. For Group 1 (above) the rule was accurate, and for Group 2 the rule was fallacious (superstitious); however, it was the same rule for both groups. The rule was "THE FASTER YOU WORK THE MORE MONEY YOU MAKE." Perhaps, it is not surprising that Group 1 subjects increased their rates of problem solving when given a rule that correctly described the relationship between fast problem solving and earning more money.

The behavior demonstrated by Group 2 students was unexpected but revealing. In the second condition, Group 2 students were given the same rule, "THE FASTER YOU WORK THE MORE MONEY YOU MAKE;" however, for this group the rule was false, and their behavior was immediately placed on extinction. That is, when they performed math problems, no money was forthcoming from the computer. After a burst of fast problem solving, students quit performing. At this point it should have been obvious that the computer was quite capable of displaying a fib (see Figure 4.2 below).

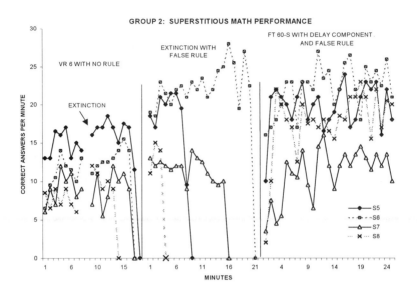

Figure 4.2. [Frequency and duration of correct math problems per minute for subjects in Group 2, as adapted from Ninness and Ninness, 1998, p.54]

At the beginning of the third session, Group 2 students (above) were re-exposed to the same false rule, but now reinforcement was delivered every 60-s independent of the students' behavior (*Now we have response-independent reinforcement plus a fallacious rule*). Under these conditions, work is completely irrelevant to earning money. Any work performed under these conditions can only be described as superstitious behavior. Nevertheless, within two to three minutes of seeing the false rule, all students in this group were performing math problems at very impressive rates *as if* the consequences described in the rule were forthcoming exactly as advertised by the computer. None of these students even attempted testing the veracity of this rule by slowing their rate of problem solving or simply watching the screen to see if money would be delivered independent of their math performance. Why should they work so hard following a rule that had just proven itself false in the previous condition? Indeed, under some conditions, delivery of response-independent reinforcement may function as a very effective extinction procedure (e.g., Hagopian, Fisher, & Legacy, 1994; Fisher, Ninness, Piazza, & Owen-DeSchryver, 1996). However, response-independent reinforcement *and* a rule that invites some minimal target behavior may change everything.

Note that at the beginning of the third session students appeared reluctant to engage in high rates of calculating. Some minimal performance apparently was prompted by the presentation of the computer-posted fallacious rule. And, even though their previous experience with the computer had just demonstrated that the computer was quite capable of posting a "bold faced lie," students all executed a few math problems which coincided with the delivery of irrelevant reinforcement. One might infer that it was this event that "triggered" their "belief" in the superstition. It appears that once we comply with an illogical rule we are in danger of falling into one form of a behavioural trap (cf. Malott et. al.). Our beliefs and behaviors may be perpetuated by the irrelevant consequences that are correlated with our actions. Acting in accordance with false belief systems interferes with our chances of finding out what might happen if we defied the superstitious rule and simply did nothing at all. As stated by Cerutti (1991), once compliance begins, it "...may engender itself by precluding opportunities to discriminate the null effects of noncompliance" (p. 63).

What about the control subjects who received response-independent reinforcement, but never viewed the fallacious rule on the computer screen?

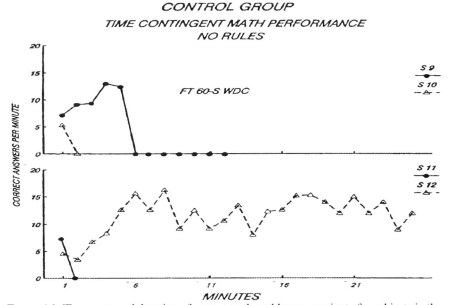

Figure 4.3. [Frequency and duration of correct math problems per minute for subjects in the control group, as adapted from Ninness and Ninness, 1998, p.55]

Figure 4.3 shows us that response-independent reinforcement in the absence of superstitious rules resulted in only one of the four control subjects demonstrating superstitious behavior. An interview with this student following the experiment indicated that he had self-generated his own superstition. This student conjured up the belief that performing math problems was somehow related to "getting more nickels on the screen." The other three students did not develop this misconception, and they stopped working. Certainly, this outcome begs the question as to why certain individuals are more likely to generate superstitious rules and behaviors than others. In fact, this very question forms the basis of much of our current research in behavioral and school psychology. Indeed, this behavioral pattern has implications for the use of functional assessment (discussed in chapter 5).

Evidence from this study suggested rather strongly that exposure to a computer-transmitted rule that seems to be consistent with a contingency may be sufficient to persuade people that a response-consequence relationship actually is in effect. Under such conditions, even students who have had a very current history of coming into contact with a conspicuous computer-generated fallacy may persist in conforming in accordance with that fallacy after a small "dose" of response-independent reinforcement. Had any of the students in Group 2 briefly tested the experimental contingencies by refraining from doing multiplication problems, they might well have concluded that they were in the midst of performing a great deal of unnecessary work, as it may be with much of our day-to-day interaction with the world. Much of what we do "customarily" may be initiated by superstitious rules and sustained by spurious correlations between our behavior and irrelevant but coincidental consequences.

Experiment 2

A second experiment was conducted to test the effects of negatively phrased superstitious rules and attempted to identify response patterns associated with the avoidance of *financial loss* while performing math problems. Two control subjects from Experiment 1 participated, and the setting and apparatus were identical to those of the previous experiment. The only exception was the exclusion of the delay component employed during experiment 1.

In the first condition, students were provided reinforcement during a VR 6 scheduled contingency that consisted of the computer posting the following phrase, "No money lost yet!" for 1s each time they completed approximately 6 problems. During the second condition (extinction with false rule), the fallacious rule was phrased in the form of an avoidance contingency. At the beginning of the session, the screen advertised, "If you work quickly, you won't lose any money. Type enter if you understand." No positive or negative consequences followed this message. During the final condition the computer posted the fallacious rule, "If you work quickly, you won't lose any money. The computer on your left will let you know if you have lost any money. Type enter if you understand." Subsequently, every 60s the second computer provided reinforcement by posting, "No money is lost yet!" for 1s.

Figure 4.4 illustrates that during the second (extinction) condition (when the computer gave no feedback whatsoever) students continued responding for some time before quitting the program. In the final condition both subjects reinitiated responding at very low rates. Perhaps, they were getting a little sceptical about their chances of earning any money. However, by the third minute of this session, rates of correct problem solving accelerated and were maintained throughout the duration of the FT 60-s response independent reinforcement condition. Keep in mind that this computer feedback was provided independent of their math performance. Had they done nothing at all they would have received the same messages on the screen.

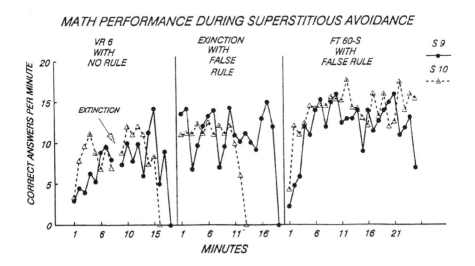

Figure 4.4. [Frequency and duration of correct math problems per minute for subjects in experiment 2, as adapted from Ninness and Ninness, 1998, p.57.]

Experiment 3

We conducted a third experiment to analyze the effects of accurate rules during extinction procedures. Again, two students who had served as control subjects in Experiment 1 participated in Experiment 3, and the experimental setting and apparatus were identical to those of the first experiment. Following scheduled reinforcement and extinction, a follow-up extinction session was initiated with the presentation of an accurate rule regarding extinction. At the beginning of the session, the computer screen displayed, "No money can be earned for solving problems during this session. Press enter if you understand." Figure 4.5 illustrates that both subjects aborted the program immediately when given an *accurate rule* regarding the forthcoming extinction contingencies.

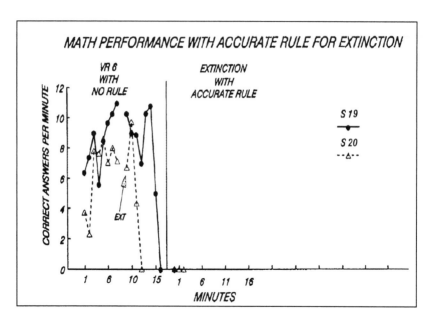

Figure 4.5. [Frequency and duration of correct math problems per minute for subjects in experiment 3, as adapted from Ninness and Ninness, 1998, p.58. Note that the subjects are identified as S11 and S12 in the original publication.]

It seems that in the world of human-computer interactions, a superstitious rule may function as well as an accurate rule *if* the superstition provides the "occasional appearance" of a cause and effect relationship. Amazingly, this appears to be true even when subjects are given substantial evidence that the computer has been "telling lies" and even when the relevant behavior includes some very labor intensive academic performance.

SELF-GENERATED SUPERSTITIONS DURING SECOND-ORDER RESPONSE-INDEPENDENT SCHEDULES

As we described at the beginning of this chapter, laboratory experiments with lower organisms have established that superstition is not exclusively a human phenomena (Skinner, 1948; cf. Staddon & Simmelhag, 1971), and continuing animal research has demonstrated the varied effects of time-based, response-independent reinforcement schedules (e.g., Lattal & Abreu-Rodrigues, 1997).

In a related set of findings, research with lower organisms has also demonstrated that a phenomenon called *second-order schedules* may generate extraordinary performances in the face of extinction. A second-order schedule is one that produces an intermittent cue (rather than a reinforcer) for the organism to perform another set of responses before actual contact with reinforcers is provided. For example, Findly and Brady (1965) were able to generate extended durations of responding in chimpanzees during fixed-ratio (FR) 4,000 by displaying a mediating food-hopper stimulus light after every 400 responses and providing tangible reinforcement after 10 displays. This contingency was described as a FR 10 (FR 400:S) where S referred to the stimulus light delivered after every 400 responses. We wondered if combining second-order schedules with response-independent reinforcement might yield *analogs* for human superstitious behavior within computer-interactive environments.

What if, rather than providing immediate access to reinforcement, we created a "chance to get money" while students sat before the computer screen. How would this affect their motivation in the face of extinction? How would this affect their tendency to develop "a false belief system." For instance, creating a coin toss graphic after every random-time (RT) 30-s and providing monetary reinforcement only when the coins matched according to RR 2 ($p = 0.5$) may be described as a second-order schedule consisting of RR 2 (RT 30-s:S) where S represents the stimulus provided in the coin toss graphic procedure.

Such a schedule seemed congenial with preparations and conceptual issues from our previous research in which we found that students who were given fallacious rules coinciding with FT contingencies showed particularly high rates and long durations of solving math problems during extinction (Ninness & Ninness, 1998). In light of our previous findings on superstitious responding, we became increasingly interested in developing a computer model of second-order response-independent reinforcement.

"Suped-Up" Superstitions Using Second-Order Random-Time Schedules

As noted earlier, RT schedules provide reinforcement independent of the subject's behavior after a "random" period of time has elapsed. For example, a RT 30-s will dispense reinforcement at the end of approximately every 30-s. The student may be working diligently or staring into space—either way reinforcement is provided after a random amount of time passes.

In this study, as in our previous study, fifth-grade students were able to respond to multiplication problems by typing answers on the keyboard. Students in experimental Group 1 were provided response-independent reinforcement according to a second-order RR 2 (RT 30-s:S) (fluctuating between 15-s and 45-s) by way of a coin toss graphic procedure. Students in experimental Group 2 were provided standard RT 30-s reinforcement. Control subjects were exposed to the same demand conditions; however, they were not provided programmed reinforcement. For this group, responding to math problems simply allowed access to a continuing assortment of multiplication problems.

Following the first 10 min, all subjects in all groups saw computer posted questions asking why they were still performing problems.

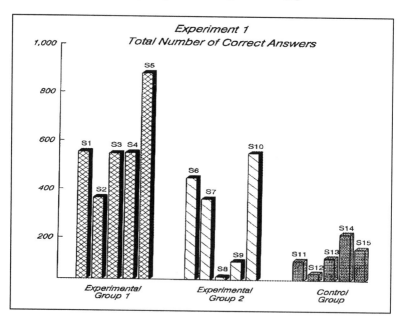

Figure 4.6. [Total number of correct answers for subjects in each group during Experiment 1, as adapted from Ninness and Ninness, 1999, p.228]

After students responded to these questions, the program continued providing response independent reinforcement to subjects in both experimental groups for 10 additional minutes. Thereafter, all forms of reinforcement ended, but math problems were still available for solving for an additional 25-min.

The group data (see Figure 4.6 above) were summarized by calculating the mean number of correct answers for subjects in each of the 3 groups. Statistical analysis via *randomization tests* revealed that the Control group achieved significantly fewer correct answers than Group 1 and Group 2. A statistically reliable difference between Group 1 and Group 2 was also found, with more problem solving performed by Group 1.

Figure 4.7 illustrates that all 5 students in experimental Group 1 performed multiplication problems at a relatively low rate during the first 3 to 5 minutes of RR 2 (RT 30-s:S) reinforcement. By the seventh or eighth minute, most subjects had reached the peak of their performance capabilities, but subject 4 continued to show a gradual acceleration throughout most of the first 20-min of his session.

Throughout the experiment, intervals in which no responding occurred were likely to be correlated with response-independent reinforcement. Consequently, it is rather surprising that none of these subjects slowed their rate or stopped performing problems and simply let the computer furnish reinforcement independent of their behavior. Contrarily, the trend lines for each subject showed a progressive acceleration of problem solving during the first few minutes of each session. Seemingly, performance rates were not altered by the brief questioning provided by the computer at the end of the tenth minute of each subject's session.

Group 2 students did not persist in performing math problems over the extended period of time demonstrated by Groups 1 students (Figure 4.8).

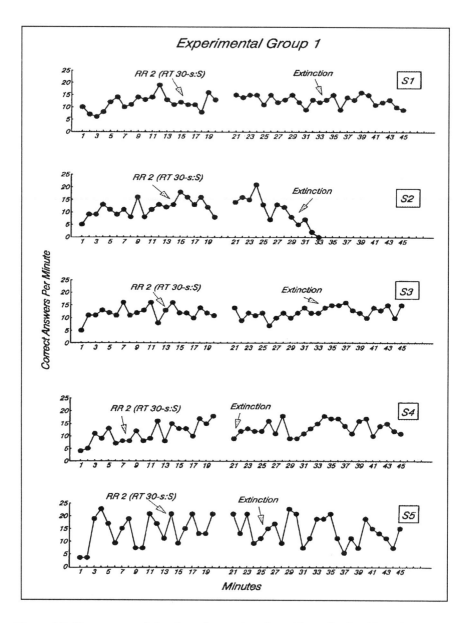

Figure 4.7. [Frequency and duration of correct math problems for 5 subjects in Group 1 receiving second-order RT 30-s reinforcement, as adapted from Ninness and Ninness, 1999, p.229]

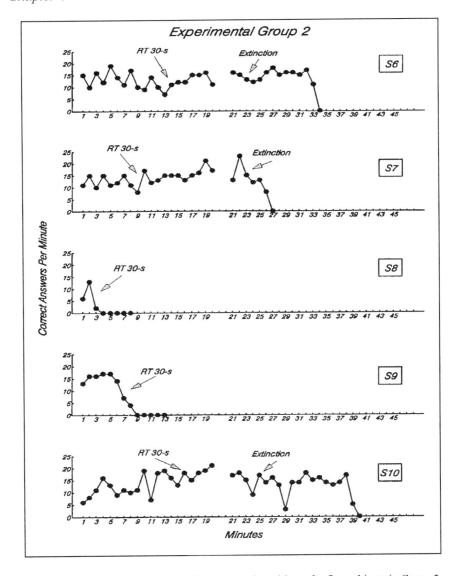

Figure 4.8. [Frequency and duration of correct math problems for five subjects in Group 2 receiving RT 30-s reinforcement, as adapted from Ninness and Ninness, 1999, p.231]

The five students in the Control Group did not have access to noncontingent financial reinforcement by way of the computer. How many multiplication problems is a 5th grade student likely to perform at the computer for the sheer joy of it? A few! However, for most people, simply doing one problem after another provides a limited level of fascination. Figure 4.9 indicates that control students were willing to perform a few problems (over a short period of time) without benefit of any form of conspicuous "extrinsic" reinforcement. What does it take to generate enthusiasm around such a mundane activity?

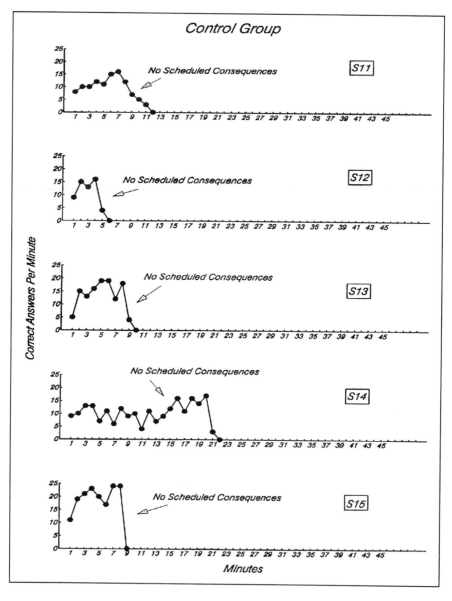

Figure 4.9. [Frequency and duration of correct math problems for five subjects in the Control Group, as adapted from Ninness and Ninness, 1999, p.233]

Superstitions During Second-Order Fixed-Time Schedules

We designed Experiment 2 to systematically replicate Experiment 1 by assessing the effects of second-order response-independent reinforcement when provided on fixed-time (FT) schedules rather than RT schedules. As noted earlier, FT schedules provided reinforcement independent of the subject's behavior after a "fixed" period of time had elapsed. For example, a FT 30-s will dispense reinforcement at the end of every 30-s even if the student is sitting on his hands. This represents one more way in which we can provide *response-independent reinforcement.* However, since FT schedules provide reinforcement according to a very predictable time pattern they will be less likely to induce superstitious behavior. In fact, previous studies have indicated that it is the "random" distribution of consequences that is the most critical to the development of superstitious behavior (Ceruttie, 1994). Thus, we anticipated that the FT schedules in the following study would prove somewhat less compelling during extinction.

As in Experiment 1, students were able to respond to multiplication problems by typing answers on the keyboard; however, for students in this experiment, response-independent reinforcement was delivered according to an RR 2 (FT 30-s:S) schedule for Group 1 and a standard FT 30-s schedule for Group 2 students. This means that, over and over again, at the end of exactly 30-s two coins flipped on the computer and screen. When and if they matched, the student won five more cents. However, as in the previous experiment, their work had no bearing on winning (or failing to win) money on the computer screen.

Again, we summarized the group data by obtaining the total number of correct answers for each subject in both experimental groups. Figure 4.10 illustrates the total number of correct answers for each subject in each group with more problem solving being performed by Group 1 students.

Individual-subject results were assessed in terms of rate and duration of correct answers/min within each student's experimental condition. Figure 4.11 illustrates that all three students in experimental Group 1 executed multiplication problems at a relatively low rate during the first few minutes of RR 2 (FT 30-s:S) reinforcement.

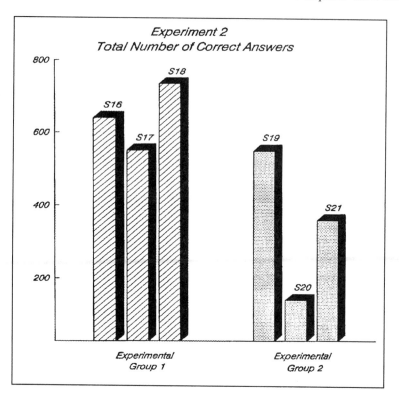

Figure 4.10. [Total number of correct answers for subjects in each group during Experiment 2, as adapted from Ninness and Ninness, 1999, p. 235]

As in the previous experiment, Group 1 students performed relatively stable rates of problem solving, with some acceleration, across the first 20-min of RR 2 (FT 30-s) schedule. All of the written responses by Group 1 students appeared to reflect their superstitious belief that performing math problems on the computer gave them a much better chance of earning more money by way of the coin-toss graphic that occurred repeatedly every 30-s. At least in this study, the more predictable FT component in the second-order schedule seemed irrelevant to the generation of superstitions.

Just as in Experiment 1 (above) the students' behavior and the inaccurate beliefs (rules) matched. That is, the students' rate of performing math problems was consistent with their "superstitious belief" that problem solving was necessary to access financial rewards. And, just as in Experiment 1, performing math problems had absolutely nothing to do with getting or failing to get money on the computer screen.

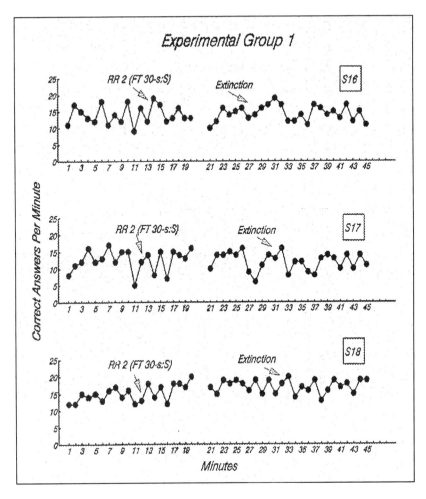

Figure 4.11. [Frequency and duration of correct math problems for 5 subjects in Group 1 receiving second-order FT 30-s reinforcement, as adapted from Ninness and Ninness, 1999, p.236]

As evidenced by Figure 4.12, Group 2 students showed much less enthusiasm for working math problems. Note however, during extinction this group did not have access to the coin-toss graphic. When extinction began on the 21st min., problems remained available for solving but the computer program provided neither money and nor an apparent chance at getting more money. This may have made all the difference. The two students who began the extinction session stopped shortly thereafter.

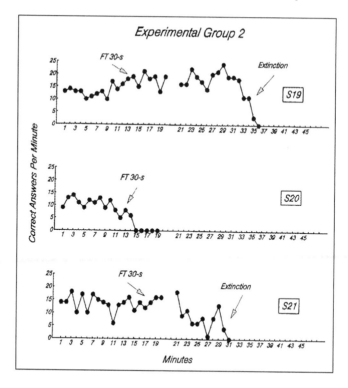

Figure 4.12. [Frequency and duration of correct math problems for 5 subjects in Group 2 receiving FT 30-s reinforcement, as adapted from Ninness and Ninness, 1999, p.238]

Second-Order Superstitions: Unnecessary Behavior And Then Some.

This analysis of second-order superstition may have important implications for human computer-interactive behavior. Indeed, these results suggest that second-order response-independent schedules of reinforcement have extremely compelling features beyond those found in simple RT or FT schedules. It is during these schedules that we find our subjects "inventing" the most outlandish interpretations of response-consequence relations where none exist.

Written responses from Group 1 students in both experiments indicate that they really "believed" there was a "cause and effect" relationship between their performances and the likelihood of accessing monetary reinforcement via the coin toss graphic. The written responses often detailed their anticipation of acquiring access to reinforcement based on being able to match HEADS or TAILS as they performed multiplication problems. Of more practical value, both RR 2 (RT 30-s:S) and RR 2 (FT 30-s:S) schedules produced higher rates and longer durations of unnecessary responding than standard RT or FT schedules. These outcomes were made particularly obvious during the extinction phase of each experiment. Four of the five students receiving RR 2 (RT 30-s:S) and all three of the students receiving RR 2 (FT 30-s:S) continued performing over a 25-min extinction condition. Concluding comments by many of these students suggested that they were willing to work even longer if the program had not ended. Moreover, our outcomes did not appear to indicate any distinction between the behavior-inducing effects of RR 2(RT 30-s:S) versus RR 2 (FT 30-s:S) schedules.

We think that the extended durations and high rates of problem solving displayed by Group 1 subjects in both experiments may be attributed to the rule-governed effects emerging from the second-order schedules. Such outcomes have parallel effects in nonverbal organisms. For example, Zimmerman (1957, 1959), shaped a FR 15 lever press to the sound of a buzzer as a discriminative stimulus that also served as a reinforcer for running an alleyway to obtain food. By incorporating this FR 15 lever press as a second-order operant, rats performed thousands of lever presses and continued responding for over 20 hr during extinction. *Analogously*, high rates and long durations of problem solving by Group 1 students of both experiments may have been due to the second-order relation between problem solving RR 2 (FT 30-s:S) and RR 2 (RT 30-s:S) established via the second-order, coin-toss graphic procedure. Interestingly, although Group 1 subjects in both experiments earned only half as much reinforcement per unit of time as did Group 2 students, they performed an average of 287 more responses (nearly a factor of 2) over the course of their experimental sessions. Even though no *response-dependent* contingency existed, the probabilistic relation between responding and time-based reinforcement in conjunction with the second-order coin-toss graphic may have increased the strength of the reinforcement contingency. Based on the comments of our subjects, at the very least we can reasonably assume that this procedure made the acquisition of reinforcement more "interesting" (see Ninness, Glenn, & Ellis, 1993, for a discussion).

It is noteworthy that, as with the findings of Ono (1993), although the students' verbal interpretations of the programmed contingencies were not consistent with the actual programmed contingencies, their interpretations of these contingencies were quite consistent with the way in which they operated on the computer. Students wrote such comments as, "If I only do a few more problems the coins will appear and I will win more nickels." Nothing could have been further from the truth, but nothing seems to have instilled more enthusiasm for high rate problem solving. It is no exaggeration to say that our students were thrilled by the chance (intermittent) monetary outcomes. In the midst of this fascination, they developed illogical but compelling rules that drove their responding through the maze of irrelevantly scattered consequences. Perhaps there is something about the allure of second-order schedules that we may be able to incorporate into therapeutic interventions? In Chapter 6 of this text we will do just that. In that chapter we will show how the above findings can be systematically employed to motivate students who have a history of academic indifference.

SHAPING HUMAN VERBAL BEHAVIOR

Much of our current research in human verbal behavior suggests that it is very difficult to separate the effects of rules and direct-acting contingencies (see Malott, Malott, & Trojan, 1999 for a discussion). Even when it appears that human behavior is under the conspicuous influence of direct-acting contingencies, other forces may be at work (Hayes et al., 1989). The issue of "awareness" is always problematic. As Hayes et al. (1989) point out, to the extent that human subjects may be able to describe the relationship between their behavior and related antecedent and consequent conditions, they may be operating under the influence of self-generated rules. Exactly how these self-generated rules develop and maintain remains the subject of some argument. Nevertheless, there may be a number of wily (but empirically verifiable) ways we can impact and measure the effects of the shaping of subjects' verbal behavior (rules) under laboratory conditions. Of course, these procedures require that we preclude subjects' awareness of treatment variables and this, you will see, makes for a somewhat challenging set of experimental preparations.

You may recall that in Chapter 2 we described *shaping* as a procedure that entails differential reinforcement of particular behaviors to the exclusion of others. The behavior that produces the reinforcing consequence (motor or verbal) is strengthened and the other behavior extinguished. In the procedure of shaping, the response that produces the reinforcing consequence keeps changing because the consequence is delivered only if later behavior more closely approximates the target behavior.

Recall that in a basic experimental arrangement, a rat may learn to press a lever--something it has never done before. When first it looks at the lever, we might provide our initial reinforcing consequence--perhaps we drop a small portion of food or water mechanically into the experimental space. Next, we will increase our criterion. Only if the rat approaches the lever will we give the reinforcer. If it moves away, we would do nothing, waiting for the rat to look at the lever and move in its direction before providing the consequence. We will reinforce next if, and only if, some behavior occurs that is getting the rat closer to the target behavior (bar pressing). At each step the criterion for reinforcement will change so that the next consequence is contingent on a closer approximation to the target.

When *shaping human behavior, instructions are not part of the procedure.* In the true sense of the term, shaping is only in progress when the individual who is being shaped has no "awareness" of the fact that his/her behavior is being influenced by a combination of differential reinforcement of some behaviors and the extinction of others. Note that individuals who have their behavior changed under the influence of verbal instructions are not being "shaped." Their behavior may change with increasing verbal standards, but such behavior is operating under the influence of "instructions" or "directions."

Recall the professor (in Chapter 2 of this text) who was shaped across the classroom by the reinforcing head nods and smiles of his conniving students. This is an excellent anecdotal example of what we mean by shaping—behavior changed under the influence of differential reinforcement. Whaley and Malott (1968, 1997) were the first to provide this entertaining but illuminating example of shaping as it may be correctly (if deviously) applied to human behavior. Recall that in their example, although the professor's behavior comes under the influence of differential reinforcers, the professor had no active *awareness* of this process as it was occurring. So it is with the shaping of all human behavior.

Experimental Settings and Interpretations

Catania and Shimoff (1985), Shimoff, Catania, and Matthews (1981), and Catania, Matthews, and Shimoff (1989) suggested that the shaping of rules, rather than specific overt behaviors, may be one of the variables that act to over-ride the effects of direct-acting contingencies. However, Catania *et al.* (1989) note that "... we can only be certain that behavior is controlled by rules when rules and contingencies are pitted against each other" (p. 121). As an illustration, Catania *et al.* (1981) pitted rules against contingencies by having subjects press buttons and respond to questions in writing regarding the most efficient way to earn points (money) while performing. When subjects were differentially reinforced for *self-generating written guesses* that ran contrary to the scheduled reinforcement contingencies, many of the subjects' response rates came under the apparent control of the verbal shaping procedure. Specifically, subjects who performed button pressing during random-ratio (RR) schedules lowered their rates of responding when differentially reinforced for writing statements, indicating that they should respond more slowly in order to access more points. Inversely, shaping *inaccurate* guesses increased subjects' rates of button pressing while on random interval (RI) schedules. Thus, shaping verbal behavior in opposition to programmed contingencies resulted in subjects performing at rates that minimized access to reinforcement during their performance on the respective schedules. In a follow-up study, Catania, Shimoff, and Matthews (1989) determined that shaping subjects' *performance descriptions* was a more powerful procedure than shaping *contingency descriptions.*

However, Torgrud and Holburn (1990) noted Catania *et al.* failed to establish schedule control before shaping guesses. They reported that prior exposure to highly differentiated schedules insulated their subjects from subsequent attempts to shape response patterns that were incompatible with programmed contingencies. Findings by Cerutti (1991) appear to support this caveat. Cerutti pitted the shaping of rules against contingencies by having subjects attempt to avoid response-independent tones by pressing panels during various mixed random-time and fixed-time schedules. In this context, subjects' inaccurate guesses (as to the best way to avoid tones) were shaped by computer feedback. Outcomes indicated that the subjects' verbal behavior in the form of guesses and panel pressing were more likely to be controlled by the shaping of guesses when response-independent tones were transmitted during highly indiscriminable random schedules. A replication by Cerutti (1994) forwarded the notion that compliance with shaped rules was most likely to occur during random indiscriminably scheduled consequences.

Shaping False Rules in "Natural" Settings

As a corollary to the above basic research, several recent findings in the literature of applied psychology have been directed at the processes by which people are induced to generate false verbal descriptions of the environment and behave accordingly. For example, Wells, Small, Penrod, Malpass, Fulero, and Brimacombe (1998) investigated the first 40 cases in the US in which DNA evidence exonerated wrongly convicted prisoners. Thirty-six of these cases involved evidence obtained from eyewitnesses who apparently were subtly shaped into incorrectly identifying and *selecting* innocent people from somewhat random and indiscriminable line-ups and photo spreads. Related research (Wells & Bradfield, 1998) suggests that subtle confirming feedback from authorities (e.g., selective head nodding and saying ahu) to witnesses during the identification process often influences (shapes) their selections and builds an *inflated false confidence* in these selections from line-ups. Interestingly, most witnesses professed that such feedback played no role in determining their "false beliefs" and inaccurate responding.

Shaping and Instructing Computer-Interactions

We have seen that simply giving instructions may have a fairly profound effect on student academic performance on the computer. For example, our previous research (Ninness & Ninness, 1998) established that many intermediate school students were willing to perform math problems at high rates and long durations when they came to "believe" inaccurate instructions regarding the best way to earn the most money while working problems on the computer. Others have found very much the same thing. For example, Dixon and Hayes (1998) showed that subjects who produced high rates of self-generated verbal descriptions of experimental preparations during computer-interactive responding performed efficiently. *Specific but obsolete* computer-posted *instructions* were associated with the *resurgence* of previously reinforced but currently ineffective patterns of responding during extinction (cf. Dermer & Rodgers, 1997).

But what manner of "transmitting" rules is most dynamic and effective—instructing or shaping? This issue is most timely because humans are spending increasingly amounts of time interacting with computers and the Internet, and it is critical to understand the dynamics of how and when computer interactions impacts human moment-by-moment decisions and performance.

We attempted to follow the lead of Catania *et al.* (1982) by pitting instructed and shaped rules against scheduled consequences. We wanted to develop a format that addressed the control exerted by scheduled consequences during computer-interactive problem solving, and we wanted to compare the relative effects of shaping verses instructing rules. Would subjects change their established patterns of answering problems just because new rules were posted on the screen? Would shaping *the selection of new rules* have any special advantage over instructions?

Shaping Selections of Inaccurate Rules

As in several of our preceding experiments, subjects in this study could respond to multiplication problems on the computer by typing answers on the keyboard (Ninness, Shore, & Ninness, 1999). And just as in previous studies, correct answers/min were calculated by the computer program and were automatically recorded to a floppy disk. However, unlike our previous studies in this area, this experiment consisted of two sessions lasting 32 min and 16 min, respectively.

Random-time (RT) 9-s schedules on the blue screen provided response-independent reinforcement. That is, working quickly served no advantage. The computer provided reinforcement at the end of approximately 9-s completely without regard to the students math performance. On the other hand, when the screen turned white, a Random-ratio (RR) 4 schedule went into effect, and the faster the students worked the more money they earned. These screens alternated every 2 min. Predictably, by the end of baseline, many students in Group 1 were working faster when the computer screen turned white. Most students had established a pattern of working on the respectively colored screens. At this point the question became, "will shaping the selection of inaccurate rules change their established response patterns?"

In the next 16 min, reinforcement continued according to the same multiple RT 9-s RR 4 schedule; however, at the end of each 2-min cycle of the multiple schedule, subjects were presented with opportunities to make selections (guesses) regarding the best way to earn the most money working problems on the respectively programmed/colored screens. Subjects in Group 1 were differentially reinforced (shaped) for making selections of rules that were "incompatible" with maximizing scheduled reinforcement. In other words, subjects now were being reinforced for selecting rules that were incorrect, and if they followed the rules, they would work to their own financial disadvantage.

At the end of each 2-min cycle, students were able to respond to the following questions: "SELECT!! THE BEST WAY TO EARN THE MOST POINTS ON THE BLUE SCREEN IS ??? TYPE 'S' WORK SLOWLY--VERY SLOWLY!!"   OR   "TYPE   'Q'   WORK   QUICKLY--VERY QUICKLY!!" Selecting descriptions of performances that *incorrectly described* reinforcement contingencies on the blue screen resulted in the acquisition of 1 cent. For example, if a subject responded *incorrectly* by typing "Q" for QUICKLY, the screen turned green and posted the following message: "CORRECT !! ADD ONE MORE CENT TO YOUR TOTAL EARNINGS. YOU NOW HAVE 38 CENTS. If a subject responded to this question *correctly* by typing "S" for "SLOWLY," the screen posted the following message, "SORRY NO MONEY THIS TIME." Next, the screen provided an opportunity to describe performance on the white screen by posting, SELECT!! THE BEST WAY TO EARN THE MOST POINTS ON THE WHITE SCREEN IS ??? TYPE 'S' WORK SLOWLY--VERY SLOWLY!!" OR "TYPE 'Q' WORK QUICKLY--VERY QUICKLY!!" Selecting descriptions of performances that *incorrectly described* reinforcement contingencies on the white screen resulted in the acquisition of 1 cent. If a subject responded *incorrectly* by typing "S" for SLOWLY, the screen turned green and posted the following message: "CORRECT !! ADD

ONE MORE CENT TO YOUR TOTAL EARNINGS. YOU NOW HAVE 38 CENTS. If a subject responded to this question *correctly* by typing "Q" for "QUICKLY," the screen posted the following message, "SORRY NO MONEY THIS TIME." A second set of the same two questions and consequences were delivered before the computer resumed the presentation of math problems and reinforcement according to the multiple RT RR schedule. Thus, at the end of each 2-min cycle, subjects could earn an additional 4 cents for making selections of performance descriptions that were incompatible with scheduled contingencies.

During the second session, subjects in Group 1 were introduced to a similar experimental preparation; however, reinforcement was contingent upon making selections of performance descriptions that were consistent with contingencies. In this session, subjects in Group 1 had their rule selection shaped again. This time, however, we reinforced rule selections that were accurate. And, to the extent that they followed the rules they selected they would really earn more money for working math problems.

Outcomes from Shaping

Generally, subjects adjusted their performances on the respectively colored screens to coincide with the number of points they received during the rule selection process (cf. Torgrud & Holburn, 1990). Most subjects required 2 or 3 cycles of rule selections before consistently obtaining all 4 available points; however, when subjects began earning all 4 points between cycles of the multiple schedule, their response rates coincided with their selection of inaccurate rules rather than the scheduled consequences for correct problem solving. Only Subject 4 consistently acquired points for selecting performance descriptions that were inconsistent with schedules and failed to come under the influence of these reinforced selections. Surprisingly, it was in the first session that Subject 3 came under the consistent control of performance descriptions that ran in opposition to schedules, but he failed to do so during the second session when reinforcement for selections of performance descriptions actually reflected the reinforcement contingencies on the respectively colored screens. His irregular point acquisition between cycles during the second session seems to suggest some level of continuing "conflict" between his selections of performance descriptions and his problem solving rates on the multiple schedule. Nevertheless, 5 of the 6 subjects did come under the apparent control of shaped selections of fallacious rules during the first session, and these subjects demonstrated remarkably inefficient (if not completely erroneous) performances during the first session.

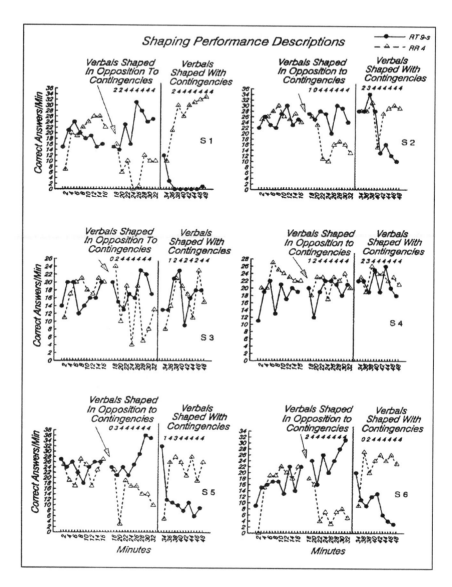

Figure 4.13. [Frequency of correct problems per minute and points earned for selected performance descriptions for 6 subjects in Group 1. Shaping selections of performance descriptions that were in opposition to scheduled reinforcement began after 16-min of baseline on the multiple RT RR schedule. In the following session, selections of performance description were consistent with scheduled reinforcement, as adapted from Ninness, Shore, and Ninness, 1999, p.636]

Instructing the Selection of Inaccurate Rules

Subjects in Group 2 performed baseline operations according to the same format as those arranged for Group 1. For 16 min, subjects received reinforcement according to the same multiple RT 9-s RR 4 schedule. As with Group 1, the RT 9-s component was assigned to the blue screen, and the RR 4 component was assigned to the white screen. However, after 16-min of baseline, students in this group were given a series of four *inaccurate instructions* regarding the best way to earn the most points. Between cycles of the multiple RT RR schedule, the computer posted the following: "INSTRUCTIONS!! THE BEST WAY TO EARN THE MOST MONEY WHILE WORKING ON THE BLUE SCREEN IS, WORK QUICKLY- VERY QUICKLY. TYPE "U" IF YOU UNDERSTAND. If the subject typed "U" within 15-s, the computer screen posted the delivery of a cumulating amount of monetary reinforcement. Next, the computer screen provided inaccurate instructions regarding how to perform most efficiently on the white screen: "INSTRUCTIONS!! THE BEST WAY TO EARN THE MOST MONEY WHILE WORKING ON THE WHITE SCREEN IS, WORK SLOWLY-VERY SLOWLY. TYPE 'U' IF YOU UNDERSTAND." If the letter "U" were not pressed within 15-s, presentation of multiplications problems resumed according to the ongoing multiple RT RR contingencies, and no "extra" money was added to the subjects' cumulating totals. These two instructions and opportunities to respond appeared twice between each 2-min cycle of the multiple RT RR schedule and allowed the subjects to earn an additional 4 cents between problem-solving cycles by typing the "U" key after each instruction. In this condition, instruction following minimized contact with scheduled reinforcement.

In the second session, instructions were reworded so as to correctly describe the performances leading to the most monetary reinforcement while solving problems on each of the colored screens. During this session, the computer posted *accurate descriptions* of programmed contingencies and reinforcement was provided for typing "U" within 15 s of each instruction. Complying with computer-posted instructions in this second condition optimized the subjects' opportunities to contact scheduled reinforcement while performing math problems in the context of the blue and white screens.

Outcomes from Instructing

Following a 16-min exposure to the multiple RT RR schedule, many of our subjects refused to change their patterns of responding when given *inaccurate instructions* regarding the best way to earn the most money while working math problems. Even subjects who were far from optimizing access to scheduled reinforcement were reluctant to shift their established mode of responding during the on-going multiple RT RR schedule. Despite the fact that all subjects in Group 2 gained monetary reinforcement for repeatedly asserting that they "understood" the best way to earn the most money *was* to work "quickly" on the blue screen/RT component and "slowly" during the white screen/RR component, the moment-by-moment behavior of 4 of the 6 subjects in Group 2 did not conform to these "understood" instructions (see Figure 14.4). The trend lines for these subjects suggested that they may *not* have found these computer-posted appeals adequately compelling. To the contrary, Subject 9 seemed to have initiated and maintained a much slower rate of problem solving while working in the context of the blue/RT screen immediately following the posting of instructions to work "quickly" in that context. Only 2 subjects in this group showed performance changes that coincided with the inaccurate instructions posted on the computer screen between cycles of the multiple schedule. It was not until the final session when instructions *accurately* described scheduled reinforcement contingencies that 5 of the 6 subjects in Group 2 came under the apparent influence of posted rules.

Implications

Shaping, in contrast to *instructing*, performance descriptions induced statistically reliable higher rates of correct problem solving during RT component and lower rates of problem solving during RR component of the multiple schedule. Group results were assessed in terms of single subject rate within each condition of the experiment. Six of the 12 subjects demonstrated sensitivity to scheduled consequences during the 16-min baseline phase of the experiment. However, these differential patterns of responding obtained during baseline were not predictive of the subjects' "sensitivity" to shaping or instructing performance descriptions. Independent of the level of differentiated responding achieved during baseline, most subjects in Group 1 performed in correspondence with the reinforcement they received while selecting performance descriptions of their own behavior.

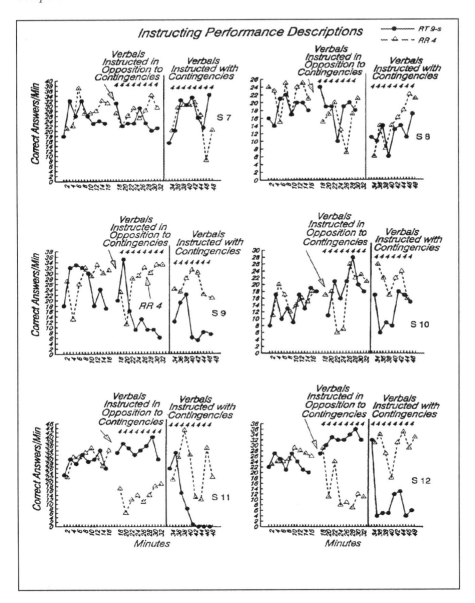

Figure 4.14. [Frequency of correct problems per minute and points earned for instructed performance descriptions for 6 subjects in Group 2. Instructing performance descriptions that were in opposition to scheduled reinforcement began after 16-min of baseline on the multiple RT RR schedule. In the following session, instruction of performance descriptions were consistent with scheduled reinforcement, as adapted from Ninness, Shore, and Ninness, 1999, p.638]

During computer interactions, shaping the selection of particular rules may lead our behavior in almost any direction. Again, our outcomes appear to run parallel to findings from the study of eyewitnesses who were given confirming "feedback" by authorities for incorrectly *selecting* innocent people from line-ups and photo spreads (Wells *et al.,* 1998). You may recall that witnesses were completely unaware of such influences and often had *inflated false confidence* in their mistaken identifications. Analogously, 5 of 6 subjects in Group 1 seemed to develop false confidence in the inaccurate rules they were differentially reinforced for selecting. Our subjects did not exhibit a false confidence as a function of reinforcement for identifying and subsequently testifying against innocent persons, but instead as a function of reinforcement for identifying inaccurate rules and subsequently performing math problems at rates that were inconsistent with accessing scheduled reinforcement. While the subjects in Group 1 did *not* display response patterns suggestive of interspecies replication during baseline, they all had baseline histories of performing at rates that were much more favorable with acquiring reinforcement in the context of the respectively colored screens. That most of these subjects were quickly shaped into performing in opposition to their present reinforcement histories stands as "testimony" to the false confidence they developed when reinforced for selecting fallacious rules.

Almost half a century ago, Greenspoon (1955) established that "unknowingly" adult human verbal behavior may come under the subtle control of shaping. Subsequently, Truax (1966) disclosed that the shaping of verbal behavior might play a veiled but critical role in therapist-patient interactions during what we know as non-directive therapy. The work of Catania et al. (1982 & 1989) isolated many of the factors related to this effect, but the potential for shifting human beliefs and performances by way of shaping verbal responding is only beginning to be recognized by applied psychologists. With the current wave of electronic information exchange in computer-interactive environments, an understanding of the variables that drive our judgments of "how and when to perform" could be invaluable. In fact, many of our most crucial judgments and performances may come down to the pressing of particular keys. The absolute impact of processes that shape our subjective "interpretations" of how and when to press these keys can hardly be overestimated. Again, we will note that although this study was conducted in a relatively "pure" computer-interactive environment, its outcome has strong implications for impacting the verbal behavior (and beliefs) of students with serious behavior problems (Chapter 6). The functionality of these procedures is not unlike procedures traditionally employed in the teaching of self-management to behaviorally disordered students. Such protocols often entail shaping selections of performance descriptors during the rehearsal of new social skills (see Ninness, Glenn, & Ellis, 1993, for a discussion). This strategy also has displayed effectiveness in the training of computer-interactive self-assessment procedures (Ninness et al., 1998). The following study on self-assessment as a learned reinforcer has similar preparations and implications.

SELF-ASSESSMENT AS A LEARNED REINFORCER: AN EXPERIMENTAL ANALYSIS

This section of the chapter addresses many of the same issues that we will revisit in Chapter 6. It is about a complex set of skills that has come to be described as "self-assessment." In common parlance, self-assessment is a learned skill that entails accurate verbal descriptions of one's own social or academic performance. Learning to correctly describe how well you are doing is an essential part of what is often called "self-control." Contrary to popular opinion though, people do not show strong academic motivation simply *because* they *have* self-control. As a summary term that describes a group of behaviors, the term "self-control" makes everyday sense; as an explanation for behavior, the term is useless in helping us solve practical problems.

One of the goals of education is that students be self-managers, but paradoxically, it is the academic and social environment that teaches the self-managing skills and identifies or specifies the behavior to be controlled. As we will point out again in Chapter 6, that is the only way the culture and its technology will be passed on to the next generation. Thus, it becomes clear that educators must somehow arrange the environment so that students will learn to assess and manage their own academic and social behavior, and the behavior that is self-assessed and self-managed will be that which the older, more experienced members of the culture designate as desirable-- reading, writing, calculating, speaking politely, cooperating to obtain group goals, playing games and musical instruments, etc. From our perspective, self-assessment is critical to every aspect of academic and social behavior.

Identifying the specific details of "behavior" involved in self-assessment is problematic since direct recordings of internal dialogue are not possible (Baer, 1984). Nevertheless, it seems apparent that external instructions interact with self-instructions and self-assessments as students generate rules regarding what they are doing and why they are doing it (Rosenfarb, Newland, Brannon, & Howey, 1992). The details of exactly what students actually say to themselves (and how they learn to say it) have been the basis for considerable argument in the literature (See Hayes, Zettle, et al., 1989). In this vein we recently conducted a study (Ninness, Ellis, &

Ninness, 1999) that attempted to determine if self-assessment could be learned in a computer-interactive environment. Our ambition was to try to identify some of the variables that influence a student's ability to correctly self-assess his or her own academic behavior. We were also interested in how learning self-assessment might function as a learned reinforcer and whether it might impact a student's potential for improved academic performance.

As in the previously described study involving superstitious math performance (Ninness & Ninness, 1998), students solved multiplication problems on a computer by typing answers on the keyboard. During this activity, reinforcement was delivered by way of a brief (.5-s) flashing message on the computer screen indicating the earning of one cent. Figure 4.15 suggests that during the pre-training experimental baseline conditions, the opportunity to self-assess and acquire accuracy feedback at 2-min intervals did not seem to promote much math problem-solving. Even though rates for 3 of the 4 subjects increased briefly, all 4 students quit the program within 5 min. Following a pre-experimental assessment of the students' maximum rate (asymptote) of solving math problems at the computer, an ABAB reversal design was employed.

During our baseline observations, earning money was not possible, but students were given an opportunity to self-assess their own math performance every 1-min. The computer provided accuracy feedback after every self-assessment. No other form of enticement was provided. At the beginning of the baseline session, the computer screen simply displayed the following message: "SCORE YOURSELF (4 to 1) ONLY WHEN THE COMPUTER ASKS, 4 = EXCELLENT SPEED & ACCURACY, 3 = GOOD SPEED & ACCURACY, 2 = FAIR SPEED & ACCURACY, 1 = POOR SPEED & ACCURACY. IF YOU SCORE YOURSELF CORRECTLY THE COMPUTER WILL TELL YOU. REMEMBER, NO MONEY CAN BE EARNED DURING THIS SESSION." Our software stipulates indexed math performance rates at or above 90% of each student's asymptote as a score of 4, 80% - 89% as a score of 3, 70% - 79% as score of 2, and 60% to 69% as a 1. Rates below 60% of the student's assessment asymptote were below all criteria for correct matches between student and computer.

Unbeknownst to the students, the computer program calculated the number of correct answers/min and kept a running record of the percentage of accurate student self-assessments. When and if the student correctly matched the computer's assessment, the word "RIGHT" appeared on the screen. If the self-assessment was inaccurate, "WRONG" appeared. Would this strategy alone be sufficiently inspiring to sustain long periods of rapid math performance? Take a look at Figure 4.15. Apparently, prior to training, opportunities to perform self-assessment, even with accuracy feedback from the computer, were not a strong source of motivation for our four students.

So now what? In the following training sessions, we put a little bait on the keyboard. This entailed a two-phase treatment plan. During *Training Phase 1*, the computer monitor displayed the following, somewhat more enticing, set of instructions: "IF YOU SCORE YOURSELF CORRECTLY YOU MAY EXCHANGE YOUR POINTS FOR PENNIES AFTER THE SESSION. PRESS ENTER IF YOU UNDERSTAND." Opportunities to self-assess were delivered at the end of every minute. Again, after each student's self-assessment that matched the computer's assessment, the word "RIGHT" appeared briefly; after an incorrect self-assessment, "WRONG" appeared. During this first treatment phase, each correct self-assessment was worth up to 4 cents--depending on how high the students scored their own behavior. This training strategy continued for 20-min sessions over two successive days, then we moved into a second level of training.

During *Training Phase 2*, we systematically faded the frequency of opportunities to self-assess by expanding the time intervals between self-assessments. The standard for widening each student's self-assessment interval was based on achieving correct problem solving/min at or above 90% of their pre-experimental performance (Fisher et al., 1996). If a student's performance sustained or improved during a given training session, the self-assessment interval was increased in the next session. Intervals were gradually extended to 1-min, 2-min, and 4-min. Student 1 needed an extra training session in order to move to the 4-min self-assessment interval; the other three students maintained their performance throughout the course of the three consecutive daily training sessions of the second training phase.

As the program progressed, our students continued swapping their self-assessment points for pennies at the end of each session, but all the while, they were obtaining ever diminishing financial returns for their efforts. In fact, by the time they attained the 4-min self-assessment interval, only five chances to self-assess were allowed. This rendered a maximum of only 20 cents for a high rate performance over a 20-min session. Evidently, by this time, money was no longer their primary source of motivation. But what was?

After training, we especially were interested in finding out if self-assessment with accuracy feedback (without financial reimbursement) was sufficient to function independently as a source of "secondary reinforcement." During this condition, the computer informed our students that self-assessments would no longer provide any financial earnings; however, it would continue displaying accuracy feedback for as long as they liked. On the screen the following message appeared: "IF YOU SCORE YOURSELF CORRECTLY THE COMPUTER WILL TELL YOU.

REMEMBER, NO MONEY CAN BE EARNED DURING THIS SESSION. PRESS ENTER IF YOU UNDERSTAND." The computer supplied a succession of multiplication problems, and students were given opportunities to self-assess and receive accuracy feedback every 2-min. Figure 5.1 suggests an obvious improvement after training. All four students exhibited higher rates of problem solving despite the fact that they were no longer earning money for performing math problems. But was it the self-assessment they had learned to like, or did they simply learn to enjoy doing math problems at the computer? There was one obvious way to find out!

In the subsequent reversal condition of the experiment, opportunities to self-assess were extracted from the program. The computer screen put our students on notice: "YOU MAY <u>NOT</u> SCORE YOURSELF OR EARN ANY MONEY DURING THIS SESSION. REMEMBER, IF YOU DO MATH PROBLEMS, YOU MAY NOT SCORE YOURSELF, AND YOU WILL NOT BE ABLE TO EARN ANY MONEY. PRESS ENTER IF YOU UNDERSTAND." The computer generated another succession of multiplication problems. Just as in the previous condition, problems popped up on the screen, one after another, but this time there was no chance for self-assessment. Figure 4.15 (reversal condition) seems to suggest that doing math problems, just for the fun of it, may not be a very entertaining activity, for at this point all math performance quickly dissipated. Well, what would happen if we put the opportunities to self-assess back into the program?

In the final condition of the experiment, opportunities to self-assess were reinstated. The computer advised our students that accurate self-assessments would not result in any financial benefits but that they could, once again, score their math performance and receive computer feedback regarding the accuracy of their self-assessments: "IF YOU SCORE YOURSELF CORRECTLY, THE COMPUTER WILL TELL YOU. REMEMBER, NO MONEY CAN BE EARNED DURING THIS SESSION. PRESS ENTER IF YOU UNDERSTAND." The final condition in Figure 4.15 suggests substantial improvement with high rates of continuous problem solving reestablished for 3 of the 4 students while self-assessing their behavior every 2-min.

Figure 4.16 shows us that computer-interactive self-assessment training was associated with improved *accuracy of self-assessments*. In fact, following training, all students demonstrated a clear improvement in the percentage accuracy of self-assessments, averaging above 90% correct self-assessments during the final post-training session.

We think that this computer interactive self-assessment study has a few important implications for interventions in natural and computer-interactive settings. By first accelerating students' opportunities to self-assess and concurrently providing financial incentives for improved *accuracy*, the "value" of *correct self-assessment* was augmented. Next, gradually fading the students' opportunities to self-assess provided a method of sustaining the high rates of academic performance in the face of progressively lower levels of compensation. After such a training history on the computer, some students may find that just the opportunity to self-assess and receive accuracy feedback was sufficiently rewarding to support continued work on this program. Thus, it appears that the opportunity to perform academic work on the computer and then have the opportunity to describe how well you have done may *acquire* reinforcing properties independent of "tangible" compensation. In the Chapter 6 we will show how similar preparations in natural environments may benefit the social and academic behavior of student with severe behavior problems.

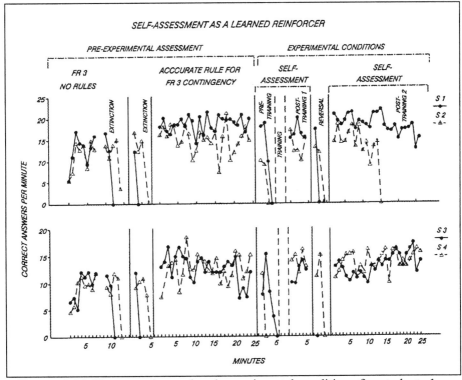

Figure 4.15. [Pre-experimental and experimental conditions for students 1 through 4, as adapted from Ninness, Ellis, and Ninness, 1999, p.412]

Improved Accuracy of Self-Assessment

It seems *unlikely* to us that our students simply gave themselves a numerical score with each self-assessment. We might speculate that over the course of repeated trials, the students "covertly" described the contingencies of self-assessment to themselves as they gave themselves a numerical self-assessment. Informal discussions with our students following the experiment supported this assumption. Indeed, it is hard to imagine anyone self-assessing (on a scale of 1 to 4) without employing additional descriptions of how well or poorly they were doing. As Skinner (1969) pointed out, "Even fragmentary descriptions of contingencies speed the acquisition of effective terminal behavior, help to maintain the behavior over a period of time, and reinstate it when forgotten" (p. 143).

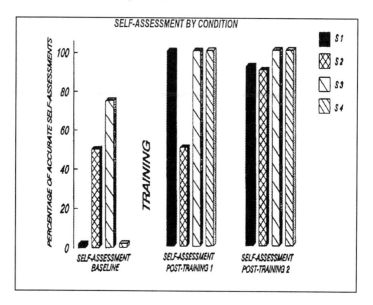

Figure 4.16. [Percentage of accurate self-assessments during baseline and posttraining conditions, as adapted from Ninness, Ellis, and Ninness, 1999, p.414]

SELF-ASSESSMENT WITH AND WITHOUT FEEDBACK

It has been suggested that providing intermittent feedback to students may be the best way to facilitate and sustain the self-assessment process (Fatuzzo & Rohrbeck, 1992). Nevertheless, the question arises from our previous research as to whether intermittent computer feedback really was a necessary feature for keeping the self-assessment process working as a strong source of reinforcement. Perhaps, after learning to self-assess, this process might maintain itself independent of any form of intermittent feedback from the computer. Maybe we could develop something of a "perpetual motion" self- reinforcement system? That is, maybe we could develop a self-sustaining reinforcement system that would require no contact with external events. (See Malott et al., 2000 for a discussion of perpetual motion in behavior analysis) It would be fascinating and even elegant if we could teach students to self-assess, gradually fade out all supporting computer feedback, and yet sustain the high level of academic work generated by our students.

As a matter of fact, several early studies have shown that feedback might not be a necessary. For example, Broden, Hall, and Mitts (1971) demonstrated that all that was necessary to improve the academic performance of one student was to simply have her self-record her own on-task behavior at various unscheduled times throughout the school day. In a similar study by Glynn, Thomas, & Shee (1973), on-task behaviors increased dramatically independent of accuracy feedback. These applied researchers had eight second-grade students place a check on a prepared data sheet at irregular intervals if they were on-task at the moment a beeper sounded. Independent observers reported that 76 percent of the students' self-assessed, on-task recordings agreed with those of trained observers. Another study found that improved academic accuracy or academic productivity was related to self-monitoring even when no feedback for correct self-recordings was provided (Maag, Reid, and DiGangi, 1993). These findings appear to support the *perpetual-motion self-assessment possibility.* On the other hand, other researchers have suggested that some sort of external feedback regarding the accuracy of self-assessment may be a very important feature (Van Houten, 1984). Connell, Carta, and Baer (1993) noted that the academic engagement of students was improved with self-assessment and accuracy feedback.

In our previous self-assessment study (Ninness, Ellis, & Ninness, 1999), we made no attempt to isolate the effects of feedback independent of self-assessment. And, at least in terms of human-computer interactions, the role of feedback in supporting accurate self-assessment and motivation to perform was unresolved (Malott, 1986; Newman, Buffington, Hemmes & Rosen, 1996; Skinner & Smith, 1992). For us, the computer feedback question seemed to be begging for a design (see Gettinger, 1985). By now, this was a study we could not resist. Thus, we developed the following study (Ninness et al., 1998) to investigate the effects of computer interactive self-assessments *with* and *without accuracy feedback.*

Our Perpetual Motion Self-Assessment Machine

This experiment was designed very much like our self-assessment experiment above; however, we developed a special strategy to train and evaluate the effects of self-assessment in the complete absence of all external reinforcement or even accuracy feedback from the computer. Essentially, this study was aimed at training students to perpetually perform math problems in the complete absence of external support.

As in the previous experiment, four regular education students participated and performed all experimental sessions during the regular school day in their homeroom. Additionally, two students identified as behaviorally disordered who also participated performed within their self-contained social adjustment class. IBM compatible computers connected to laser printers were utilized for all experimental conditions.

Following a pre-experimental assessment of our students' pre-treatment rate of doing math problems on the computer, we arranged a somewhat unique A-BC-D-BC withdrawal of treatment design (Hersen & Barlow, 1976). This is a fairly complex single-subject design that allowed us to see how students would perform *with* and *without feedback*. Following baseline (A), we ran a series of computer-interactive self-assessment tutorial programs. Then, in the BC phase, we tested the effects of self-assessment training *without feedback* (B) and *with feedback* (C). During the reversal phase (D) we gave students opportunities to perform math problems on the computer; however, this time there were *no opportunities for self-assessment* (with or without feedback). In the last phase of the study, we returned to the BC conditions. Here, once again, students were provided opportunities to self-assess with (B) and without (C) accuracy feedback from the computer. All of this was necessary to determine whether or not our students could learn the "pure" value of self-assessment and thus sustain their high rates of problem solving in the complete absence of any form of feedback.

Self-Assessment Tutorials: Three Phases

During the baseline sessions, students were given the chance to self-assess at 2-min intervals. During this condition, self-assessment was accompanied by accuracy feedback. At the beginning of the session, the computer screen displayed the following message: "THE COMPUTER WILL TELL YOU IF YOU HAVE SCORED YOURSELF CORRECTLY, BUT YOU WILL NOT EARN ANY MONEY [OR OTHER REWARDS] FOR SCORING YOURSELF CORRECTLY. PRESS ENTER IF YOU UNDERSTAND."

Then the tutorial programs began. During these training sessions, students were advised (by the computer) to score themselves on a scale ranging from 1 to 4. Just as we used in the previous experiment (Ninness, Ellis, & Ninness, 1999), 4 indicated perfect performance and so on.

At the beginning of each tutorial session, the computer screen posted the following instructions: "IF YOU SCORE YOURSELF CORRECTLY, YOU MAY EXCHANGE YOUR POINTS FOR AN EQUAL NUMBER OF PENNIES [OR OTHER REWARDS] AFTER THE SESSION. PRESS ENTER IF YOU UNDERSTAND." Although students were informed as to *how fast* they had performed math problems during the pre-experimental session, they were not specifically told of the particular problem/min requirement that corresponded with each point on the Lykert scale.

Student self-assessments that matched the computer's calculations resulted in the screen displaying the word, "RIGHT" for .5-s; non-matching self-assessments resulted in the screen strobing the words, "THE CORRECT ANSWER IS [correct answer]." for 1-s. After the session, the total number of correct self-assessment points were exchanged for pennies, and the student's average correct answers/min was printed. This outcome was then used in setting the students' individual response criteria for the next tutorial session. The students' self-assessment standards for scoring speed and accuracy were gradually raised as they performed problems more quickly. When students reached 90% correct self-assessment and 90% of their required correct problems/min for at least 3 consecutive training sessions, they moved to the next phase of the tutorial program. Tutorials lasted for approximately 20-min each day (or semi-daily) over a period of 3 to 4 weeks.

Students in the self-contained classrooms performed under slightly different conditions. Rather than pennies, these students exchanged their points for tangible (e.g., cokes or comic books) or activity-based (e.g., free-time or games) reinforcers. Because these two students functioned at a lower level of math proficiency, they required additional training sessions before advancing through each tutorial phase with the tutorial sessions occurring over a period of about 2 months. Although these students advanced through the self-assessment tutorials more slowly than the regular education students, their individualized criteria for advancing through the tutorials was the same.

During training Phase 1 (shaping self-assessments), the program enabled students to evaluate their own performances at the end of every 2-min interval. Students were differentially reinforced (*shaped*) for correctly identifying their own performances in the preceding 2 min. In Phase 2 (leaning self-assessments), the number of opportunities to self-assess was gradually leaned (Mace, Brown, & West, 1987) by expanding self-assessment intervals from 2-min, to 4-min, and, finally, 8-min in duration (Fisher et al., 1996). Finally, in Phase 3 (terminating feedback), students were again given opportunities to self-assess their math performances at 2-min, 4-min, and 8-min intervals, respectively. However, during these tutorial sessions, the computer did not furnish any accuracy feedback of self-assessments. Correct self-assessment points were still tallied by the computer and exchanged for an equal number of pennies (or tangible/activity-based reinforcers). Thus, in this condition, students had no way of knowing how many points they had earned until the session was concluded.

Data in Figure 4.17 seem to progress the theory that computer-interactive tutorials may provide a vehicle to substantiate self-assessment as a learned reinforcer while enhancing academic performance in the absence of exchange for financial or tangible/activity-based reinforcement. Furthermore, these outcomes provided that the *rules* regarding correct self-assessment gradually become somewhat more effective following a particular history. Hayes, Zettle, and Rosenfarb (1989) proposed that a rule that functions to increase the reinforcing effectiveness of a given event is an *augmental*. However, Hayes, Zettle, et al. added that "...it is not clear how various psychological processes could combine to produce augmenting, even after the rule is understood." (p. 207). Perhaps, elements of the training history acquired by our tutorials recommend one format by which this process might occur.

Phase 1 tutorial programs increased student opportunities to self-assess and provided *differentially reinforced approximations* of correct matches between student and computer assessments. This process may have established the initial value of *correct self-assessment* as a reinforcing activity. Phase 2 tutorial programs gradually enlarged the intervals between opportunities to self-assess and allowed us to lean the density of reinforcement per problem while maintaining the relative value of feedback for correct self-assessments. In Phase 3 there was no accuracy feedback from the computer but there was continued compensation based on the accuracy of self-assessments. Following this particular history the words, "YOU MAY SCORE YOURSELF...," may have served as a rule that increased the reinforcing effectiveness of self-assessment--especially, when the rule advised the students that accuracy feedback was forthcoming.

Upon completing these tutorials, students were gauged in terms of their rate and duration of performing math problems while self-assessing their own performances *without and with* accuracy feedback in the absence of financial (or tangible/activity-based) compensation. We had anticipated that Phase 3 of our tutorial program would set up the reinforcing effects of self-assessment independent of accuracy feedback. However, our data only

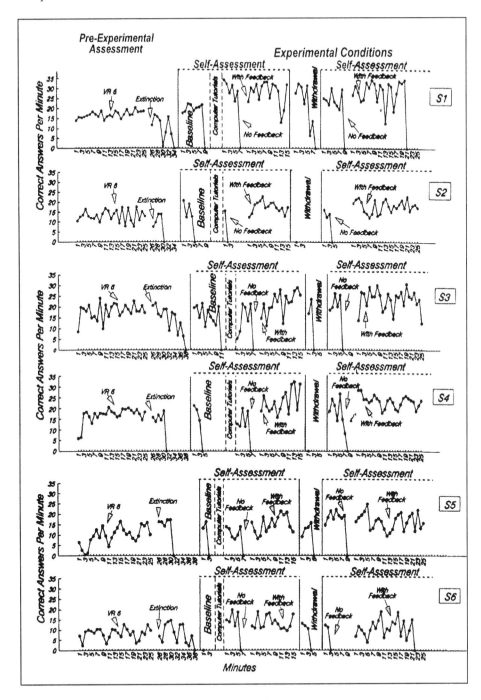

Figure 4.17. [Pre-experimental and experimental conditions for Subjects 1 through 6, as adapted from Ninness, Ninness, Sherman, and Schotta, 1998, p.609]

showed very limited support for this outcome. While Subjects 1, 3, 4, and 5 demonstrated elevations in their rates of responding following tutorials, their *enthusiasm* for performing multiplication problems *while self-assessing without feedback* was short-lived. All students terminated responding within 7-min during the first experimental condition that began by advising students that they would not be given accuracy feedback or compensation while performing math problems. However, the next experimental session in which students were given opportunities to engage in self-assessment and receive accuracy feedback from the computer was sufficiently *enticing* to support relatively higher rates and longer durations of math behavior.

During the withdrawal condition, math performance quickly diminished across students when we removed all occasions for self-assessment. Opportunities to self-assess did not appear to "reinvigorate" their enthusiasm until the computer displayed the rule stating it would provide *accuracy feedback for correct self-assessment* of math performance. While our tutorial programs seem to have *augmented* the effectiveness of rules regarding the opportunity to *self-assess with feedback*, this was not true of rules that described opportunities to *self-assess without feedback*. Clearly, some form of intermittent feedback seems to be critical to long-term maintenance of our self-assessment strategy. These findings are consistent with outcomes from many applied settings in which termination of feedback for correct self-assessment resulted in withdrawal of self-managed behaviors (e.g., Smith, Nelson, Young, & West, 1992).

As Malott et al. (2000) point out, "Everyone wants the perpetual-motion machine, but no perpetual-motion machine exists." (p. 441). Malott et al. forward the following poignant commentary on perpetual-behavior intervention, "Behaviorists often get sucked into their own similar futile quest. Behaviorists search for the perpetual-behavior intervention: **You modify the behavior, the modified behavior maintains itself, and you never have to deliver another behavioral consequence.** That's the myth of perpetual behavior." (p. 441). Based on our above findings, we could not agree more! Nevertheless, there is quite a bit to be said for the beneficial effects of *self-assessment with feedback*.

Accuracy of Self-Assessments

Tutorial training had a favorable influence on the *precision of student self-assessments with accuracy feedback*. While Subjects 2 and 4 produced 100% accurate self-assessments throughout baseline, Figure 4.18 illustrates that Subject 1 obtained 50% accurate self-assessment, and that Subjects 3, 5 and 6 were inaccurate throughout all baseline self-assessments. After 3 to 4 weeks of training, students illustrated noticeable progress in the percentage of accurate self-assessments. The final experimental condition is the most striking. Although Subject 5 achieved only 50% accuracy during the *self-assessment without feedback condition*, he was 100% accurate during the *self-assessment with feedback condition*. Moreover, 5 of the 6 students obtained 100% correct self-assessment throughout the duration of this final session.

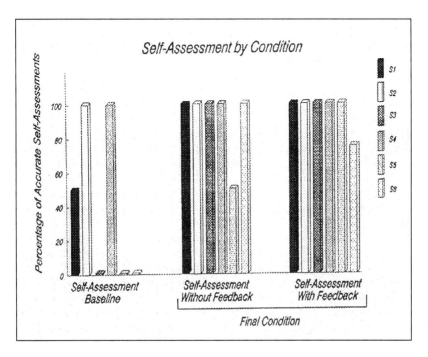

Figure 4.18. [Percentages of accurate self-assessments during baseline and the second experimental condition for Subjects 1 through 6, as adapted from Ninness, Ninness, Sherman, and Schotta, 1998, p.611]

Maybe, this should not be so surprising. Dickinson (1989) points out that all forms of *self-motivated behavior* may be rooted in some form of social exchange. She adds that behavior that is intrinsically reinforcing is often a form of learned reinforcement which has been established by approval from others. The reinforcing value of such rules may become strengthened by the individual's coming to understand and manipulate the environment, but the environment usually persists as, at least, an occasional source of acknowledgement.

Following the experiment, students were questioned as to why they had stopped solving problems during the *self-assessment without feedback* condition and why they had continued performing during the *self-assessment with feedback condition.* Subject 3 remarked, "doing problems and not knowing how well I was doing got very boring." When asked why he had performed when the computer gave him feedback, he said, "the whole thing got to be more like a game." The other students all provided answers that reflected essentially the same theme. It is interesting to note, however, that these students did not appear to "enjoy this game" until after they had finished the tutorial process.

The Behaviorally Disordered Students

Importantly, this process seems to have been as effective with students identified as behaviorally disordered as it was with regular education students. Although both behaviorally disordered students began at lower rates of correct problems/min and lower levels of self-assessment accuracy, they both demonstrated substantial progress subsequent to tutorial training. This was especially apparent in the case of Subject 5 who almost doubled his rate of correct problems/min and tripled the number of minutes he continued to perform math problems in the absence of tangible reinforcement. Even though Subject 6 did not achieve such overwhelming gains, he clearly benefited from learning to self-assess his own performance.

These results may have implications for self-assessment strategies in applied settings. Shaping rule-following behavior regarding self-assessment procedures appeared to generalize across time *only when* supported by some level of feedback. Chapter 6 places considerable emphasis on using self-assessment as a vehicle for developing generalization across settings and across time. Outcomes from this study will prove very useful in understanding how and why self-assessment with feedback blends with the teaching of social skills to behaviorally disordered students.

IN SUMMARY

This chapter has reviewed some of the classic and current literature from analogues to direct-acting contingencies such as instructional control, superstitious behavior, stimulus equivalence, and computer-interactive behavior. We have pointed out that schedules of reinforcement may function quite differently in humans than infrahumans.

Current research (e.g., Rosenfarb et al., 1992) suggests that students often develop rules in accordance with the circumstances in which they find themselves. As their environments change, so do their rules and their behaviors. With this contemporary perspective on rule-governed behavior and direct-acting contingencies, we are better positioned to consider problem behaviors as they occur under the influence of various school conditions. First, Chapter 5 provides a system for functionally assessing the conditions that evoke problem behaviors. Then, Chapter 6 shows how these functional assessment outcomes may be used to develop effective and efficient intervention systems.

Chapter 5

COMPUTER-INTERACTIVE FUNCTIONAL ASSESSMENTS

You may have some recollection of a young track star who had an intense fear of flowers. In Chapter I, Nelda Hudson had come to Larry Pritchard, a school psychology intern, at the behest of one of her teachers. Nelda had no clue as to why she felt such intense anxiety and trepidation upon encountering sunflowers--of all things. Her fear was "totally irrational and without logical foundation," she had told herself many times. Nelda was a very logical person, but her irrational panic was real, as real as the auto accident she had nearly caused when suddenly trying to avert coming close to a cluster of sunflowers on the highway. Clearly, her phobia was getting out of control, and something had to be done.

Larry listened to Nelda's explanation of her "condition." At first, he thought the whole thing was some kind of bizarre high school prank. Maybe, Nelda thought it was "time to tease the new shrink." But with Nelda's description of sunflowers came the recognition of her sincerity. And while she had no specific recall of how or when she had first become so terrified of these plants, she could not remember a time when she could tolerate being anywhere near them. At the recommendation of Dr. Manning, Larry's supervisor, Nelda was administered a traditional psychological assessment battery. She responded to a personality inventory, a series of questionnaires, and a thematic apperception test. She answered a long series of questions about herself and her family history. She drew pictures of various designs as well as producing sketches of herself and her various family members. Finally, she found herself trying to describe what she thought she saw in the peculiar patterns of ink blots. None of this was making Nelda feel any better about sunflowers, and increasingly, she was coming to believe that psychologists and their methods were more than a little mystical.

Nelda's personality assessment was eventually scored. It was noted that she actually made reference to a sun flower while describing a particular amorphous ink blot.

Dr. Manning shook her head, "This could be serious!"

"But most of her responses look pretty standard," Larry objected.

"Exactly my point," said Dr. Manning, "That's usually a very bad sign." continuing to shake her head.

Nelda immediately was referred to Dr. Hamilton for more intensive psychological assessment, evaluation, and "interpretation." So it goes.

CONSTRUCTS

As previously described in Ninness et al. (1993) and Ninness, Ellis, et al. (1999), traditional assessment strategies use standardized testing procedures such as behavior rating scales, projective techniques, personality inventories, and drawings in an attempt to develop "psychological constructs." In common parlance, these psychological constructs are roughly equivalent to personality characteristics or traits. In psychological testing, constructs are based on clusters of answers to test questions that are standardized on large samples of subjects. Certain types of answers are highly correlated with those produced by individuals who actually demonstrate particular types of maladaptive behavior. The predictive validity of personality assessment is predicated on statistical correlations between specific test profiles and the incidence of people showing the same profiles and who manifest various forms of maladaptive behavior. However, it is generally understood that correlations do not prove causation (Hopkins, Hopkins, & Glass, 1996). At best, correlations are only preliminary indicators of the way in which certain types of measures may be associated.

With the use of these instruments, personality traits, characteristics, and attributes are further refined into diagnostic categories. However, unlike standardized intellectual or medical assessments, no "real" maladaptive behavior is actually seen by the examiner. Rather, the examinee's diagnosis is inferred from answers to test items that are produced during the course of the person's assessment. If the examinee's profile matches those of others who have behaved "badly," so much the worse for the examinee. It will be assumed that he/she is very likely to behave in a similar fashion. This will be inferred despite the fact that the reliability and validity of such testing procedures has long been understood to be inadequate (e.g., Anastasi, 1968; Sattler, 1992).

In a circumstance in which a student is referred for psychological assessment based on his/her well documented record of frequently performing unnecessary, risky, and inappropriate behaviors, we may find that this student agrees with personality test statements suggesting that it is "fun to take risks" and that "most rules are silly." A few agreements with test statements such as these, and the referred student probably will score very high on the "impulsivity scale." The student has correctly identified and reported his own behavior. His pattern of agreements and disagreements with various test items is correlated with other individuals who agree with the same statements and who happen to show particular types of problem behaviors. This same student may respond to a projective technique in the form of an amorphous ink blot with a comment such as "that's two rams colliding head-on." Again, such a statement is correlated with those made by people who demonstrate inappropriate and impulsive behaviors--again, so much the worse for the examinee. This is more evidence that he/she is likely to do the same. The forthcoming diagnostic description of the child represents a statistical version of "guilt by association," but it does not explain the student's problem behavior. It only gives the referral question (Why is this student continually talking without permission or continually out of his/her seat?) a more interesting and technical sounding label--"High Impulsivity."

To write a psychological report indicating that a student is spontaneously disruptive in class because he has "poor impulse control" is equivalent to suggesting that a maladaptive behavior by a given label is caused by that label. Moreover, determining that a student behaves impulsively because he/she "has poor impulse control" obscures any functional analysis of the variables that interact with the student's problem behavior by advancing a circular logic built on pseudoscientific jargon. In fairness, these personality instruments may be useful in developing a very general and preliminary description of the way a person "might" behave. But a more reasonable commentary regarding someone who agrees with personality inventory statements such as, "most rules are stupid," and who also describes ink blots performing impetuous activities is simply "this person may be at risk for demonstrating impulsive behaviors."

Independent of supercilious diagnostic codes, labels, or constructs, the person charged with developing an intervention plan must still identify when, where, and why the referred student performs problem behaviors in the classroom and throughout the school. This requires ascertaining the real world conditions under which the student is most likely to display various forms of the problem behavior, the conditions under which he/she is less likely to do so, and what the target behavior looks like when it occurs.

To reiterate, the questionnaires, projective tests, personality inventories, and rating scales may establish the existence of a general category of problem behavior. But, finding that a student has a learning disability, a personality disorder, or an attention deficit hyperactive disorder does not tell us enough to enable us to design an effective intervention. Unless we can do more than classify problems into important sounding categories, we may be unable to justify the time and expense of assessment. In order to design efficient and effective intervention plans, we will need to reliably identify 1) the specific conditions in which the problem is most likely to occur, 2) how frequently it occurs, 3) what happens in the environment immediately before and after it occurs, and 4) what is its effect on the behavior of other students and the teacher in that setting. Unless we understand how these and other variables interact with the child's behavior, we will be very unlikely to provide a useful behavior intervention plan.

FUNCTIONAL ASSESSMENT

Behavioral school psychologists have employed their grounding in behavioral processes to develop a specialized technology for assessing problem behaviors in experimental and natural settings. Rather than personality tests and projective techniques, direct observers serve as "transducers between the behavior and the record of that behavior" (Repp, Roberts, Slack, Repp, & Berkler, 1976, p. 501). This chapter will introduce and define the functional analysis and functional assessment of maladaptive behavior, provide a brief review the current literature, and review the public schools' attempt to incorporate this system within special education and psychological services. In addition, we will look at a computer interactive strategy to facilitate functional assessment called Functional Observation of Classrooms And Learners (FOCAL Point).

The common function of functional assessments and functional analyses is to reliably identify particular antecedent and/or consequent events that interact with and sustain maladaptive behaviors (Iwata, Dorsey, Slifer, Bauman, & Richman, 1982). In the past two decades, this procedure has become one of the most powerful and controversial individual assessment procedures in school psychology and behavior analysis. Furthermore, Steege (1999) points out that functional assessment procedures have been recognized as critical features for implementation of effective treatment plans for students/children with serious behavior problems by

Association for Behavior Analysis (Right to Effective Treatment, 1989) and the National Institute of Health (NIH Conference Report, 1989).

Steege goes on to suggest that functional assessment "…is a student-centered and empathic assessment model. An empathic relationship with the student and his or her support network is a fundamental aspect of behavioral assessments and interventions. Moreover, as scientist-practitioners, behavior analysts *care* enough about the student to offer reliable and valid assessment methodologies. We collect reliable and socially meaningful data, test our hypotheses, design individualized habilitative interventions and systematically evaluate the effectiveness of these interventions." (p. 14).

Unfortunately, the terms functional assessment and/or functional analysis also have become increasingly "generic." To make matters worse, the law does not state what a functional assessment actually entails. IDEA simply asserts that schools must conduct a functional behavioral assessment and implement a behavior intervention plan for children who violate school rules or codes of conduct either before or not later than 10 days after disciplinary action is taken. Within public schools, the procedural details have become so vague, inconsistent, all encompassing, and ambiguous that the term seems to mean everything and nothing to everybody who claims to be conducting this method of assessment. Moreover, the United States Department of Education currently has no plans of defining these terms (Paul Steenen, personal communication, June 1999). Given the current state of administrative, legal, and bureaucratic revision and diversified reinterpretations of this classic procedure, the reader might benefit from a few points of clarification.

Analogs as Simulations of the Natural Environment

Functional analysis procedures were initially developed in the 1980's beginning with the work of Iwata and his associates (Repp, 1994). They are based on the belief that behavior serves a purpose for the individual and is maintained by certain environmental conditions. Thus, the assessment procedures attempt to ascertain the variables for which the behavior is a function. Historically, a functional analysis procedure entails constructing, in controlled environments, analog conditions which simulate how problem behaviors are being reinforced in the natural environment (Umbreit, 1995). During simulations or analogs, changes in targeted behaviors are recorded as various antecedent and consequent conditions are systematically presented and withdrawn contingent on the escalation of maladaptive behaviors (Fisher *et al.,* 1995). Most researchers reserve the term extended functional analysis to refer to the more rigorous experimental methodology of simulating natural environments (analogs) in which antecedents and consequence are systematically presented and withdrawn contingent on increases in targeted behaviors. Certainly, the vast majority of studies that employ extended functional analyses have been conducted in university affiliated hospital settings with the help of highly trained professional and academic staff.

Extended functional analysis entails objective data collection of target behaviors and demonstrates high levels of internal validity. And, even though the system has high precision, it is rarely used in cases involving low rate problem behaviors or behaviors that are potentially dangerous to others or potentially illegal. Extended functional analysis procedures usually entail at least 4 (and sometimes 5 or 6) analog conditions within simulated experimental settings (session rooms). The session rooms are specifically structured to approximate the environments in which the child may demonstrate various maladaptive behaviors. Sessions usually require at least 10 min to run, and each of the analog conditions is presented in a randomly assigned sequence 10 times over at least 40 sessions. The functional analysis literature reveals five analogs that are particularly valuable in assessing behaviorally disordered and developmentally disabled children. These include, but are not limited to the following: a) demand, b) social attention, c) toy play, d) alone, and e) tangible (Iwata, et al., 1982; Iwata et al., 1994).

Demand

It has been found that a large number of behaviorally disordered and developmentally delayed children initiate maladaptive behaviors in an attempt to escape or avoid complying with instructions provided by adults. During this analog, requests are continually presented according to verbal, gestural, and physical prompts every 10 s. That is, if the child does not follow the verbal request, a gestural prompt is invoked. (The therapist models the requested behavior for the client.) If the child does not follow the gestural prompt s/he is physically guided through the requested task. If a problem behavior occurs at any time during the presentation of demand, the experimenter/therapist immediately desists; however, a new request begins within 10 s of allowing the child to escape the previous demand. Repeatedly simulating these instructional demands in a session room allows the behavior analyst to confirm or disconfirm this circumstance as one variable interacting with child's problem behavior.

Social Attention

This analog grew out of the empirical observation that behaviorally disordered children often exhibit problem behaviors in an apparent attempt to solicit social attention from nearby peers or adults. This possibility is assessed during an analog in which the client is given free access to preferred toys in the session room in the presence of a therapist who is reading a book (or otherwise involved in a solitary activity of some form). However, in the event that the child performs some maladaptive behavior while playing, the therapist provides an immediate verbal reprimand. Studies have demonstrated that particular children exhibit gradually accelerating rates of serious destructive responding under the influence of verbal reprimands (e.g., Fisher, Piazza, Zarcone, O'Conner, & Ninness, 1995).

Toy Play

This analog is often employed as a control condition. Here the therapist simply plays with the client and gives brief response-independent social reinforcement at the end of every 30 s interval. This condition frequently has been employed to assess the degree to which the child may behave maladaptively or appropriately under fairly optimal conditions

Alone

Many developmentally disabled children have learned self-injurious behaviors that are sustained as a function of endogenous opiates released during severe tissue damage (Cataldo & Harris, 1982). In order to test this hypothesis, the client is left alone in the session room; however, s/he is well covered in protective apparel to preclude the possibility of actually self-inflicting any real physical harm.

Tangible (Toy Removal)

Much the same as in the social attention analog, it has been observed that many children have learned to access desired objects or events by initiating a tantrum. To test this hypothesis, the client is permitted to play with a preferred toy (or other highly preferred item) for 1 min. The therapist takes the toy away and returns it for 20 s only if the child exhibits any targeted problem behaviors. Toys are repeatedly removed and returned contingent on the occurrence of maladaptive behaviors.

In the Literature

It is interesting to note that Iwata et al. (1994) extensively reviewed 152 emotionally/behaviorally disordered and developmentally disabled children who had well documented histories of self-injurious behavior (SIB). This retrospective analysis revealed that 38.1% of the clients showed increased SIB during demand analogs. Social attention analogs or other variations of positive reinforcement accounted for 26.3% problem behaviors, and self-stimulating reinforcement maintained another 25.7%. Various combinations of these same analogs accounted for only 5.3% of the maladaptive behaviors. Important to point out is the fact that this form of rigorous functional analysis was able to reliably identify the controlling variables pertaining to SIB in all but 4.6% of the cases reviewed. Such dramatic findings are literally unprecedented in the history of psychology and behavior analysis.

To cite only a few of the multitude of examples from the literature, functional analysis has been employed to identify specific consequences that previously maintained target behaviors that can be transformed into procedures for learning prosocial and adaptive behaviors (Carr & Durand, 1985; Steege, Wacker, Berg, Cigrand, & Cooper, 1989; Hagopian et al., 1994). Functional analysis is used to ascertain extinction procedures for aggressive and destructive behaviors (e.g., Iwata, Pace, Kalsher, et al., 1990). Recently, customized analogs have simulated clients' unusual reinforcement histories and clearly identified the types of consequences associated with these unusual histories (Piazza, Fisher, Hagopian, Boman, & Toole, 1996). Functional analysis has demonstrated a facility for identifying variables relating to maladaptive verbal behavior. For example, Mace, Webb, Sharkey, Mattson, and Rosen (1988) performed a functional analysis of schizophrenic behaviors exhibited by a woman during controlled analog conditions. Maladaptive comments escalated under conditions in which contingent attention was provided and when task demands were terminated following the occurrence of bizarre comments. Durrand and Crimmins (1987) have used analogs to show how contingent termination of demands were associated with escalating rates of bizarre verbalizations by a 9-year-old autistic boy.

Functional assessments are being employed in a widening population that now includes normal functioning students with serious behavior problems (Dunlap, Kern, Clarke, Robbins, 1993; O'Neil, Horner, Albin,

Sprague, Story, & Newton, 1997). In public school settings, analogs now include the presentation of academic requests by teachers (Carr, Newson, & Binkoff, 1976) and peer social attention (Carr & Durrand, 1985). The list of important outcomes goes on and on (see Neef & Iwata, 1994 for a review). Moreover, multiple law suits are pending and have been brought against school districts that fail to implement appropriate FBA and behavior plans for students with disabilities (Jones & Jones, 1998).

Ironically, the term, *functional assessment*, has been "revised" to suggest an assortment of preliminary data collection strategies for conducting *functional analysis*. (Note that even in the behavioral literature the two terms are often used interchangeably.) In the early literature, the term functional assessment was used to describe the initial stages of developing hypotheses for analogs to be later tested in the actual functional analysis. However, at some point it was determined that functional assessments alone were sufficient for certain settings. Moreover, preliminary functional assessments are comparatively easy to conduct and the strategy acquires a certain amount of face validity by virtue of its association with the extended functional analysis literature. Unfortunately, functional assessment procedures, as they are currently practiced in many school districts, show an extremely wide range of integrity and reliability.

PUBLIC SCHOOLS' INTERPRETATIONS OF FUNCTIONAL ASSESSMENTS

Perhaps due to the influence of research on the effectiveness of functional analysis, the general acceptance of the functional assessment strategy found its way into the Individuals with Disabilities Education Act Amendments (IDEA) of 1997. As part of the assistive technology service (Sec 602, 2, A), in order to increase, maintain, or improve the functional capabilities of a child with a disability the law includes a "functional evaluation of the child in the child's customary environment." In Sec 614(b)(2)(A) it is stated that the local education agency should include relevant functional information as part of the variety of assessment tools and strategies to determine a disability or to develop the individualized education program (IEP). As a behavior management tool, functional behavioral assessment (FBA) is discussed in Sec 615(k)(1)(B)(i) under Authority of School Personnel. It is mandated that the IEP team implement behavioral interventions, strategies and supports if the student with disabilities manifests serious behavior problems. Public schools are mandated to perform an FBA if they move toward placing a student with disabilities in an alternative setting for 10 days, or remove a child from his current placement and into an alternative setting for a period not to exceed 45 days. It is stated that if a FBA was not conducted prior or within 10 days for a behavior that results in a suspension, then an IEP must be convened to develop an intervention plan based on functional assessment.

Public schools appear to be responding to the IDEA mandate. However, the lack of guidance in IDEA in proper use of functional assessment is reflected in the inconsistent methodology and rigor in the format used by schools. Systematic procedures are central to effective functional analysis procedures in the foundation literature. However, depending upon the sophistication of the particular functional assessment strategies employed and the training of those who employ them, functional assessments have demonstrated everything from highly refined and efficient analyses of behavior problems to wasteful, time-consuming, paper trails that do nothing more than exacerbate the existing bureaucratic and procedural demands placed on school psychologists and related professionals. A look at samples of functional assessments used by public schools illustrates the disparity between the true functional assessment methodology and what many schools currently use in response to the federal mandate.

ABC Formats

One example uses what has typically been called an ABC Analysis. This is a narrative analysis form with four columns in which to record informal observations. The observer records relevant information concerning setting events, antecedents, behavior, and consequences. For setting events, information is recorded concerning physical elements of the setting, the child's health, and other potential environmental events such as occurrences before school. For antecedents, the observer records information about what is occurring immediately prior to the behavior such as who is present, the ongoing activity, and actions by others. For behavior, the target student's specific actions and verbalizations are listed. For consequent events, what the teacher and others say or do is recorded. This system has been used for decades as a very preliminary step in developing functional assessment analogs.

Defining Tasks

Another functional assessment used by schools involves defining the tasks of the classroom teacher and the school counselor. The teacher's job of data gathering is to review the student's file and to meet with parent, prior teacher, and the child to brainstorm and provide insight. In addition, the teacher should make sure the discipline folder is current, keep anecdotal records using functional analysis sheets, and assess academic skills. The school counselor's job in this assessment is to begin seeing the child regularly and to meet with the teacher and parents on new strategies.

File Review and Narrative Descriptions

Other schools have adopted published or commercially available functional assessment forms. In one example, the school district incorporated an example published in a journal. This form calls for a review of files and a three line description of behaviors by school staff, three lines for the parent(s)' description, and a three line summary. There is also a list of possible preceding events and following events where the assessor checks possibilities and gives a one line description of each.

Checklists and Worksheets

One commercially available functional assessment targeting public school usage incorporates a behavior rating checklist, a mental health screening, an assessment of interpersonal strengths and weaknesses, and a behavior worksheet. The worksheet is completed by the school psychologist and requires a description of the behavior, its severity, and its function. Possible functions include communication, attention-getting, seeking power or revenge, and establishing sense of self.

Retrospective Inferences

To further illustrate the quagmire that currently saturates functional assessment terminology within school psychology, Nelson, Roberts, Bullis, Roberts, Albers, & Ohland, (1999) state that, "The products of a functional assessment are the (a) identification of an individual's strengths and weaknesses in a number of functional areas and (b) identification of environmental demands and support services and practices." (p. 8).

Functional assessment is not a process of finding support services and practices, completing check sheets, or filling out summary statements on a functional-assessment worksheet. As pointed out by Steege (1999), "Simply completing a form does not constitute a sound functional assessment." (p. 14). Essentially, procedures and broad conceptualizations such as those described above are retrospective inferences based on anecdotal accounts. Whether such details are obtained in the form of narrative descriptions of behaviors, anecdotal records, interestingly designed checklists, or strategies for locating support services, these data collection procedures can only be described as preliminary stages for a functional assessment, i.e., getting background information. Clearly, retrospective data collection can be useful in developing functional assessments, but it does not provide independently reliable information regarding the *function* of any student's maladaptive behavior.

EXTENDED FUNCTIONAL ASSESSMENT STRATEGIES FOR THE PUBLIC SCHOOL

Recently, however, functional assessment procedures have been successfully extended to school settings. For example, Broussard and Northup (1995) describe the use of a functional assessment for three students referred for disruptive behavior in regular education classrooms. Prior to the functional assessment, a descriptive assessment led to the selection of one of three possible variables maintaining the disruptive behavior: teacher attention, peer attention, or escape from academic tasks.

For the first student, it was hypothesized from the descriptive assessment that teacher attention maintained the disruptive behavior. Contingent and noncontingent teacher attention conditions were conducted in the classroom in order to evaluate the hypothesis. During contingent teacher attention, the therapist made disapproving remarks following the target behavior. During noncontingent teacher attention, praise was given every 60 seconds independent of the student's behavior while all occurrences of the target behavior were ignored.

It was hypothesized that peer attention was maintaining the disruptive behavior for the second student. During this analog the student was asked to complete an easy academic task in a nearby empty classroom with only the observer present. For the peer present condition, two peers accompanied the participant to the other classroom, and all were given the instruction to work quietly on worksheets.

For the third student it was hypothesized that the object of the behavior was to provide an escape from academic tasks. The first condition conducted contained a difficult academic task; the second condition contained an easy academic task. Following the occurrence of the target behavior, the worksheet was removed and all behavior was ignored for one minute. At that time, the worksheet was reintroduced. Instructions were repeated until the participant resumed working or another target behavior occurred.

For all three students, the functional analysis confirmed the selected hypothesis, and contingency reversal resulted in increased academic work and significantly reduced target behaviors. However, it must be noted that the experiments were conducted by a trained therapist and required considerable time and effort. The use of these procedures in the regular classroom would not be simple, cheap, or easily adaptable for use by untrained personnel. The assessment procedures are very doable but not easily invoked for general use in the classroom environment.

DESCRIPTIVE ANALYSIS: AN ALTERNATIVE FORM OF FUNCTIONAL ASSESSMENT

As an alternative to extended functional analysis designs (or brief functional analysis), *descriptive analyses* have been advanced as a relatively equivalent, cost effective, and less labor intensive strategy for collecting data in real time on antecedent and consequent events (Ninness, Ellis, et al., 1999). Rather than analogs, this type of functional assessment relies exclusively on in vivo direct observations of target behaviors in natural settings. Using computer-interactive recording systems, target behaviors are operationally defined and antecedent and consequent events are identified in real time in real settings.

However, unlike traditional functional assessment designs, this type of functional assessment is not capable of unequivalently specifying cause and effect relationships. Lerman and Iwata (1993) point out that even though the descriptive analyses have clear advantages in that they allow immediate access to target behavior in the natural context in which they occur, the procedure has limitations. For example, descriptive analyses are inefficient at identifying problem behaviors sustained by intermittent reinforcers, the presence of observers in natural settings may be conspicuous and obtrusive, and important variables may be obscured by inadvertent and distracting features of natural settings. Lerman and Iwata note that even when such contaminating variables can be ruled out, descriptive analysis are only capable of providing correlational data.

Nevertheless, behavioral analysts have successfully employed descriptive analyses to develop treatment plans for specific maladaptive behaviors. For example, the above cited study by Broussard and Northup (1995) employed a descriptive analysis prior to initiating analogs to test various hypothesis regarding the controlling variables. Outcomes from the preliminary descriptive analyses were highly correlated with the findings of the functional analysis. Mace and Lalli (1991) combined descriptive and functional analyses to facilitate the identification of the evasive variables relating to the bizarre verbal behavior of a severely handicapped client. The descriptive analysis yielded important outcomes used in refining experimental analogs that subsequently identified the most critical variables maintaining the client's bizarre speech. Mace and Lalli suggest that a descriptive analysis often might be particularly useful as a vanguard in the production of specialized analogs. Using a descriptive assessment procedure, we (Ninness, Fuerst, & Rutherford, 1995) isolated the antecedent and consequent events correlated with adolescent disruption and off-task behavior of two junior high students identified as SED. And, as we will describe in greater detail in Chapter 6, descriptive analyses of students with behavior disorders demonstrated that aggressive behaviors were correlated with provocation by classmates, self-initiated disruption, or continuing interactive disruption among students (Ninness, Ellis, Miller, Baker, & Rutherford, 1995). In both of these studies, using a descriptive analysis to identify the antecedents and consequences of student disruption, off-task behavior, and aggression gave us a special advantage in developing efficient and effective behavior intervention plans.

RUNNING FUNCTIONAL ASSESSMENTS IN A DESCRIPTIVE ANALYSIS FORMAT

A good place to begin is by observing the student across a number of settings and making a list of things the referred student actually does that represent a problem. Although a review of student academic records and discipline reports and a discussion with parents and teachers is useful as a source of background information, nothing can provide a clearer picture of the actual problem than a discrete direct observation. Here, the observer can find exactly what the student is saying or doing that represents a problem. Now, the observer is well positioned to develop an operational definition of the problem behavior in the context in which it occurs. An operational definition is nothing more than a very clearly written description of what the student's problem behavior actually looks like. But, an operational definition has some important features for observing and understanding behavior. It provides a means whereby we may group related topographies (movements) into larger response classes that represent precise details and examples of the target behavior. For example, the referred student who acts-out impulsively may "talk out of turn in class," "get out of his seat without permission," "run across the classroom or cafeteria," and manifest five or six similarly inappropriate target behaviors that reasonably fall within the same general category of impulsive behavior. Although each of these target behaviors represents a different topography, each is clearly recognizable as an example of spontaneously inappropriate behavior. A precise, clearly written description of the various topographies of the student's impulsive behaviors should make them easily distinguishable from other classes of problem behaviors such as aggression.

An operational definition of the response variations subsumed under "impulsive behaviors" is not intended to convey any information regarding causative factors. It merely provides a system for consistently recognizing the target behaviors as they occur in real time. Listing and describing these topographies provides a means whereby two observers concurrently may watch the same student perform a wide range of impulsive behaviors and agree or disagree as to how the student is acting at any given moment in time.

Moreover, an operational definition of the problem behavior precludes the necessity of separately counting twenty-five or more behaviors simultaneously. Throughout the literature in applied behavior analysis, it has been consistently demonstrated that well written operational definitions allow two observers to obtain intra-observer agreement regarding the occurrence and nonoccurrence of classes of target behavior (See Ninness, Glenn, & Ellis, 1993, for details on calculating intraobserver reliabilities). In our experience we have found that it is easier to obtain high intraobserver agreements and demonstrate dramatic impacts on problem behaviors while measuring only one well-defined problem behavior or dependent variable at a time. Using an operational definition of problem behavior allows observers to demonstrate the reliability of their observations before and after an intervention plan has been implemented. We would suggest that it is precisely because traditional assessments frequently fail to demonstrate the reliability of their measurements that they also fail to measure the effectiveness of their associated treatments.

FOCAL POINT FUNCTIONAL ASSESSMENTS WITH NOTEBOOK COMPUTERS

As previously described, functional assessments have a unique characteristic separating them from traditional psychological assessment--emphasis on accountability. Functional assessments are mandated and conducted with an eye toward locating the variables that interact with the student's maladaptive behavior. Once these variables are identified, the success of intervention can be based on the student demonstrating improved performance under the same (and more general) conditions. Thus, functional assessments serve as a guide for developing efficient behavior plans, and they provide criteria for demonstrating effective treatment outcomes.

FOCAL Point software is designed for making direct observations of the target behaviors in natural settings. The assessment strategies in this software package take behavior assessment well past the collecting of anecdotal data on diversified and undefined behavior problems. They provide the observer with information as to "when", "why", and "where" baseline data is occurring. Rather than using retrospective teacher logs, office records, Lykert scales, or personality profiles, this software provides the school psychologist, diagnostician, counselor, or behavior specialist with a direct observation format that tracks problem behaviors as they occur across real time. And, it allows the observer to select the observation procedure that is best suited to operationally define and reliably identify particular types of problem behaviors in the contexts in which they are most likely to be exhibited.

Observation Protocols

Generally, the literature suggests that direct observations in natural settings are most easily and reliably conducted by way of partial interval observation (Ninness, Glenn, & Ellis, 1993). Partial-interval observations are usually employed when attempting to identify and compare various forms of erratic, chaotic, and a very wide range of maladaptive behaviors across school settings. By far, this observation system is the one most often used in the applied literature of school psychology. A recent review of the literature demonstrates that 72% of the current studies use some form of partial-interval observation.

Using Windows 95 or newer operating systems, the *FOCAL* Point partial-interval subroutines allow each observation to be set according to the operational definition of the problem behavior. Depending on the type of behavior the student may be exhibiting, the observer may select 5-s, 10-s, 30-s, 1-min, or 5-min partial intervals. A good rule of thumb is the faster the problem behavior occurs, the shorter the interval should be (Ninness et al., 1993).

Output

Output specifies the percentage of intervals in which maladaptive behaviors occur across conditions. Each data session provides more information as to when, where, and why the student is most likely to demonstrate some form of the target behavior. Following each data session, the data can be easily transferred to Excel spreadsheets and calculations of interobserver reliabilities as well as graphing in the forms of histograms or time-series line graphs can be performed. Figure 5.1 illustrates a sample graph derived from *FOCAL* Point Observations and graphed in Excel. In this example, an elementary student appears to exhibit particularly high rates of inappropriate behavior during Escape from academic demands.

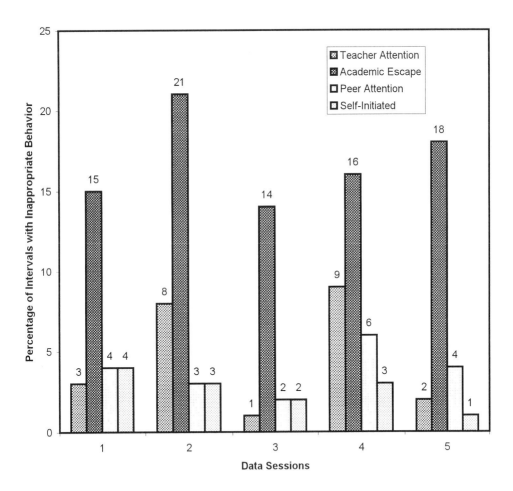

Figure 5.1. [Sample data depicting disruptive behavior during a functional assessment across 5 sessions and 4 conditions.]

Moreover, the above data suggest that this student's problem behavior was *less likely* to occur during teacher attention, peer attention, self-initiation, or any combination of these circumstances. Therefore, it is reasonable to assume that academic demands (more than any of the other conditions that occur in the classroom context) are key variables that interact with this student's likelihood of performing problem behavior.

Relatively few intervals were identified as ones in which spontaneous "self-initiated" problem behavior occurred. This itself is an important finding. It allows us to rule out "internal causes" of the student's maladaptive behavior. We recommend that a self-initiated condition be included in most classroom functional assessment procedures. When this condition (spontaneous problem behaviors) can be ruled out, Behavior Intervention Plans (BIP's) are much easier to develop and implement.

INSTALLING *FOCAL* POINT FOR WINDOWS 95/98/NT AND ABOVE

1. Normally *FOCAL* Point will automatically initiate installation upon placing it directly in the appropriate CD drive. Just follow the on-screen directions and make the appropriate selections that are provided during the installation process.
2. If *FOCAL* Point does not automatically install upon inserting the CD into the appropriate drive, select RUN from your START BAR and type **e:setup.exe**. Hit the return key and the loading process will begin.

RUNNING PARTIAL-INTERVAL OBSERVATIONS ON *FOCAL* POINT

1. Configure Buttons: Partial-interval observations contain six condition buttons and three control buttons. Before initiating a session, up to six of these condition buttons can be set by tapping the mouse on the configure box in the upper left-hand corner of the screen. Immediately, a form appears that will allow you to specify a long (twenty-five characters) name for up to six conditions in which problem behaviors may emerge. Adjacent to each condition, you may specify a short (seven characters) name for each condition. The short name and the occurrence or nonoccurrence of the behavior will appear on the lower portion of the screen as the program runs. In this way, you are continually updated on the moment-to-moment behavior changes that occur across environmental conditions throughout the observation session.
2. Beginning the session: The upper left control button is labeled "Begin Session." Tapping this button brings up a form asking for details

regarding the student's identification. Also, this form will allow you to specify the interval width to be used throughout the session. A general rule of thumb regarding the selection of an appropriate interval width is, "the faster the behavior occurs, the shorter the interval width" (Ninness, Glenn, & Ellis, 1993). After specifying the interval width, tap "OK" and a final form will let you validate all previous entries before initiating the program. Tap "Yes" to begin the session, tap "No" to go back to the previous form and make any necessary changes, or simply cancel the program. When "Yes" is tapped, the program begins and a digital clock in the middle of the screen is activated. The top line specifies the Starting Time. The line below indicates Running Time.

3.   During the partial-interval observations, the program displays the word "Record" inside a blue box. If the student performs the problem behavior any time during the partial-interval, tap the button that describes the condition in which the behavior occurs. At the end of each interval, the computer beeps (beeper volume may be set on the bottom control panel), the screen turns black for one second, and the program updates a running record of the student's moment-by-moment performance. Immediately, a new interval begins and the process is repeated throughout the observation session.

4.   At any time during the program, you may view the current percentage of intervals in which the student is demonstrating problem behaviors across all conditions. To obtain this information, simply tap the "Display Percent" button and the current percentage of problem behaviors across all conditions is posted as the program continues to run in real time.

5   To end the program, press "Quit." At this point, session data may be printed, sent to Excel for graphing, or both.

6.   After tapping the "Quit" button, go to File on the upper-left side of the screen and select Print, Save, or Exit. Print will directly output the aggregated session data and total percentages of problem behavior within each condition to your selected printer. Save will store the current session data as an ASCII file and allow you to retrieve it in Excel (usually as a .csv file). Within Excel your data can be graphed or aggregated by whatever format best suits your special interests and needs. We should point out that the raw data on your .csv file will appear to have one extra interval. This was the interval in which the session was terminated. This last interval is not used in calculating the percentage of target behaviors that are recorded just below these raw data points. Session data is provided at the bottom of each spreadsheet as the percentage of target behaviors that were identified by the observer within each of the conditions. Note: Simply highlighting this

output and then typing **F11** will automatically generate most of what is needed to produce a comprehensive graph for an individual session.

7. Tapping E̲xit will end your program without saving your data; however, your condition buttons will remain the same until you change them during the following session. Generally, it is recommended that all six condition buttons be used only on the first functional assessment session. During subsequent sessions at least two conditions can be eliminated on the basis of having relatively low percentages of problem behaviors. The applied research demonstrates that 4 conditions are sufficient for making contrasts across sessions (Ninness, McCuller, & Ninness, 1999).

8. To produce a complete functional assessment graph showing a series of conditions across several sessions as in Figure 5.1 above, simply cut and paste data from previous session on to one spreadsheet. Place each condition value (for each successive session) across rows. Do the same for each session so that each session has a series of values representing the percentage of intervals with target behaviors identified within a row. This way, each row represents a new session. Provide condition names (e.g., Teacher Attention, Academic Escape, etc.) at the top of condition/column, and provide session numbers (e.g., 1, 2, 3, etc.) at the far left of each session (see Figure 5.2 above). Now, select (darken) the area to be graphed and go to the **Chart Wizard**. Within the Chart Wizard, select **"Column."** **Next,** from the **"Series in:"** pick Co̲lumns. Next, select **"Titles and Categories"** for the categories for X values and Y values. **Next** (and most importantly), select **"new s̲heet."** Now, hit **F11** and your functional assessment graphs is ready. From here, you can add other features according to your preference. (Actually, in order to become really proficient at this process, we recommend that you buy an Excel manual to help you in refining your graphs.).

	Teach Att	Acad Esc	Peer Att	Distraction
1	3	15	4	4
2	8	21	3	3
3	1	14	7	2
4	9	16	6	11
5	2	16	4	2

Figure 5.2. [Sample data depicting information entered into Excel when creating a graph]

Intraobserver Agreement

Reliability coefficients for concurrent observations are easily derived on Excel spreadsheets. (See Ninness et al., 1993 for details on standardized procedures for obtaining intraobserver agreements.)

IN SUMMARY

Functional assessment has been acknowledged as the standard for behavior analysts, special educators, school psychologists and other professionals providing behavioral intervention systems to children with disabilities. Students and clients have a right to methodologically valid and reliable assessment procedures and now this right is mandated within our public law. This chapter has introduced and defined the functional analysis and functional assessment of maladaptive behavior, provided a brief review of the current literature, and reviewed the public schools attempt to incorporate this system within special education and psychological services. Additionally, we examined a computer interactive strategy to facilitate functional assessment in public school settings. In the next chapter we will develop and implement specific individual education programs and behavior intervention plans based on functional assessments.

Chapter 6

LEARNING TO BEHAVE YOURSELF

It was a hot summer in Pittsburgh, and Herbie and the "flushing furies" spent every possible moment alleviating their stress by flipping from the high board at the Greenfield public pool. Performing rolling cannon balls from the ten-foot tower seemed to offer substantially less risk than Herbie had encountered performing aerial gymnastics in Saint Rosalia's boys' room--even when he managed to drench the teenage girls sunning at the water's edge. Ah, but those carefree days of summer were over all too soon. And with the falling leaves of September came the inevitable supplementary Latin lessons, diagrams of complex sentences, enigmatic verb conjugation, intricate mathematical operations, and so on. But where was Sister Servula? On that first day, Herbie anticipated her mandate, "Take your hands out of your pockets and come with me--you fresh article." By noon, the stress was peeking, and he risked asking Sister Mary Agnus if Sister Servula had been transferred. "She's here, Herbert, and I believe Mother Felicitous and she would like a word with you." Herbie tried to smile at Sister Mary Agnus. Miraculously, the bell rang, and Herbie hurried off to the lunch room as if nothing had happened.

But there in the lunch room, in the basement of the church, at the end of the lunch line, stood Sister Servula. Her arms were folded, and she was staring down the long lunch line as if she were waiting for 'someone.' Suddenly, Herbie didn't feel very hungry. As he took a quick scan of the nearest and least conspicuous exits, he detected dark movement in his direction.

"Herbert!"

Herbie pretended not to hear as he looked nonchalantly around the lunch room, but the walls were closing in around him.

"Herbert!!!"

FUNCTIONAL ASSESSMENTS AND PRESCRIPTIVE INTERVENTIONS

So there are circumstances where students may go undetected in their mischievous conduct, and there are other settings where they are fairly conspicuous. For the most part, students who have long and complex histories of creating difficulties (for themselves and others) are fairly conspicuous. Most often the students' difficulties are literally "in your face." The problem for the school psychologist is not one of detecting and diagnosing the maladaptive behavior but finding out what to do about it. What do we do with a student who creates problems *because s/he is trying to avoid the inherent irritations of academics* versus a student who is being seriously problematic *because he enjoys the attention he gets for doing so?* How do we know why the student is doing what s/he is doing? Clearly, labeling the student takes us no closer answering this question or to changing his/her maladaptive behavior/s.

The same question may be more systemically phrased, "Under what conditions does the student become most likely to exhibit seriously inappropriate behavior?" Another version of this excellent question might be phased, "What are the variables that interact with the student's problem behavior?" These are questions that may be addressed by employing the functional assessment strategies described in the previous chapter. Moreover, after conducting this functional assessment, one is well positioned to implement a particular type of intervention based on the functional assessment outcome. Again, this system doesn't give us a label. It gives us a way to identify the variables that are correlated with the student's problem behavior. Once these variables are identified, the necessary treatment may be fairly conspicuous.

Imagine a student who "acts out" disruptively throughout various parts of the school day. A casual observer may notice that s/he seems to have awkward social skills and poor work habits. S/he is easily distracted by the incidental activities of those around him, and, occasionally, s/he seems to enjoy asking inane questions of the teacher. To the casual observer, there may be a multitude of events and settings that seem to precipitate the student's erratic inappropriate behavior. Or, the maladaptive behavior may seem to occur spontaneously. It is tempting to suggest that the student has some sort of emotional/behavioral disorder and be done with it. However, a systematic observer may arrive at another conclusion. A series of relatively short but systematic observations may yield a pattern of problem behaviors that are consistently correlated with particular conditions.

For example, a referral to psychological services suggests that a fourth-grade student "is not using his time wisely," "does not work or play well with others," continually interrupts the teacher with irrelevant commentary, often disrupts classroom activities by making loud and unnecessary noises, and occasionally and unpredictably performs a range of nonsensical and bizarre activities. These problems behaviors may seem to emerge haphazardly across every conceivable circumstance. This is a student who is creating problems for himself and others, and the teacher has had just about enough! She has tried *everything* and *nothing seems to work.* This is a student who may soon receive a diagnosis. From here, things can only get worse. On the other hand, this is a student who might benefit from a functional assessment. What an idea!

A Hypothetical Example

A review of this student's records shows that he has been sent to the office frequently for performing a host of "disruptive" behaviors. A teacher survey/check list shows us that he is frequently off-task, disruptive, loud, annoying, does not use his time wisely, and does not work or play well with others. However, it is generally agreed that the student is not hyperactive. Rather, he is described by most as "impulsive." A meeting with the student's parents and his teachers is held; this further confirms the laundry list of unhappy descriptors. For example, he gets out of his seat without permission, calls out unsolicited replies to teacher interrogatives, teases students who respond appropriately, and so on. It is noted that this child has previously been placed on various forms of medication (including psychostimulants), and, of course, nothing seems to help! It's an all too common story. It's such a shame and everyone agrees this student has such potential. Maybe this is just not the right "location" for him. Maybe he needs some kind of "special help" someplace where they know how to work with students who have "special problems."

Wait! Has anybody conducted a functional assessment--in real time? Perhaps, we should give it a try before we conduct a series of personality tests, make a diagnosis, and decide on his "alternative" placement. With some reluctance and skepticism, the committee agrees to have a functional assessment conducted before moving forward with the battery of personality inventories, rating scales, projective techniques, and subsequent "placement."

The school psychologist conducts a few preliminary observations in order to develop an operational definition of the problem behavior. Most of these behaviors fall well within the realm of *disruption.* The school psychologist then conducts a series of five, 15-min, observations using *FOCAL* Point. Something of a pattern becomes apparent. What's more, the

probability of this particular pattern occurring by chance is calculated, and it
is very, very small. Figure 6.1 illustrates the functional assessment outcome.

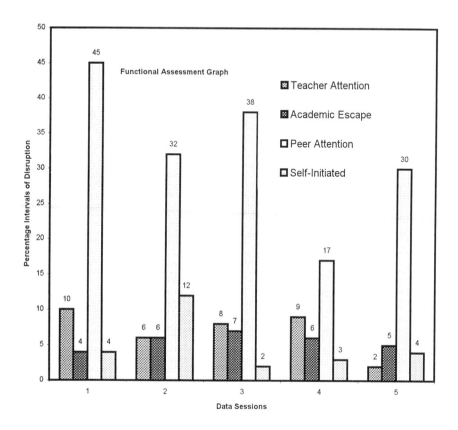

Figure 6.1. [Sample data depicting disruptive behavior during a functional assessment across
5 sessions and 4 conditions. Note that this graph specifies the statistical probability of the
problem behavior continually occurring within a specific context.]

Another meeting is held to describe the above results, and everyone
agrees that there certainly seems to be a pattern associated with the student's
disruptive behavior. Clearly, the student is most likely to act-out disruptively
under circumstances that lead to *peer attention.* This is not to suggest that
other events never correlate with disruption; however, peer attention is by far
the most significant. More importantly, the data suggest that his disruptions
and off-task behavior seldom occur in spontaneous or "self-initiated"
conditions. But there are conditions that are consistently correlated with
problem behavior. This pattern of problem behavior may have emerged
under the influence of rules, direct-acting contingencies, or some interaction

of both. Nevertheless, there is a pattern that suggests the conditions associated with maladaptive behavior and our intervention will be most effective if it is directed at the student as he behaves under those conditions. Figure 6.2 shows us the same graph collapsed across sessions.

At this point someone might ask, "So what can we do now that we could not have done before?" A good deal! Functional assessments don't diagnose, but they allow us to be prescriptive. For the past two decades, functional analysis and functional assessments have been used to guide interventions (Neef & Iwata, 1994). The professional literature is replete with procedures based on successful outcomes developed from various functional assessments. The particulars are far beyond the scope of this book; however, in the case of a student who shows us a pattern of responsiveness to peer attention, an intervention based on group-contingencies has well documented success (e.g. Broussard & Northrup, 1995). Since this procedure is classic and it has proven to be especially effective in working with students who are "peer-attention seekers," we will give it detailed consideration.

Again someone might ask, "So what can we do now that we could not have done before?" A good deal! The above graph reveals that peer attention is highly correlated with the student's disruptions. On the other hand, teacher attention, academic escape, and self-initiated conditions that are not highly correlated with the problem behavior. Importantly, employing the self-initiated condition allows us to rule out the possibility that the student's problem behaviors are entirely "spontaneous" and unrelated to environmental events. Certainly, this may not always be the case. Many students do, in fact, show high rates of "self-initiated" problem behavior. When this is found to be true, we must adjust our behavior intervention plans accordingly. In fact, in the latter part of this chapter we elaborate extensively on self-management procedures that grew out of functional assessments of students who demonstrated high levels of "self-initiated aggressive behavior." We feel that it is almost always advantageous to employ this self-initiated condition during functional assessments in order to rule out or rule in environmental events that interact with the student's problem behaviors.

Occasionally, students do not show problem behaviors that are correlated with any specific conditions across sessions. When this is the case, we are no better off than we were before the assessment began. But this is a relatively rare finding. More often, functional assessments give us considerable insight into when, where, and why students are exhibiting target behaviors.

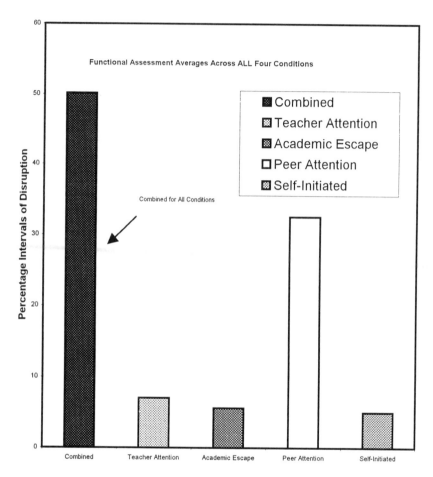

Figure 6.2. [Sample data depicting disruptive behavior during a functional assessment across 5 sessions and 4 conditions. Note that this graph displays the same information as Figure 6.1; however, the data is collapsed across conditions.]

Once again, functional assessments don't provide diagnosis, but they do allow us to be prescriptive. For the past two decades, functional analysis and functional assessments have been used to guide interventions for a multitude of client populations. The long list of prescriptive interventions growing out of functional assessments is far beyond the scope of this book. Suffice to say that the professional literature is replete with procedures based on successful outcomes developed from diversified functional assessment profiles (see Neef & Iwata, 1994 for a discussion). However, in the case of the above hypothetical student, an intervention based on group-contingencies makes a good example of a treatment generated from a particular functional assessment profile. Since the intervention procedure is classic, and it has proven to be especially effective in working with students who are "peer-attention seekers," (Broussard & Northrup, 1995) we will give it detailed consideration.

GROUP CONTINGENCIES AND PEER ATTENTION

In Chapter 3, we pointed out that Hayes, Zettle, et al. (1989) describe a particular type of rule-following governed by the "apparent correspondence" between the rule and the way the environment appears to be organized as *tracking.* To reiterate, a person who "believes" a particular verbal statement to be true may perform in accordance with, or track, the particulars of that rule even in the absence of guidance or supervision. In any given circumstance tracking may or may not work to a person's advantage, but it is most likely to be demonstrated by individuals who have a certain history. According to Hayes, Zettle, et al., tracking is influenced by the listener's history of making contact with the consequences of following directions, the similarity between the rule and other rules in the person's repertoire, and the gravity of the consequences for violating or following the rule.

Remember that tracking stands in contrast to *pliance,* which has been defined as a type of rule-following that is contingent on the correspondence between the rule and the *socially mediated consequences* provided during *supervision* of the relevant behavior. A person who performs in accordance with a rule due to pliance may or may not believe in the merits of the rule per se. More important is the person's belief in the forthcoming consequences for violating or following the rule (Hayes, Zettle, et al., 1989). Individuals who follow rules in the form of pliance do so primarily because they anticipate consequences (negative or positive) will be provided by someone who is aware of their behavior as well as the rules for what they should be doing. Note that both in the case of tracking and pliance our conclusion that a particular person "believes" a rule is predicated on their performance in compliance or opposition to the rule. A student who follows rules only under the influence of social mediation (supervision) is performing according to pliance. Group-contingencies are a classic example generating rule-following by way of pliance. That is, the dramatic and immediate improvements we see with the implementation of this strategy occur because students anticipate consequences will be provided by someone who is aware of their behavior as well as the rules regarding that behavior.

Group-contingencies operate so that all members of the group profit or lose according to a group standard. These procedures are very well suited for students who appear unusually responsive to the influence of peer attention.

In group-contingencies the whole class suffers or gains when particular students are targeted.

The Good Behavior Game

One of the most repeatedly described classroom management procedures ever to hit behavior analysis literature proved to be the Good Behavior Game. There are numerous reasons for the popularity of this type of programming. Just a few include the simplicity, the strength, and the positive results of group-contingencies . Group-contingencies usually require very little instruction, and they are simple to operate. Because they take advantage of peer pressure, they are a very powerful reinforcer, and the positive results of this strategy are evident almost immediately.

The Good Behavior Game was originally produced by Barrish et al. in 1969. The classroom circumstances included seven students with records of serious disruption and classroom violations. Although there was a behavior plan in effect which involved the teacher repeatedly advising the students of the classroom rules, it did not adequately motivate the students to behave properly.

All twenty-four students in this classroom were unobtrusively observed through ten sessions in both math and reading. Inappropriate talking-out behavior occurred during 96 percent of the observed intervals; out-of-seat behavior occurred during 82 percent of the intervals. After baseline, a multiple baseline and series of reversals were implemented in the experimental analysis of several contingencies. The math class was initially divided into two teams of twelve players. The teacher explained that when any member of a team was seen violating classroom rules, that person would cause his team to receive a mark. At the end of math class, the team with the fewest marks would be the winner, and if both teams received less than five marks, both teams would win concurrently.

The reward system in this program was particularly important. Because this type of classroom management program appealed to a sense of competition, Barrish et al. believed that the Good Behavior Game permitted a reinforcement procedure that made use of opportunities intrinsic to the classroom environment. Winners of the day's Good Behavior Game were permitted to "(1) wear victory tags, (2) put a star by each of its members' names on the winner's charts, (3) line up first for lunch if one team won or early if both teams won, and (4) take part at the end of the day in a 30min free time during which the team(s) would have special projects" (Barrish et al., 1969, p.121). While the winners were enjoying their special projects, losers of the day's game were required to continue working during the last half hour of the day. If one or both teams received fewer than twenty marks in the course of an entire week, they were permitted to go to recess four minutes early each day. Purposefully, the contingencies for the game were arranged so that both teams could win most of the time; and that is precisely what they did.

The resulting data for the first six days of math period were exceptional. Inappropriate talking out instantly dropped to a median 19 percent of the observed intervals, and out-of-seat behavior dropped to 9 percent. The internal validity of this intervention was verified with the concurrent multiple baseline. Reading periods, which occurred on the same days, maintained baseline levels for both dependent measures. For four days the contingencies were reversed so that the game was withdrawn in math and implemented during reading. This established further validation of the independent effects of this program. Baseline rates for talking-out and out-of-seat behaviors returned during math periods, while the immediate reduction and continued low level of inappropriate behavior resulted during reading periods. Both talking-out and out-of-seat behaviors during reading stayed below 20 percent during this phase of the study.

The game was implemented in both math and reading in the fourth phase of the study. Expectedly, the disruptive behavior rates during reading remained at low levels, and math once again occurred in a classroom nearly devoid of inappropriate talking or walking about the room. The sequential series of experimental reversals and the use of a multiple baseline showing that the effects occurred only in the target subject areas allow for little doubt that the drastic change in student behavior was primarily a function of the game.

It is important to remember that this game can and should be arranged so that both teams win most of the time. Both teams won the game more than 82 percent of the time in this experiment. Yet the disruptive behavior of particular students at any given time during the operating of the game was punished by it causing their team to receive a mark. Evidently, this mild form of punishment produced rather strong peer pressure to cease and desist. Thus, the teacher was cleared from her previous obligatory repetitions of punishment and scoldings.

During the experiment, two students appeared to try to gain social reinforcement by sabotaging their own teams. These students were simply removed from their teams and earned individual marks that detracted from their own individual free-time period in order to terminate this antisocial behavior.

Electronic Version of the Game

The first reproduction appeared three years after the Good Behavior Game was first released. Medland and Stachnik (1972) produced the same powerful effects when they deviated from the original study by using certain technological innovations. They used essentially the same set of game rules as Barrish et al.'s procedure, but they arranged a typical reading group of twenty-eight fifth-graders into a series of electronically controlled game conditions.

Five forty-minute baseline (1) sessions revealed that both teams had an especially high rate of disruptive, out-of-seat, and talking-out behaviors. Baseline (1) data reveal averages of about 75 to 100 occurrences of the target behaviors per session. Electronic contingencies were initiated with the introduction of game (I), and the class was told that the two teams were now competing for free time. As in the previous experiment, any time any member of either team was out of his or her seat, talking out, or causing any form of disruption, their whole team would earn a mark. Electronic feedback enabled the class to judge their performance, thus making competition possible. Students could constantly monitor marks against the teams by means of red and green lights stationed at the front of the class. The green light meant that all behavior was acceptable, and the red light was a warning that meant someone was behaving in an unacceptable manner.

The team with the fewest marks at the end of the reading period won the game for that day and received free time which consisted of three minutes of extra morning recess. Extra activity time was earned on a weekly basis if a team made fewer than twenty marks during an entire week. As always, any disruptive individual or one who intentionally attempted to undermine his own team was removed from the game for a period of one day. Both groups 1 and 2 showed an immediate and consistent reduction in target behaviors and maintained this behavior throughout the ten-day course of game (1).

The next phase of the experiment involved simultaneous instating of rules + lights. Again in this phase, classroom rules were described to the class on a daily basis, and the lights used in game (1) as a form of group feedback were reinstated. In this phase, however, there was no "backup" consequence comparable to the feedback provided by the lights or the student's appropriate behavior. Once again, group rates of disruption, talking-out, and out-of-seat behaviors were at near-zero during the reading period. Little further change was apparent when game (2) was finally reinstated during the last five days, but there was little room for additional improvement.

An All Positive Version of the Game

The above systems have been used so often and, for the most part, so successfully that applied researchers have not bothered looking at too many alternatives or variations on the primary thrust of the game. However, the primary thrust is taking points away from a team when an individual student demonstrates maladaptive or noncompliance behavior. This is a powerful form of peer pressure but for some individuals this may not be the most advantageous way to approach their problem. As you may know, there are some individuals who really don't mind causing their colleagues and classmates to suffer a little—particularly if it brings them some social attention in the process. The solution here can be simple but effective.

The game can be modified easily such that *points are never deleted* from a team or individual. Rather, the emphasis is placed exclusively on the delivery of earned points contingent on small improvements in target student's behavior. This innovation requires a little advanced planning in group dynamics. Usually, we recommend that the whole class is told that "special student/s" will be selected to earn points on behalf their team (or for that matter the whole class). Of course, these students are deviously selected precisely because they are the ones who are most in need of the most improvement. The class is told that as these special students show even slight improvements their whole team (or class) will gain points. The points are for everyone's benefit but the target student is in the enviable position of earning points for the group. Particularly in the first few days of this new system, the teacher needs be especially sensitive to the this student's smallest attempt to comply. As the student is caught being good, the class is repeatedly notified that he/she has earned another point for his team's benefit.

This version of the game removes the punishment contingency and replaces it with a more powerful group reinforcement procedure. There are few reinforcers in our culture that are as influential as group appreciation. The version of the game allows students to come into contact with group appreciation for the type of behavior change that also is sincerely appreciated by most teachers.

Limitations

Given the Good Behavior Game's record of success one might be tempted to suggest it as an "all purpose" intervention strategy. However, this might not be good planning. Under some conditions, the game has been known to show less spectacular results. Generally, this has happened when the students' problem behaviors were not related to attempts to gain peer attention. Also, the game is likely to be less effective when working with student/s who have longer and more complex histories of behavior disorders. Nevertheless, the game has its place and its place *can be identified* with a well planned functional assessment. The idea is to conduct a real time functional assessment, see what the behavioral literature has suggested for similar problems, and proceed with interventions that are most likely to address the variables that have been identified in the this student's functional assessment.

UNDER DIFFERENT CONDITIONS WITH DIFFERENT STUDENTS

Sometimes functional assessment outcomes bear little or no resemblance to those seen anywhere in the literature. We are still better positioned than we were before the procedure was implemented. Knowing the variables for which the problem behavior is a function tells us a lot about where to begin treatment. It tells us something about why the student behaves as s/he does and it tells us a little about who else may be interacting with the student's problem/s.

The good news is that there is no shortage of problems to be addressed with real time functional assessments. However, this may only be real good news if everyone is in the mood to actually implement treatments based on functional assessment outcomes. But otherwise, why do a functional assessment?

We are not so ambitious in this chapter as to attempt to suggest an array of interventions emanating from volumes of functional assessment publications. However, we will offer a relatively recent study in which we used functional assessment to develop interventions for students who had long and complicated histories of aggressive behaviors in public school settings.

Aggression, Functional-Assessment, and Self-Assessment

Although Herbie may not be the best example, everyone probably knows at least one model of "self-control." For example, some individuals are able to shun instant gratification and pursue long-term goals until the larger and more significant rewards arrive. In their everyday lives, they may actively avoid tasty fats and sugars, throw away their cigarettes, exercise regularly, and stick to a reasonable budget while saving or investing their money. In saying that someone has "good self-control", we are describing many different behaviors that have something in common: the behaviors do not bring an immediate gratification, but they often lead to important outcomes in the future. Contrary to popular opinion, people do not behave in such ways *because* they *have* self-control. As a summary term that describes a group of behaviors, the term "self-control" makes everyday sense; as an explanation for behavior, "self-control" is useless in helping us solve practical problems, and it is scientifically nonsensical. The behavior involved in self-control might be more easily understood if the term self-management were used. Everyone is familiar with the notion of management as the manipulation of the environment.

This section of the chapter is about a complex set of skills that has come to be termed "self-management" and how functional assessment may contribute to its development. Self-management skills are acquired in the context of a social environment, and when those skills are insufficient, we must look to the social environment as the means of remediating those skill deficits. One of the goals of education is that students be self-managers, but paradoxically, it is the social environment that teaches the self-managing skills and identifies or specifies the behavior to be managed. That is the only way the culture will be passed on to the next generation. Thus, it becomes clear that educators must somehow arrange the environment so that students will learn to manage their own behavior, and the behavior managed will be that which the older, more experienced members of the culture designate as desirable--reading, writing, calculating, speaking politely, cooperating to obtain group goals, and playing games and musical instruments, etc. From our perspective, self-management is fundamental to every academic and social behavior.

Once students have good self-management skills, educational personnel will only have to maintain those skills, rather than manage all the behavioral contingencies themselves. Of course, the job of teaching the self-management skills has to be done in the first place, and for many students, that learning must occur in the schools.

Nevertheless, it seems that it is often difficult for many people to believe that self-management is a learned skill. In this chapter, we will try to show how the behavior of rule-governed self-management emerges from interactions with the environment.

The Evolution of Self-Management

For several decades, behavior analysts have sought to identify the kinds of interactions that produce self-managing behavior. Almost twenty years ago, O'Leary and Dubey (1979) stated that the goal in this research has been to teach children to manage on-task behavior so that teacher-maintained contingencies are minimized. Since then, research in this area has begun to create a "self-management" technology (Baer, 1984; Fowler, 1984; Glynn & Thomas, 1974; O'Leary & Dubey, 1979; Rosenbaum & Drabman, 1979; Young, West, Morgan, Smith, Glomb, & Haws-Kuresa, 1987) that has been analyzed in terms of scheduled reinforcement (e.g., Neef, Mace, & Shade, 1993) and rule-governed behavior (e.g., Kern-Dunlap, Dunlap, Clarke, Childs, White, & Stewart, 1992). Ironically, conflicting models of self-management have utilized somewhat similar procedures. Nevertheless, they all require learning to follow particular types of rules for self-management. To cite just a few examples, self-recording has augmented student academic achievement (Knapczyk & Livingston, 1973; McLaughlin & Truhlicka, 1983); reduced "talking-out" behavior in class (Broden et al., 1971); enhanced student on-task behavior (Glynn et al., 1973); improved academic efficiency among students with learning disabilities in regular education classroom (Maag et al., 1993); and has been incorporated into a strategy to encourage teacher praise for improved academic performance (Connell et al., 1993).

Self-management studies have illustrated that even junior high school students with behavior disorders are capable of learning to self-manage social skills and increase on-task behavior (Houghton, 1991; Kern-Dunlap et al. 1992; Smith et al., 1992) when functional assessment are employed. Self-management has proven an especially important tool in the transfer of students' on-task behavior across environments when each setting contained adult supervision (Rhode, Morgan, & Young, 1983) and in the absence of adult supervision (Ninness, Fuerst, Rutherford, & Glenn, 1991). Recently, Newman, Buffington, Hemmes, & Rosen, D. (1996) provided an excellent overview and critique of current self-management-related issues and concepts. However, there are other strategies for teaching students to control their own behavior.

Christmas in Detention

Following what can only be described as a very long first day in fourth grade, Herbie was assigned to an indefinite stay in after school detention-- the "black hole." For those who were not condemned to the black hole, school was over at 3:30. For those unlucky souls who were caught committing transgressions, school ended sometime after 5:00

But at Saint Rosalia's, the good sisters did not believe in wasting time-- anybody's time. Rather than having recalcitrant students print perfunctory and redundant sentences as a form of penance, the Sisters of Charity insisted on putting such students to the task of completing any and all academic assignments to supreme perfection. Each math operation was scrutinized by the "prefect of detention," corrected and recalculated by the student. Each sentence was examined for mechanical inaccuracies and rewritten to precision. Herbie had several of these, and hour after hour, day after day, in the black hole, he revised and resubmitted his daily assignments to the supreme satisfaction of Sister Servula. When his daily assignments were brought up to her specifications, homework assignments were initiated, completed, evaluated, revised, and resubmitted for further evaluation.

This prolonged and intensively structured tutelage was a new experience for Herbie. But, under these highly structured and inescapable academic conditions, a small metamorphosis was taking place. For the first time in his academic life, Herbie was actually prepared for the next day's lessons! More than that, after a few months of this supplementary structure with Sister Servula, Herbie began to really work during the regular part of the school day.

The semester was ending as the holidays approached and, finally, on the last day of his first semester of fourth grade, Sister Servula asked Herbie if he had finally learned how to *behave himself in the absence of supervision.* "Yes Sister," he replied meekly.

"You know, Herbert, if you go back to your old ways I'll be waiting for you."

"Yes, Sister," and Herbie's eyes were gleaming. He asked himself, "Could it be over?"

"Well, your time in detention is over--for now."

"Yes, Sister," and the bell rang as Herbie picked up his books and darted for the door.

"One moment Sir--I've got one more thing for you!"
Herbie turned and s l o w l y walked toward the Ice Nun. As he approached, she told him to hold out his hand. He winced in anticipation. But as he held out a nervous palm, she did something quite unexpected. She gently placed in the center of his hand a white book marker inscribed with the words, "Little Sisters of Charity."

Herbie smiled as only a fourth grader can, "Thank you Sister." Taking a very deep breath he said, "I'll really try to behave myself in the future Sister."

"You're a fresh article, Herbert--but have a Merry Christmas."

RULE-FOLLOWING IN THE ABSENCE OF SUPERVISION

Evidently, Herbie required an intensive history of coming into contact with the consequences for following and not following certain rules. What are the chances that such a history is sufficient to sustain his rule-following in the absence of supervision? Will Herbie's limited rule-following repertoire show elements of *tracking* or will he only demonstrate *pliance.*

Herbie's behavior was not the worst the Sisters of Charity had seen. By today's standards in the public school, Herbie would be considered a minor annoyance. Presently, many of our public schools offer much more impressive challenges. Perhaps, one of the worst scenarios involves students who are identified as having "behavior disorders" (BD) or "emotional disturbance" (ED). These students, identified as ED, indulge in serious problem behaviors much more often than their regular education peers (Dwyer, 1991), and even though many people are very "concerned," there are no easy answers here. As Malott *et al.* (2000) put it:

> Everyone wants a quick fix. The preacher wants to preach an hour on Sunday and have the parishioners lead lives of virtue the rest of the week. The psychologist wants to psychoanalyze an hour on Monday and have the patients lead lives of mental health the rest of the week. The teacher wants to lecture an hour on Wednesday and have the students lead lives of intellectual inquiry forever.
>
> Everyone's naive. It ain't that easy. (p. 441).

Because many of these students are physically dangerous, many of them are relegated to "alternative settings" (see Ninness, Glenn, & Ellis; 1993 for a discussion) where intensive social skills training packages are implemented (e.g., Argyle, Trower, & Bryant, 1974; Crane & Reynolds, 1983). However, in order to produce any real, long-term improvements in behavior we must find a way to make sure that the students' regular education environment supports the social skills we teach. Improved social skills will not sustain very long in the absence of natural or structured contingencies that continue to support such training.

Transfer of Social Skills Training

The primary problem has always revolved around the issue of *transfer*. That is, it is not unusual for students with severe behavior disorders to demonstrate prosocial skills in one classroom setting where they were learned; however, it is extremely unusual for these students to demonstrate *transfer* improvements across locations and time. Thus, a second set of skills may be required to support the tracking of newly learned prosocial behavior across environments (teachers, classroom, and other campus settings).

Self-management procedures would seem like a good candidate for supporting tracking rules for appropriate behavior across settings; however, self-management strategies have had mixed results in the school systems, particularly among behaviorally disordered adolescents. Research in this area appears equivocal at best (Hughes, Ruhl, & Misra, 1989; O'Leary & Dubey, 1979). Particularly, studies provide scant evidence to substantiate the generalized effects of self-management in the absence of direct or apparent supervision by authority figures (see Wilson, 1984 for a review). For example, Smith, Young, West, Morgan, & Rhode, (1988) found that self-monitoring and self-evaluation skills of behaviorally disordered junior-high adolescents in resource classrooms did not transfer to regular education classrooms. On the other hand, Ninness, Fuerst, Rutherford, and Glenn (1991) were relatively successful in demonstrating that behaviorally disordered junior high school students could learn to self-manage appropriate behavior in and between classes in the absence of direct supervision. We managed to accomplish this, in part, by teaching self-management under conditions which "simulated" the absence of supervision. Shortly thereafter, Smith, Nelson, Young, and West (1992) demonstrated the transfer of self-management skills by behaviorally disordered and learning disabled high school students from their training/resource setting to regular classrooms. These researchers structured this generalization by conscripting regular education peers to co-assess the behavior of the "self-managing" students.

Nevertheless, until 1995, there had been little evidence to support the social validity or generalization of aggression control procedures in the absence of supervision. At that time, we (Ninness, Ellis, Miller, et al., 1995) set about the business of using what we knew about self-assessment procedures with a population of students who offered a real challenge. In this study we sought to examine the effect of self-assessment procedures on the generalization of aggression replacement skills by junior high students who had been identified as SED. This study contrasted with previous research in that generalization was measured by covertly filming students in an out-of-class, unsupervised setting.

SHAPING RULES FOR SELF-MANAGEMENT AND SOCIAL SKILLS

Almost half a century ago, Greenspoon (1955) demonstrated that "unknowingly" adult human verbal behavior might come under the subtle control of shaping. Shortly thereafter, Truax (1966) revealed that the shaping of verbal behavior might play a veiled but critical role in therapist-patient interactions during what has come to be known as non-directive therapy. The work of Catania *et al.* (1982) isolated many of the factors contributing to this effect, but the potential for changing human beliefs and performances by way of shaping verbal responding is only beginning to be recognized by applied psychologists. The following experiment illustrates the value of shaping when used with other procedures.

Participants for this study were four males, ages 14-15 years. These students were all of average intelligence who, prior to training, spent their school day in a self-contained special education classroom serving eight junior high school students identified as SED. One teacher and an aide directed the special education class. These four subjects were selected because of their well documented and exceptional histories of disruptive, aggressive behavior throughout the junior high campus. Moreover, they had all been identified as SED using the guidelines provided by IDEA PL 105-17 (USDOE, 1997). The selection criteria for the four subjects were based on office referrals regarding physical aggression. All eight students in this class had "certified" histories of severe aggressive episodes during the weeks and months prior to the study.

Target Behaviors

First, we had to know exactly what we were measuring. Aggressive behavior was operationally defined as striking, pulling, kicking, hitting, shoving and/or throwing objects at another student. Our definition also included any behavior that approximated but did not result in complete and direct contact with another student (e.g., boxing, karate kicking, jabbing, and/or poking in the direction of a nearby student). All of these types of aggressive behavior were scored in a single category because they were all functionally similar, considered socially inappropriate, and had potential for escalating into more serious behavioral problems. The percentage of aggressive behavior was calculated by dividing the number of 10-s intervals in which these behaviors occurred by the total number of 10-s intervals in the 10-min observation period for each observation session/day and multiplying the number obtained by 100%. This partial interval observation system has become a somewhat standard strategy for measuring aggressive behaviors (Ninness, Glenn, & Ellis, 1993).

Assessment of Conditions Leading to and Maintaining Aggression

We also wanted to know something about when, where, and why these problem behaviors emerged. Using a functional assessment, we *operationally defined* each 10-s interval in which an aggressive behavior occurred as having been *provoked by another student, self-initiated* by the target students, or the *continuing interaction between or among students once an episode had begun.* Because the telephoto lens was located at some distance from the location in which the students were located (about 40 yards), it was not possible to detect verbal provocations; however, antagonistic gestures and initiations of physical assaults were fairly distinct. An aggressive episode was considered *provoked* if another student performed any aggressive gesture that approximated contact or made contact with another student. An aggressive episode was identified as *self-initiated* if the target student was the first to perform any of the above behaviors. When some form of physical exchange was already in progress, both students were scored as *continuing* aggression. (Note, these aggression behaviors were almost always low intensity "scuffles.") In the event that a serious exchange of physical contact ever occurred, it was instantly terminated by nearby staff located just inside the cafeteria.

All of these behaviors were directly observed and recorded as the four targeted students (and their classmates) stood "unsupervised" in front of the school cafeteria for at least 10 min/day. This location was selected to assess generality of training effects for three reasons: (1) students did not receive self-management or aggression control training in this location; (2) unsupervised standing and talking occurred here under ordinary school conditions; and (3) the site yielded an excellent position for covert camera placement and filming.

Some of this may strike the casual observer as being somewhat extreme and perhaps invasive of these students' privacy. Bear in mind the following points: these students were at serious risk of being placed in more restrictive environments; others were at risk of just dropping out of school; and all of the students and their parents gave informed consent for their children's participation and for filming of their children's behavior. We explained the study's procedures to the eight students, revealing to them that at various unpredictable times during the school year they would be filmed from a concealed location. Also, the students and their parents were assured that special education services would be provided irrespective of whether or not they decided to take part in the training and covert filming.

Experimental Design

We employed an ABAB design to assess changes in the percentage of intervals in which aggressive behaviors occurred in the absence of direct supervision. The 6-week baseline phase was succeeded by 11 weeks of the aggression control intervention package, followed by a 9-week reversal-to-baseline condition. An 11-week reinstatement of the aggression control package concluded the experimental procedures.

During baseline, the teacher instructed the students to walk unchaperoned from their self-contained classroom to the front of the cafeteria--a distance of approximately 100 yards. They were asked to stand quietly in that location until the lunch bell rang. They were given no other details respecting how they were to conduct themselves in this area. It was at this time and location that their activities were covertly captured on videotape.

Self-Assessment of Social Skills

Formal aggression-replacement and self-assessment training with the school psychologist was conducted at least once a day for 30 to 60 min/session in the self-contained classroom; however, student self-assessment of all classroom behaviors was maintained by the classroom teacher throughout the entire school day. Just as in the previous computer-interactive studies, students learned to score themselves regarding their own prosocial and aggression replacement skills using a Lykert scale ranging from 1 (poor) to 4 (excellent). Both students and teacher recorded their points on the same daily point sheets placed on each student's desk. Following the students' self-assessment, the teacher provided a "matching" assessment of the student's behavior. If the students' assessment matched the teacher's assessment, (plus or minus one point), the student was permitted to keep his/her points and an extra bonus point was added; however, in the event that there was more than a 1-point discrepancy between teacher and student assessment, no points were awarded for that interval. Rather than using money as a reinforcer, as in the previous study, positive consequences were furnished by means of tangible and activity-based reinforcers according to a "leveling system" and a "wheel of fortune." The details of these two reinforcement procedures are particularly germane to our overall intervention plan and they deserve special consideration.

In Chapter 4, we pointed out that shaping verbal rules (performance descriptions) was more powerful than giving instructions or simply reinforcing overt behavior (Ninness, Shore, & Ninness, 1999). Here again, we see that shaping our students, verbal interpretation of how they performed was an especially powerful procedure. Consider the self-assessment strategies we employed during the computer-interactive self-assessment programs of Chapter 4 (Ninness, Ellis, & Ninness, 1999; Ninness & Ninness, 1999). The primary intervention was differential reinforcement for improved correspondence between how students "described themselves" and how they "performed." Essentially, we shaped improved self-assessments by our students as they performed math problems. In this study we attempted to shape improved self-assessment by our students as they performed aggression replacement skills. Both studies share the common but powerful strategy of shaping verbal behavior.

Leveling

Many programs for emotionally disturbed students entail a graduated hierarchy of social prerogatives tied to the learning and maintaining of critical prosocial skills. For students who are a serious physical threat to themselves and others, a leveling/reinforcement system places these students in a sequestered environment so that they and others in the school are physically protected.

A second purpose of the leveling system is directed at engineering motivation. Very often, severely disturbed students are said to be "unmotivated to improve their behavior," but this need not be the case. Deprivation of commonplace campus activities often increases the value of mundane behaviors (Konarski, Johnson, Crowell, & Whitman, 1980). Routine school prerogatives such as unescorted passage to restrooms, unconstrained seating within the cafeteria, having a personal locker, and being in regular education classes usually gain power as strong reinforcers following a few weeks of deprivation. The purpose of such denial is not retribution; rather, it is the essential behavioral condition of having extremely "at-risk" students placed in structured and safe settings until they learn to control their own behavior. These activities and options are restored gradually as the students learn and demonstrate the necessary social skills across a wide-range of campus settings. As students demonstrate improved prosocial and academic behaviors, they are given access to an increasing array of privileges (e.g., regular education classes, unsupervised breaks, unchaperoned movement between scheduled classes, regular lunch privileges, etc.).

Following procedures from Ninness et al. (1991), the leveling system specifies the conditions for upward mobility through the hierarchy of academic options and social privileges. And, just as in the previously described computer-interactive self-assessment study (Ninness et al., 1998), at each plateau of the leveling system, the frequency of each self-assessment interval was lengthened. The working assumption was that those at the bottom of the leveling system, with the weakest skills, needed the most rehearsal and the most frequent opportunity to acquire feedback for their self-assessments. When these skills improved, the self-assessment window gradually opened wider.

Beyond gradual readmission to regular education classes, other tangible and activity-based reinforcers were obtainable on the reinforcement menu at each stage of the leveling system. However, there were no particular tangible components of this menu. The general theme was to diversify the reinforcers (mix and match) on a monthly (or sometimes weekly) basis. Developing new and unique items and activities seemed to make the acquisition of these reinforcers more "interesting"--and thus more compelling--than they might otherwise be. Table 6.1 illustrates one series of potential reinforcers accessible on the leveling system. Note however, that although particular components might be replaced at various times throughout the semester, gaining access to outside classes on a graduated basis remained a constant.

Table 1. [Deprivation and Reinforcement by Level]

1. Red: must sit in assigned seat during lunch; break spent working at desk; must walk in quiet/supervised line to lunch, restroom, etc.; no access to special privileges accessible at upper levels.

2. Orange: chooses seating location for lunch; may walk alone to restroom during breaks; may go on field trips.

3. Green: may walk alone to a greater number of locations; may use computer games; issued a locker; placement in one regular class.

4. Blue: placement in additional regular or resource classes.

Note: Adapted from Ninness, Fuerst, Rutherford, and Glenn, 1991.

When students began the program at the red level, they self-assessed three times per period. The student's self-assessment was followed immediately by a teacher assessment, and a bonus point "might be" added for correctly anticipating the teacher assessments within plus or minus one point. However, student self-assessments were not tallied. These were exclusively employed to obtain *matching* scores with the teacher. It was the teacher's score assessment that was actually computed for the daily point count. At the red level, students could obtain a maximum of 100 possible daily points. In order for students to move to the next (orange) level, they had to secure a minimum of 90% of the possible 100 points over the course of a two week period. After a student had reached the orange level, points were averaged at the end of every week; however, the average was always calculated by counting all daily points over the previous two-week period. When students attained the orange level, they self-assessed only at half hour intervals and could acquire only a maximum of 70 total points per day. This was adjusted by dividing daily totals by .7, bringing maximum daily points up to 100. In order for students to move to the next (green) level, they had to acquire 95% of the potential daily points averaged over the course of the previous two weeks. At the green level, students only self-assessed at the end of every period (about 55 minutes) and could earn only 40 points per day. Dividing by .4 brought the score back up to a possible 100. Movement to the blue level required obtaining a 97% average over a two-week period; however, blue-level students, like Green level students, scored themselves at the end of every period with a maximum of 40 possible points. As students exhibited improved performance, they moved up the leveling system and gained access to outside classes. However, even in these outside classes, they had a period progress report on which they continued to self-assess at the end of every academic period. In fact, students continued to have their self-assessment sheets co-scored by the regular education teacher for at least one semester after matriculating from the self-contained social-adjustment classroom.

Reinforcement on a Double Intermittency

As just described, access to reinforcement by way of the leveling system does not occur on a daily basis. Students must obtain a specified average score over a 2-week period before being placed on the next higher level. This extended period of time is a necessary precondition to upward mobility on the leveling system, as we must have evidence that a student can sustain his improvement in social skills and self-management before providing him with access to settings in which he will have more free, unsupervised movement. However, from a personal and a behavioral perspective, this is a long time for a child or adolescent to wait for a positive consequence following the demonstration of improved behavior. In order to compensate for this delay we have developed other methods to supplement the effects of the reinforcers provided in the leveling system.

Predicated on the basic research described in Chapter 4, we have developed reinforcement techniques which have proved to be particularly compelling. In Chapter 4 we proposed that the extended durations and relatively high rates of problem solving attributed to the rule-governed effects emerging from the second-order schedules. In that study we demonstrated that high rates and long durations of problem solving by students (in both experiments) may have been a function of the second-order relation between problem solving RR 2 (FT 30-s:S) and RR 2 (RT 30-s:S) established via the second-order, coin-toss graphic procedure. Interestingly, although Group 1 subjects in both experiments obtained only half as much reinforcement per unit of time as did Group 2 students, they performed an average of 287 more responses (nearly a factor of 2) over the course of their experimental sessions. Even though no *response-dependent* contingency existed, the probabilistic relation between responding and time-based reinforcement in conjunction with the second-order coin-toss graphic may have augmented the strength of the reinforcement contingency. Based on the comments of our subjects, at the very least we can reasonably assume that this procedure made reinforcement acquisition more "enticing" (Ninness & Ninness, 1999).

Interestingly, these outcomes fall in line with some rather dated laboratory research by Zimmerman (1957, 1959) who noticed that a reinforcer which is unpredictable tends to produce "enthusiasm" and resistance to extinction. Zimmerman's early research demonstrated that laboratory animals showed extreme resistance to extinction and relatively high rates of responding in the face of extinction when they had been exposed to schedules of reinforcement which provided for intermittent, interlocking contingencies. Zimmerman (1957, 1959) shaped a FR 15 lever press to the sound of a buzzer as a discriminative stimulus that also functioned as a reinforcer for running an alleyway to obtain food. By incorporating this FR 15 lever press as a second-order operant, rats emitted thousands of lever presses and continued responding for over 20 hr during extinction.

Specifically, if rats were first trained to run alleyways for food reinforcement at the sound of a buzzer and subsequently placed on a variable ratio schedule of reinforcement, a first order of intermittency was provided. If then, the opportunity to hear the buzzer was made contingent on a second variable ratio schedule for bar pressing an interlocking double intermittency related to ultimately running the alleyway to obtain food as a reinforcer was provided. Under these conditions, bar pressing during extinction was maintained over thousands of responses working for 20 hr spaced over several sessions. Place this in contrast to the commonly understood finding that organisms on simple variable ratio schedules will emit only about 50 presses within roughly 45 minutes before extinction takes place. This basic research illustrates the behavioral fact that when a reinforcer is made exceedingly unpredictable, but seemingly accessible, its power as a reinforcer is dramatically increased. This sort of power is demonstrated clearly in the effects game shows have on their contestants and audience. This same system can be used within the behavioral engineering of a classroom. Furthermore, we have found that this system can be used to compensate for the necessary delays inherent to a leveling system.

We are not going to suggest that our students are operating at the level of laboratory animals in a highly controlled experimental setting. Clearly, the fact that students have extensive verbal behavior complicates the effects of any direct acting contingencies irrespective of the level of intermittency of reinforcement. Nevertheless, it has become increasingly apparent to us that students (and for that matter, staff) are particularly enthusiastic about the delivery of any reinforcer which can be placed on an unpredictable and interlocking, intermittent schedule. In order to produce this effect we have developed a system which in some ways parallels the double intermittent contingencies demonstrated in Zimmerman's design.

The manner in which this system approximates (or perhaps to some extent extends) our research on second-order schedules and Zimmerman's procedures relates to the acquisition and delivery of additional reinforcers as an adjunct to the weekly rewards provided in the leveling system. Rather than have students wait until the end of each week so that a retrospective two week average can be obtained and possible promotion to the next level provided, we add the feature of giving each student, regardless of his/her current level, an opportunity to obtain a daily reward. This daily reward is tied very closely to the individual student's current running average during the previous 2 days of class. Each student is individually assigned a relatively easy and attainable short-term goal which is just slightly above the average for the previous two days. For example, if a given student has scored an average of 85 points during the previous 2 days of class, the short term goal for this student might be set at 88. In most cases this would be attainable by a student who has previously averaged 85 in the previous 2 days; however, the acquisition of a 88 points is by no means a certainty for the student, and it can be posited that he has a current intermittent history of obtaining these short term goals. Thus, the possibility of the student acquiring a sufficient number of daily points is somewhat analogous to an individual who has an intermittent (variable ratio) history of winning various games. In both cases, the individuals have a relatively current history of success and failure for achieving short term goals. But we can interlock our student's actual acquisition of the daily reinforcer with another intermittency. This can be done by making sufficient point acquisition contingent on a second behavior which is that of spinning a wheel in order to determine what type of short term reinforcer is to be made available on that specific day. For this second level of intermittency, typically, we arrange 6 numbers on a facsimile of a roulette wheel. Each number is tied to a different daily back-up reinforcer, and we have gone to great lengths to make these back-up reinforcers uniquely interesting--but not expensive. We use activity based reinforcers, concrete reinforcers, and social reinforcers for our back-up rewards. Such diverse and ridiculous items as arcade toys (plastic vomit, fly in a plastic ice-cube), baseball cards, cokes, computer time, and an opportunity to visit individually with the teacher for 10 minutes have been variously hidden behind the numbers on our roulette wheel. We find that the fact that our daily reinforcers are attainable, doubly intermittent, and "interestingly unpredictable" has added a special dimension to the effectiveness of what might otherwise be a series of rather mundane reinforcers. We have also found that this daily reinforcement system has been especially helpful for students who are just starting on the program and who have not yet come under the influence of the more sophisticated and intrinsic reinforcers associated with successful self-management and upward mobility on the leveling system.

Aggression Replacement Training

Our assessment of conditions leading to aggression showed us one thing very clearly. These students were aggressive and disruptive almost everywhere on campus and much of time they actively solicited and initiated these physical encounters. It became obvious that our intervention package had to address two very important issues simultaneously: 1) teaching students new aggression replacement skills, and 2) incorporating a strategy to make these new aggression control skills "portable." Our functional assessment told us that these students had to learn how to overcome the provocations (tauntings) of others, and they had to learn how to avoid the temptation to initiate aggression when given the opportunity to do so. Moreover, they had to learn how to carry these critical social skills with them to a wide variety of diversified school settings.

Thus, we began a period of intense social structure and training. Our aggression replacement procedures were introduced within the self-contained classroom. During the 11-week intervention phase, all eight students in the social adjustment classroom were instructed in the principles and procedures of aggression control. These skills were trained almost everywhere on campus and with a wide variety of regular and special education peers, teachers, and administrators. Our students practiced modeling aggression control in the cafeteria and in the hallway, and they performed role playing aggression replacement behavior in conjunction with self-management training in the classroom, the library, and gymnasium. Everywhere we had seen aggression take place, we took our training. We trained "to generalize" (Stokes & Baer, 1977). Formal training periods lasted from 30-60 min/day; however, training was continued throughout the entire academic school day and even in the bus line. There was almost no time during the school day when some form of training was not in progress; however, there was one place where we intentionally did not train. This was the location just in front of the school cafeteria at lunch time. Ultimately, this would be the location where we would test the generalization of our treatment.

Response classes of aggression replacement skills consisted of disregarding the "inappropriate" remarks made by other students (and staff); bypassing disagreements among, or with, other students; not being "responsive" to aggressive physical gestures by other students; resisting the "temptation" to initiate aggressive physical contact with other students; and controlling anger when taunted by other students. During the first part of training, all social skills instruction was provided within the self-contained classroom in the following order:

1. The teacher specified the rules regarding the relationship between the behavior of avoiding or initiating conflict, and the delayed beneficial outcomes associated with correct self-assessment of this behavior (e.g., the wheel of fortune).

2. The teacher demonstrated (modeled) the posture, gestures, and overt self-instructions while continuing to work in the midst of distractions and provocations of other students. The teacher overtly modeled self-instruction rules to stay on-task in the face of these distractions.

3. Students practiced the behavior just demonstrated by the teacher and overtly verbalized their self-instructions to stay on task even while being provoked. While avoiding eye contact with those who annoyed them, they repeated aloud their self-instructions such as, "I'm not going to let this person bother me, and I will be able to give myself a high score." Simultaneously, the students practiced using a gesture (palm open, small wave) to suggest that they did not want to be bothered while they were working.

4. The teacher, psychologist, and associate psychologist attempted to shape the students' increasing approximations of correct self-assessments by providing social reinforcement contingent on improving performances (cf. Ninness, Ninness, Sherman, & Schotta, 1998).

5. Gradually, students were instructed to fade self-instructions to a covert level by whispering the same aggression control statements; although, they continued to grade themselves (scale of 1 to 4) as to the adequacy of their individual performances under these simulated conditions (self-assessment and self-recording).

6. Peers and teachers provided concurrent assessments of the student's performance. These assessments served as feedback only and were not used as part of the daily scoring system.

7. Students rotated the role-playing of on-task performance while various students and teachers served as sources of minor provocations. Self-assessment with feedback from teacher and peers continued (Ninness et al., 1995, pp.476-477).

Starting somewhere around the fourth week of social skills training, we began leaving these students alone in the classroom while they rehearsed these social skills routines independently. We didn't go very far! In an adjoining room, we had installed a one-way mirror along with a camera. In the event that anything did "go wrong," we were able to intervene immediately, but things never did go wrong (in a serious way).

Keep in mind that by this time, our students were becoming very proficient at performing aggression replacement skills in our presence, as well as under conditions that *simulated* our absence. Thus, leaving the classroom briefly while they rehearsed did not represent a very substantial change in their training regimen. Moreover, to guarantee continued successful performances, these "unsupervised" rehearsals initially were practiced for only 3 to 5 min at a time. However, as with the training of any new social or academic skill, we steadily increased the response requirements. Rehearsals were gradually expanded to 10 min, 15 min, and eventually up to 20 min in duration. All the while students practiced avoiding provocations of others, they practiced avoiding the "temptation" to initiate provocations, and they continued doing their work in the apparent absence of adult supervision. Students self-assessed their performances following our return to the classroom. Here's a very important point:

> *Since we had been watching them through the one-way mirror, we were*
> *well positioned to identify particular students who might need a little "extra*
> *training" in the fine art of <u>accurate</u> self-assessment.*

When our students finally started getting really good at performing these skills in the classroom, even while there was no direct supervision of their behavior, we began instructing, modeling, and rehearsing aggression replacement skills in a wide variety of *other settings throughout the campus*. Again, we remained well positioned to observe their behavior covertly. As in the training conducted in the classroom, initially, these skills were instructed, modeled, and rehearsed with direct supervision and feedback. Students were coached on the subtle details of body language, eye contact, and verbal behavior associated with avoiding altercations.

Altercation scenarios were often based on real confrontations previously encountered by our students. In these same locations, we *simulated* and rehearsed the correct performance of assertively avoiding altercations. For example, if one of our students had been taunted, or was even pushed while walking upstairs, the entire class practiced "assertively ignoring" irritating remarks, and physical "jarring" while walking up the stairwell. As in our classroom simulations, all the students modeled and role-played the correct responses for one another while peers, the teacher, and the psychologist provided performance feedback. This skill also entailed the use of self-instructions (rules) such as, "I'm not going to get angry here. If I keep it together, I can give myself a high score." This particular skill was not one that came naturally, and for several of our students, it took quite a bit of serious rehearsal before mastery was achieved. Nevertheless, we believe this is a skill which is well worth mastering by many junior high students.

Teaching to Generalize

Slowly, direct supervision was faded, and teachers and psychologists monitored the students covertly. That is, we instructed the students to practice their aggression control skills should the occasion arise "spontaneously" as they walked to assorted settings around the campus. The students were told that they might confront provocation from prearranged props (confederate students or school staffs) we had positioned around the campus. As always, they were instructed to self-assess their ability to refrain from initiating or responding to belligerent behaviors or verbalizations of others while moving from one campus location to the next (or while being left alone in the classroom). At about this point, training really intensified!

As our students became increasingly proficient at dealing with interpersonal confrontations and avoiding the temptation to initiate problems, we structured spontaneous behavioral probes. That is, during the latter part of training, students were given spontaneous challenges or "red flags" (McGinnis, 1984). These were prearranged replications of problem conditions that had been mastered during instruction, modeling, role-playing and unsupervised rehearsal. This training procedure made it extremely difficult for students to differentiate fabricated social aggravation from "real life" obstacles (cf. Stokes & Baer, 1977). Red flags were scheduled randomly throughout the school day and in diversified classroom and nonclassroom environments. Let us emphasize, however, that students were informed that they would not be expected to endure actual physical mistreatment from anyone under any circumstances. During these red-flag practice sessions, each student's behavior was recorded by hidden cameras and direct observers. Our students self-assessed their behavior following their return to the classroom. Again, we were well positioned to identify students who might need a little "extra training" in precision self-assessment in a particular out-of-class setting.

After eight weeks of instruction, modeling, rehearsal, and red-flag challenges, we arranged a series of covert filmed observations of our students as they stood unsupervised in front of the school cafeteria. We did this every day at lunch time for nine days. Students were asked to score themselves regarding their behavior just as they had done throughout all of their training. They were told that their self-assessed points would be tallied with their daily points and become exchangeable for progress on the social pyramid as well as opportunities to play the wheel-of-fortune. This was consistent with strategies we had employed all throughout the previous eight weeks of training. Figure 6.3 shows a drastic reduction in the percentage of aggressive behaviors during this time.

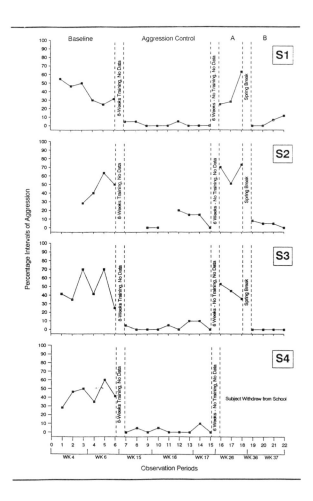

Figure 6.3. [Percentage of episodes of aggressive behavior under baseline, treatment, reversal, and reinstatement conditions for Subjects 1 through 4, as adapted from Ninness, Ellis, Miller, Baker, and Rutherford, 1995, p.482]

Following these observations, we terminated training entirely for nine weeks. Students were specifically instructed that all training exercises would be completely terminated in all out-of-class settings, and they should cease and desist scoring their own behavior while they were not in the classroom setting. This may seem somewhat abrupt, but we had to find a way to assess the effect of completely discontinuing out-of-class self-assessment procedures. We needed to know if self-assessment was the critical variable supporting their improved behavior. In the last three days of this reversal-to-baseline phase, we filmed our students as they stood, unsupervised, in front of the school cafeteria. Three days was enough to show us all we needed (or wanted) to know!

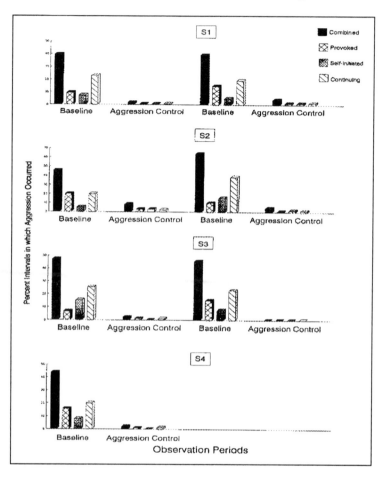

Figure 6.4. [Percentage of episodes of aggressive behavior under combined conditions as well as under conditions of provocation, self-initiation, and continuation of ongoing aggressive behavior for Subjects 1 through 4, as adapted from Ninness, Ellis, Miller, Baker, and Rutherford, 1995, p.484]

On the following day, we reinstated treatment. Students were given condensed instructions to self-assess their behavior everywhere on the campus, but detailed rehearsals of aggression-replacement skills were not conducted. In fact, formal training time was cut down to about 20 min/day, and role-playing was conducted exclusively as unsupervised rehearsal and red flag challenges. This represented a very abbreviated training scheduled when compared to all that we had done in the initial stages of the training. Of course, we were interested in seeing how they would conduct themselves when standing in front of the school cafeteria in the absence of supervision.

Figure 6.4 suggests that before we introduced the aggression control package and self-assessment, all four of our students had rather high levels of aggressive behavior. This changed dramatically following eight weeks of aggression replacement and self-assessment training. Nevertheless, during reversal-to-baseline conditions, these maladaptive behaviors reemerged. But, when an abbreviated form of treatment was reinstated in the final condition, our students once again demonstrated very low level aggressive behaviors.

Examination of the circumstances in which our students demonstrated aggressive behaviors suggests some diversity of antecedents (Figure 6.4); however, after reinstituting self-assessment contingencies, maladaptive behaviors became so infrequent that differences can no longer be detected.

Verbal Antecedents of Aggression

Using a functional assessment allowed us to direct our treatment to the antecedent conditions of aggression. Nevertheless, certain caveats present themselves. Particularly among students with good verbal skills, self-initiated aggression (or other maladaptive social behaviors) may be attributed to the development of self-instructed rules that are tied to a wide range of verbal antecedents and consequences (Hayes, Kohlenberg, & Malancon, 1989). Clearly, it was not possible to access the specific verbal repertoires of these students prior to treatment. We had no way of knowing what they were saying to themselves about their own aggressive behavior. However, we did learn something about the conditions in which they were most likely to act-out aggressively. Unbeknownst to us prior to the filmed functional assessment, these students were not just responding aggressively to other people's taunting and provocations. Our students were just as likely, if not more likely, to initiate aggressive episodes whenever and wherever the chance presented itself. Moreover, once an episode began they were very unlikely to stop. Most of the baseline and reversal intervals were composed of a combination of self-initiated, provoked, and continuing aggression. Therefore, it became eminently clear to us that our intervention needed to include equal amounts of emphasis in all three area of potential volatility. This is something we would not have anticipated and would not have introduced into our social skills program had we not conducted a functional assessment prior to training.

Rule-Following After Functional Assessment and Treatment

The students in this study continued following rules for aggression control even when it appeared to them that they were not being supervised. As previously described in this chapter, this is compatible with an account of rule-following described as *tracking* (Hayes & Wilson, 1993). This kind of self-managed behavior, in the absence of direct supervision of authority figures, stands in contrast to *pliance*, which we previously described as a type of rule-following that is a function of the correspondence between the rule and the socially mediated consequences provided during *supervision* of a particular target behavior.

These conspicuous and extreme changes in aggressive behavior beg the question: "Why did such rule-governed behavior discontinue during the nine-week reversal phase of our study?" Catania (1992) points out that rules that are functional are maintained in the individual's repertoire; those rules that are not useful lose their capacity to govern behavior. During the reversal phase, our students were no longer able to acquire any reinforcement (direct or indirect) contingent on correct self-assessments. By the end of nine weeks, these rules no longer served any useful purpose (in fact, they probably became somewhat irrelevant), and these rules gradually dropped out of the students' repertoires. On the other hand, indulging in rough "horseplay" and outright aggression provided substantial and immediate social reinforcement.

With the reinstatement of self-assessment contingencies, our students "believed" that they could once again gain access to the positive consequences of following rules for aggression control. This ABAB reversal-of-treatment design gave us a picture that would otherwise remain very elusive. It allowed us to see the limitations associated with even intensive social skills and self-assessment training. Just as we discovered in our previously described computer-interactive self-assessment study (Ninness et al., 1999), when the contingencies supporting self-assessment were removed, so were the students' improved behaviors. Such limitations were not as apparent in our previous self-management research (Ninness et al., 1991).

Even though these results showed us that aggression control strategies are most compelling while self-assessment and other aggression control procedures are in effect, they are, nevertheless, functional in a multitude of environments and in the complete absence of authority figures. These learned, prosocial skills generalize very nicely across settings, but like everything else, these strategies have their limitations. Generalization across time is one of these limitations. Yet, once these skills become firm in the students' repertoire, it is not especially difficult to develop and sustain a maintenance program.

Let us restate our general theory regarding functional assessment and self-assessment. Functional assessments provide real time information on the circumstances in which students are at the highest risk for demonstrating maladaptive behaviors. Without this information, the school psychologist is operating at a serious disadvantage in trying to develop useful behavior intervention plans. Without this information, one literally does not know the targets for treatment. Indeed, were it not for the functional assessment we conducted prior to aggression replacement training, we would not have known the targets for student self-assessment.

After initial training, fading the density of opportunities to self-assess may furnish a means to sustain rule-following behavior, even with progressively fewer opportunities to self-assess. Following such a training history, even sporadic opportunities to self-assess while having another person (or computer as we discussed in Chapter 4) corroborate the accuracy of self-assessment seem to provide additional reinforcing value. Moreover, it seems fair to speculate that the student who gives him or herself a high self-assessment score at the end of a given interval may well render other self-descriptive comments that elaborate (however briefly) on how well he or she has just done. With special training, these self-descriptive statements may gain additional reinforcing value. Simply put, people like to tell themselves how well they have done--particularly if they can really believe what they say.

IN SUMMARY

These are only a few of the immense number of applied research studies in which functional assessment strategies have contributed to the development effective and efficient behavior intervention plans. As noted earlier, functional assessments have a unique characteristic separating them from traditional psychological assessments--emphasis on accountability. Again, functional assessments are mandated and conducted with an eye toward locating the variables that interact with the student's maladaptive behavior. Once these variables are identified, the success of intervention can be based on the student demonstrating improved performance under the same (and more general) conditions. Thus, functional assessments serve as a guide for developing efficient behavior plans, and they provide criteria for demonstrating effective treatment outcomes.

Epilogue

As noted in the prologue, this book ends where it begins. But we have described only a few of the emerging functional and scientific methods of helping people to improve their own behavior. In this book, we have placed a special emphasis on strategies that surround rule-governed behavior, functional assessments, self-assessments, and the shaping of verbal behavior. Our book has highlighted the many ways in which our verbal description of contingencies may be as influential and dynamic as the "actual" contingencies that exist in our worlds. However, to requote Skinner (1969), "Even fragmentary descriptions of contingencies speed the acquisition of effective terminal behavior, help to maintain the behavior over a period of time, and reinstate it when forgotten" (p. 143). Indeed, *learning to correctly describe* our behavior and the contingencies into which our behavior falls may be one of the more critical links in the continuing evolution of human learning.

Goodnight Sister Servula

Many decades after leaving the black hole, Herbie sits in a large leather chair with his feet propped on the desk before him. His fingers dance about the keyboard of the tiny computer resting on his lap. Somehow, the screen has managed to capture his complete and undivided attention. In the background a radio is playing.

Lucy in the sky with diamonds...

In the distance, phones are ringing and a dog is barking. A new CD is being burned and a fax machine drops fresh data in a basket beside him, but Herbie appears focused on the small computer and relatively impervious to these minor distractions. Perhaps, some of Herbie's behavior has evolved. After several hours of tapping the keyboard, he stretches and looks at the clock on his desk--11:30 p.m.! His tired eyes fall on a very old yellow bookmark inside an ornate wooden frame. Inscribed on it are the words, "Little Sisters of Charity." Quietly contemplating the chronology of his species, and his own interesting journey through time, he smiles and whispers, "Goodnight Sister Servula--wherever you are!"

The End

Bibliography

Anastasi, A. C. (1968). *Psychological testing: Third edition.* New York: Macmillan.

Argyle, M., Trower, P., & Bryant, B. (1974). Explorations in the treatment of personality disorders and neurosis by social skill training. *British Journal of Medical Psychology, 47,* 63-72.

Azrin, N. H. (1958). Some effects of noise on human behavior. *Journal of the Experimental Analysis of Behavior, 1,* 183-200.

Baer, D. M. (1984). Does research on self-control need more control? *Analysis and Intervention in Developmental Disabilities, 4,* 211-218.

Baron, A., Perone, M. & Galizio, M. (1991). Analyzing the reinforcement process at the human level: Can application and behavioristic interpretation replace laboratory research? *Behavior Analyst, 14,* 95-105.

Barrish, H. H., Saunders, M., & Wolf, M. M. (1969). Good behavior game: Effects of individual contingencies for group consequences on disruptive behavior in a classroom. *Journal of Applied Behavior Analysis, 2,* 119-124.

Belfiore, P. J., Lee, D. L., Vargas, A. U., & Skinner, C. H. (1997). Effects of high-preference single-digit mathematics problems completion on multiple-digit mathematics problems performance. *Journal of Applied Behavior Analysis, 30,* 327-330.

Bentall, R. P., & Lowe, C. F. (1987). The role of verbal behavior in human learning: III. Instructional effects in children. *Journal of the Experimental Analysis of Behavior, 47,* 177-190.

Bentall, R. P., Lowe, C. F., & Beasty, A. (1985). The role of verbal behavior in human learning: II. Developmental differences. *Journal of the Experimental Analysis of Behavior, 43,* 165-180.

Breland, K. and Breland, M. (1961). The misbehavior of organisms. *American Psychologist, 61,* 681-684.

Broden, M., Hall, R. V., & Mitts, B. (1971). The effects of self-recording on the classroom behavior of two eighth-grade students. *Journal of Applied Behavior Analysis, 3,* 191-199.

Broussard, C. D. & Northup, J. (1995). An approach to functional assessment and analysis of disruptive behavior in regular education classrooms. *School Psychology Quarterly, 10*(2), 151-164.

Bruner, A., & Revushky, S. H. (1961). Collateral behavior in humans. *Journal of the Experimental Analysis of Behavior, 4,* 349-350.

Carr, E. G. & Durand, V. M. (1985). Reducing behavior problems through functional communication training. *Journal of Applied Behavior Analysis, 18,* 111-126.

Carr, E. G., Newson, C. D., & Binkoff, J. A. (1976). Stimulus control of self-destructive behavior in a psychotic child. *Journal of Applied Behavior Analysis, 13,*101-117.

Cataldo, M. F. & Harris, J. (1982). The biological basis for self-injury in the mentally retarded. *Analysis and Intervention in Developmental Disabilities, 2,* 21-39.

Catania, A. C., (1993). *Learning: Second edition.* Englewood Cliffs, NJ: Prentice-Hall.

Catania, A. C. (1992). *Learning: Third Edition.* Englewood Cliffs, NJ: Prentice Hall. Catania, A. C. (1994). The natural and artificial selection of verbal behavior. In S. C. Hayes, L. J. Hayes, M. Sato, & K. Ono. (Eds.) *Behavior Analysis of Language and Cognition.* Reno, NV: Context Press.

Catania, A. C., Matthews, B. A., & Shimoff E. (1982). Instructed versus shaped human behavior: Interactions with nonverbal responding. *Journal of the Experimental Analysis of Behavior, 38,* 233-248.

Catania, A. C., Shimoff, E., Matthews, B. A. (1989). An experimental analysis of rule-governed behavior. In S. C. Hayes (Ed.), *Rule-governed behavior: cognition, contingencies, and instructional control.* (pp. 119-150). New York: Plenum Press.

Cerutti, D. T. (1994). Compliance with instructions: Effects of randomness in scheduling and monitoring. *The Psychological Record, 44,* 259-269.

Cerutti, D. T. (1991). Discriminative versus reinforcing properties of schedules as determinants of schedule insensitivity in humans. *The Psychological Record, 41,* 51-67.

Connell, M. C., Carta, J. J., & Baer, D. M. (1993). Programming generalization of in-class transition skills: Teaching preschoolers with developmental delays to self-assess and recruit contingent teacher praise. *Journal of Applied Behavior Analysis, 26,* 345-357.

Conner, J. M. & Ferguson-Smith, M. A. (1987). Essential medical genetics: Second edition. Oxford: Blackwell Scientific Publications.

Crane, C., & Reynolds, J. (1983). *Social skills and me.* Houston, TX: Crane/Reynolds, Inc.

Davis, H., & Hubbard, J. (1972). An analysis of superstitious behavior in the rat. *Behaviour, 3,* 1-12.

Dermer, M. L. & Rodgers, J. G. (1997). Schedule control over following instructions comprised of novel combinations of verbal stimuli. *The Psychological Record, 47,* 243-260.

Dickinson, A. M. (1989). The detrimental effects of extrinsic reinforcement on intrinsic motivation. *The Behavior Analyst 12,* 1-15.

Dixon, M. R. & Hayes, L. J. (1998). Effects of differing instructional histories on the resurgence of rule-following. *The Psychological Record, 48,* 275-292.

Dunlap, G., Kern, L., Clarke, S., & Robbins, F. (1993). Functional assessment, curricular revision, and severe behavior problems. *Journal of Applied Behavior Analysis, 24,* 387-397.

Durand, V. M. & Crimmins, D. B. (1987). Assessment and treatment of psychotic speech in an autistic child. *Journal of Autism and Developmental Disorders, 17,* 17-28.

Dwyer, K. P. (1991). Making the least restrictive environment work for children with serious emotional disturbance. *Preventing School Failure, 34,* 14-21.

Eaton, S. B., Shostak, M., & Konner, M. (1988). *The Paleolithic Prescription.* New York: Harper & Row.

Edgington, E. S., (1995). *Randomization Tests.* New York, NY: Marcel Dekker, Inc.

Fatuzzo, J. W. & Rohrbeck, C. A. (1992). Self-managed groups: fitting self-management approaches into classroom systems. *School Psychology Review, 21,* 255-263.

Ferster, C. B. & Skinner B. F. (1957). *Schedules of reinforcement.* New York: Appleton-Century-Crofts.

Findly, J. D., and Brady, J. V. (1965). Facilitation of large ratio performance by use of conditioned reinforcement. *Journal of the Experimental Analysis of Behavior, 8,* 125-129.

Fisher, W. W., Ninness, H. A. C., Piazza, C. C. & Owen-DeSchryver, J. S. (1996). On the reinforcing effects of the content of verbal attention. *Journal of Applied Behavior Analysis, 29.* 235-238.

Fisher, W. W., Piazza, C. C., Zarcone, J. R., O'Conner, J. & Ninness, H. A. C. (1995, May) *On the clinical and theoretical implications of molar and molecular functional assessment.* Paper presented at the 21st

Annual Convention of the Association for Behavior Analysis International, Washington, DC.

Flora, S. R., Pavlik, W. B., & Pittenger, D. J., (1990). Effects of a masking task on schedule discrimination and extinction in humans. *The Psychological Record, 40*, 83-104.

Fowler, S. A. (1984). Introductory comments: The pragmatics of self-management for the developmentally disabled. *Analysis and Intervention in Developmental Disabilities, 4*, 85-89.

Galizio, M. (1979). Contingency-shaped and rule-governed behavior: Instructed control of human loss avoidance. *Journal of the Experimental Analysis of Behavior, 31*, 53-70.

Gettinger, M. (1985). Effects of teacher directed versus student directed instruction and cues versus no cues for improving spelling performance. *Journal of Applied Behavior Analysis, 18*, 167-171.

Glenn, S. S. (1995). Units of interaction, evolution, and replication: organic and behavioral parallels. *The Behavior Analyst, 18*, 237-251.

Glynn, E. L., & Thomas, J. D. (1974). Effects of cueing on self-control of classroom behavior. *Journal of Applied Behavior Analysis, 7*, 299-306.

Glynn, E. L., & Thomas, J. D., & Shee, S. M. (1973). Behavioral self-control of on-task behavior in an elementary classroom. *Journal of Applied Behavior Analysis, 6*, 105-113.

Greenspoon, J. (1955). The reinforcing effect of two spoken sounds on the frequency of two responses. *American Journal of Psychology, 68*, 409-416.

Hackenberg, T. D., & Joker, V. R. (1994). Instructional versus schedule control of human choices in situations of diminishing returns. *Journal of the Experimental Analysis of Behavior, 62*, 367-383.

Hagopian, L. P., Fisher, W. W., & Legacy, S. M., (1994). Schedule effects of noncontingent reinforcement on attention-maintained destructive behavior in identical quadruplets. *Journal of Applied Behavior Analysis, 27*, 317-326.

Harzem, P., Lowe, C. F. & Bagshaw, M. (1978). Verbal control in human operant behavior. *Psychological Record, 28*, 405-423.

Hayes, S. C., Brownstein, A. J., Zettle, R. D. Rosenfarb, I., & Korn, Z. (1986). Rule-governed behavior and sensitivity to changing consequences of reponing. *Journal of the Experimental Analysis of Behavior, 45*, 237-256.

Hayes, L. J., Dixon, M. R., Caslake, D. L., Beckwith, J. L., & Schurr, C. S. (1997). Deviations from animal standards in human schedule performances through self-generated verbal behavior. *Mexican Journal of Behavior Analysis, 23*(1), 53-65.

Hayes, S. C. & Hayes, L. J. (1989). The verbal action of the listener as a basis for rule-governance. In S. C. Hayes (Ed.), *Rule-governed behavior:*

Cognition, contingencies, and instructional control (pp. 135-190). New York: Plenum Press.

Hayes, S. C., Kohlenberg, B. S., & Melancon, S. M. (1989). Avoiding and altering rule-control as a strategy of clinical intervention. In S. C. Hayes (Ed.), *Rule-governed behavior: Cognition, contingencies, and instructional control* (pp. 359-385). New York: Plenum Press.

Hayes, S. C., & Wilson, K. G. (1993). Some applied implications of a contemporary behavior-analytic account of verbal events. *The Behavior Analyst, 16,* 283-301.

Hayes, S. C., Zettle, R. D., & Rosenfarb, I. (1989). Rule following, In S. C. Hayes (Ed.), *Rule-governed behavior: Cognition, contingencies, and instructional control.* (pp.191-220). New York: Plenum.

Hefferline, R. F. & Keenan, B. (1963). Amplitude induction gradient of a small-scale (covert) operant. *Journal of the Experimental Analysis of Behavior, 6,* 307-315.

Heltzer, R. A., & Vyse, S. A. (1994). Intermittent consequences and problem solving: The experimental control of "superstitious" beliefs. *The Psychological Record, 44,* 155-169.

Hersen, M. & Barlow, D. (1976). *Single-case Experimental Designs: Strategies for Studying Behavior Change.* New York: Pergamon Press.

Holland, A. L. & Matthews, J. (1963). Application of teaching machine concepts to speech pathology and audiology. *American Speech and Hearing Association, 5,* 474-482.

Holland, J. G. (1958). Counting by humans on a fixed-ratio schedule of reinforcement. *Journal of the Experimental Analysis of Behavior, 1,* 179-181.

Homme, L. (1974). *How to use contingency contracting in the classroom.* Champaign, IL: Research Press.

Hopkins, K. D., Hopkins, B. R., & Glass, G. V. (1966). *Basic Statistics for the Behavioral Sciences: (3rd edition).* Needham Heights, MA: Allyn & Bacon.

Houghton, S. J. (1991). Promoting generalization of appropriate behavior across special and mainstream settings: A case study. *Educational Psychology in Practice, 7,* 49-54.

Hughes, C. A., Ruhl, K. L., & Misra, A. (1989). Self-management with behaviorally disordered students in school settings: A promise unfulfilled? *Behavior Disorders, 14,* 250-262.

Hyten, C. & Madden, G. J. (1993). The scallop in human fixed-interval research: a review of problems with data description. *The Psychological Record, 43,* 471-500.

Iwata, B. A., Dorsey, M., Slifer, K., Bauman, K., & Richman, G. S. (1982). Toward a functional analysis of self-injury. *Analysis and Intervention in Developmental Disabilities, 2*, 3-20.

Iwata, B. A., Pace, G. M., Dorsey, M. F., Zarcone, J. R., Vollmer, T. R., Smith, R. G., Rodgers, T. A., Lerman, D. C., Shore, B. A., Mazaleski, J. L., Goh, H., Cowdery, G. E., Kalsher, M. J., McCosh, K. C., & Willis, K. D. (1994). The functions of self-injurious behavior: An experimental-epidemiological analysis. *Journal of Applied Behavior Analysis 27*, 215-240.

Iwata, B. A., Pace, G. M., Kalsher, Cowdery, G. E., & Cataldo, M. F. (1990). Experimental analysis and extinction of self-injurious escape behavior. *Journal of Applied Behavior Analysis, 23*, 11-27.

Johanson, D. C. & Edey, M. A. (1981). *Lucy, The Beginnings of Humankind.* New York: Simon & Schuster.

Jones, V. F. & Jones, L. S. (1998). *Comprehensive classroom management: Creating a positive learning environment for all students.* Needham, MA: Allyn & Bacon.

Kaufman, A., Baron, A., & Kopp, R. E. (1966). Some effects of instructions on human operant behavior. *Psychonomic Monograph Supplements, 1*, 243-250.

Kern-Dunlap, L., Dunlap, G., Clarke, S., Childs, K. E., White, R. L., & Stewart, M. P. (1992). The effects of a videotape feedback package on peer interactions of children with serious behavioral and emotional challenges. *Journal of Applied Behavior Analysis, 25*, 355-364.

Knapczyk, D. R., & Livingston, G. (1973). Self-recording and student teacher supervision: Variables within a token economy structure. *Journal of Applied Behavior Analysis, 6*, 481-486.

Konarski, E. A., Johnson, M. R., Crowell, C. R. & Whitman, T. L. (1980). Response deprivation and reinforcement in applied settings: A preliminary analysis. *Journal of Applied Behavior Analysis, 13*, 595-609.

Kurten, B. (1993). *Our Earliest Ancestors.* New York: Columbia University Press.

Lattal, K. A. & Neef, N. A. (1996). Recent reinforcement-schedule research and applied behavior analysis. *Journal of Applied Behavior Analysis, 29*, 213-230.

Lattal, K. A. & Abreu-Rodrigues, J. (1997). Response-independent events in the behavior stream. *Journal of the Experimental Analysis of Behavior, 68*, 375-398.

Lerman, D. C. & Iwata, B. A., (1993). Descriptive and experimental analysis of variables maintaining self-injurious behavior. *Journal of Applied Behavior Analysis, 26*, 293-319.

Lewin, R. (1984). *Human Evolution:An Illustrated Introduction.* New York: W. H. Freeman & Co.

Lippman, L. G., & Meyer, M. E. (1967). Fixed-interval performance as related to instructions and to subject's verbalizations of the contingency. *Psychonomic Science, XXX,* 135-136.

Locke, J. (1950). *Essay concerning human understanding.* New York: Dover. (Original work published 1690).

Long, E. R., Hammack, J. T., May, F., & Cambell, B. J. (1958). Intermittent reinforcement of operant behavior in children. *Journal of the Experimental Analysis of Behavior, 1,* 315-339.

Lowe, C. F. (1979). Determinants of human operant behaviour. In M.D. Zeiler & P. Harzem (Eds.), *Advances in analysis of behaviour: Vol. 1. Reinforcement and the organization of behaviour* (pp. 159-192). Chichester, England: Wiley.

Lowe, C. F., Beasty, A., & Bentall, R. P., (1983). The role of verbal behavior in human learning: Infant performance on fixed-interval schedules. *Journal of the Experimental Analysis of Behavior, 39,* 157-164.

Maag, J. W., Reid, R., & DiGangi, S. A. (1993). Differential effects of self-monitoring attention, accuracy, and productivity. *Journal of Applied Behavior Analysis, 26,* 329-344.

Mace, F. C., Brown, D. K. & West, B. J. (1987). Behavioral self-management in education. In C. A. Maher and J. E. Zins (Eds.), *Psychoeducational interventions in the schools. Methods and procedures for enhancing student competence* (pp. 160-176). New York: Pergamon.

Mace, F. C. & Lalli, J. S. (1991). Linking descriptive and experimental analysis in the treatment of bizarre speech. *Journal of Applied Behavior Analysis, 24,* 553-562.

Mace, F. C, Webb, M. E., Sharkey, R. W., Mattson, D. M., & Rosen, H. S. (1988). Functional analysis and treatment of bizarre speech. *Journal of Behavior Therapy and Experimental Psychiatry, 19,* 714-721.

Madden, G. J., Chase, P. N., & Joyce, J. H. (1998). Making sense of sensitivity in the human operant literature. *The Behavior Analyst, 21,* 1-12.

Malott, R. W. (1986). Self-management, rule-governed behavior, and everyday life. In H. W. Reese & L. J. Parrott (Eds.), *Behavioral Science: Philosophical, Methodological, and Empirical Advances* (pp. 207-228). Hillsdale, N. J. Lawrence Erlbaum.

Malott, R., Whaley, D., & Malott, M. E. (1993). *Elementary principles of behavior. (2nd ed.).* Englewood Cliffs, NJ: Prentice Hall.

Malott, R. W., Whaley, D. L., & Malott, M. E. (1997). *Elementary Principles of Behavior (3rd ed.).* Upper Saddle River, New Jersey: Prentice Hall.

Malott, R. W., Malott, M. E.. & Trojan, E. A. (2000). *Elementary Principles of Behavior (4th ed.).* Upper Saddle River, New Jersey: Prentice Hall.

Marx, B. P., & Gross, A. M. (1995). An analysis of two contextual variables. *Behavior Modification, 19,* 451-463.

Matthews, B. A., Catania, A. C. & Shimoff, E. (1985). Effects of uninstructed verbal behavior on nonverbal responding: Contingency descriptions versus performance descriptions. *Journal of the Experimental Analysis of Behavior, 43,* 155-164.

Max, L. W. (1934). An experimental study of the motor theory of consciousness. I. History and critique. *Journal of General Psychology, 11,* 112-125. [233].

McGinnis, E. (1984). Teaching social skills to behaviorally disordered youth. In *Social/affective intervention in behaviorally disordered youth* (pp. 87-120). Des Moines, IA: State Board of Public Instruction.

McLaughlin, T. F., & Truhlicka, M. (1983). Effects on academic performance of self-recording and matching with behaviorally disordered students: A replication. *Behavioral Engineering, 8,* 69-74.

Medland, M. B. & Stachnik, T. J. (1972). Good-behavior game: A replication and systematic analysis. *Journal of Applied Behavior Analysis, 5,* 45-51.

Michael, J. (1982). Distinguishing between discriminative and motivational functions of stimuli. Journal of the Experimental Analysis of Behavior, 37, 149-155.

Morgan, D. L. (1998). Selectionist thought and methodological orthodoxy in psychological science. *The Psychological Record, 48,* 439-456.

Mulinksy, A. (1989). *Choices not chances: An essential guide to your heredity and health.* Boston: Little, Brown, and Company.

Neef, N. A. & Iwata, B. A. (1994). Current research on functional analysis methodologies: An introduction. *Journal of Applied Behavior Analysis, 27,* 211-214.

Neef, N. A., Mace, F. C., & Shade, D. (1993). Impulsivity in students with serious emotional disturbance: The interaction effects of reinforcer rate, delay, and quality. Journal of Applied Behavior Analysis, 26, 37-52.

Nelson, J. R., Roberts, M. L., Bullis, M., Albers, C., & Ohland, B. (1999). Functional behavioral assessments: Looking beyond applied behavior analysis. *Communique, 27,* 1 & 8-9.

Newman, B., Buffington, D. M., & Hemmes, N. S. (1995). The effects of schedules of reinforcementon instruction following. *The Psychological Record, 45,* 463-476.

Newman, B., Buffington, D. M., Hemmes, N. S., & Rosen, D. (1996). Answering objections to self-management related concepts. *Behavior and Social Issues, 6,* 85-95.

Ninness, H. A. C., Ellis, J., & Ninness, S. K., (1999). Self-assessment as a learned reinforcer during computer interactive math performance: An experimental analysis. *Behavior Modification, 23*(3), 403-418.

Ninness, H. A. C., Ellis, J. Miller, B., Baker, D., & Rutherford, R. (1995). The effects of self-management of the transfer of aggression replacement skills in the absence of supervision. *Behavior Modification, 19,* 464-490.

Ninness, H. A. C., Fuerst, J., & Rutherford, R. (1995). A descriptive analysis of disruptive behavior during pre- and post-unsupervised self-management by students with SED: a within study replication. *Journal of Emotional and Behavioral Disorders, 3,* 230-240.

Ninness, H. A. C., Fuerst, J., Rutherford, R. D., & Glenn, S. S. (1991). Effects of self-management training and reinforcement on the transfer of improved conduct in the absence of supervision. *Journal of Applied Behavior Analysis, 24,* 499-508.

Ninness, H. A. C. & Glenn, S. S. (1988). *Applied Behavior Analysis and School Psychology: A Research Guide to Principles and Procedures.* Westport, CT: Greenwood Press.

Ninness, H. A. C., Glenn, S. S., & Ellis, J. (1993). *Assessment and treatment of emotional or behavioral disorders.* Westport, CN: Praeger.

Ninness, H. A. C., McCuller, G., & Ninness, S. K. (1999). Functional analysisutilizing a four-term contingency. In D. A. Sabatino & B. L. Brooks (Eds.), *Contemporary Interdisciplinary Interventions for Children with Emotional/Behavior Disorders* (pp. 505-531). Durham NC: Carolina Academic Press.

Ninness, H. A. C. & Ninness, S. K. (1998). Superstitious math performance: Interactions between rules and scheduled contingencies. *The Psychological Record, 48,* 45-62.

Ninness, H. A. C. & Ninness, S. K. (1999). Contingencies of Superstition: Self-Generated rules and responding during second-order response-independent schedules. *The Psychological Record, 49,* 221-243.

Ninness, H. A. C., Ninness, S. K., Sherman, S., & Schotta, C. (1998). Augmenting self-assessment during computer-interactive problem solving. *The Psychological Record, 48,* 601-616.

Ninness, H. A. C., Ozenne, L., McCuller, G., Rumph, R., & Ninness, S. K. (in press). Fixed-interval responding during human computer-interactive problem solving. *The psychological Record.*

Ninness, H. A. C., Shore, T., & Ninness, S. K. (1999). Shaping verses instructing verbal rules during computer-interactive problems solving. *The Psychological Record, 49,* 625-644.

O'Leary, S. G., & Dubey, D. R. (1979). Applications of self-control procedures by children: A review, *Journal of Applied Behavior Analysis, 12,* 449-465.

Ono, K. (1994). Verbal control of superstitious behavior: Superstitions as false rules. In S. C. Hayes, L. J. Hayes, M. Sato, & K. Ono (Eds.), *The Behavior analysis of language and cognition.* (pp. 181-196). Reno, NV: Context Press.

Ost, L. & Hugdahl, K. (1985). Acquisition of blood and dental phobia and anxiety response patterns in clinical patients. *Behavior Research and Therapy, 23,* 27-34.

Pavlov, I. P. (1927). *Conditioned reflexes.* (trans. G. V. Anrep). London: Oxford University Press. (22, 42, 187, 352)

Piazza, C. C., Fisher, W. W., Hagopian, L. P., Bowman, L. G., & Toole, L. (1996). Using a choice assessment to predict reinforcer effectiveness. *Journal of Applied Behavior Analysis, 29,* 1-9.

Premack, D. (1965). Reinforcement theory, In D. Levine (Ed.), *Nebraska symposium on motivation,* Lincoln: University of Nebraska Press, 123-180.

Repp, A. (1994). Comments on functional analysis procedures for school-based behavior problems. *Journal of Applied Behavior Analysis, 25,* 409-411.

Repp, A. C., Roberts, D. M., Slack, D. J., Repp, C. F., & Berkler, M. S. (1976). A comparison of frequency, interval, and time-sampling methods of data collection. *Journal of Applied Behavior Analysis, 9,* 501-506.

Rhode, G., Morgan, D. P., & Young, K. R. (1983). Generalization and maintenance of treatment gains of behaviorally handicapped student from resource room to regular classroom using self-evaluation procedures. *Journal of Applied Behavior Analysis, 16,* 171-188.

Rosenbaum, M. S., & Drabman, R. S. (1979). Self-control training in the classroom: A review and critique. *Journal of Applied Behavior Analysis 12,* 467-485.

Rosenfarb, I. S., Newland, M. C., Brannon, S. E., & Howey, D. S. (1992). Effects of self-generated rules on the development of schedule-controlled behavior. *Journal of the Experimental Analysis of Behavior, 58,* 107-121.

Sattler, J. M. (1992). Assessment of Children *(3rd ed.). San Diago, CA:* Jerome M. Sattler, Publisher, Inc.

Schlinger, H., & Blakely, E., (1987). Function-altering effects of contingency-specifying stimuli. *The Behavior Analyst, 10,* 41-45.

Sidman, M., (1960). *Tactics of Scientific Research.* New York: Basic Books.

Sidman, M., & Tailby, W. (1982). Conditional discrimination vs. matching-to-sample: An expansion of the testing paradigm. *Journal of the Experimental Analysis of Behavior, 37,* 5-22.

Skinner, B. F. (1938). *The behavior of organisms.* New York: Appleton-Century-Crofts.

Skinner, B. F. (1948). "Superstition" in the pigeon. *Journal of Experimental Psychology, 38,* 168-172.

Skinner, B. F. (1969). *Contingencies of reinforcement: A theoretical analysis.* New York: Appleton-Century-Crofts.

Skinner, C. H. & Smith, E. S. (1992). Issues surrounding the use of self-management interventions for increasing academic performance. *School Psychology Review, 21,* 202-210.

Slavin, R. E. (1994). *Educational Psychology: Theory and Practice.* Boston: Allyn and Bacon.

Smith, D. J., Nelson, R. J., Young, K. R., & West, R. P. (1992). The effect of a self-management procedure on the classroom and academic behavior of students with mild handicaps. *School Psychology Review, 21,* 59-72.

Smith, D. J., Young, R., West, R. P., Morgan, D. P., & Rhode, G. (1988). Reducing the disruptive behavior of junior high school students: A classroom self-management procedure. *Behavior Disorders, 13,* 231-239.

Staddon, J. E. R. & Simmelhag, V. L. (1971). The "superstition" experiment: A reexamination of its implications for the principles of adaptive behavior. *Psychological Review, 78,* 3-43.

Steege, M. W. (1999). Functional assessment: An odyssey. *Communique, 27,* 14-15.

Steege, M. W., Wacker, D. P., Berg, W. K., Cigrand, K. K., & Cooper, L. J. (1989). The use of behavioral assessment to prescribe and evaluate treatments for severly handicapped children. *Journal of Applied Behavior Analysis, 22,* 22-33.

Stokes, T. F., & Baer, D. M. (1977). An implicit technology of generalization. *Journal of Applied Behavior Analysis, 10,* 349-367.

Timberlake, W., & Lucas, G. A. (1985). The basis of superstitious behavior: Chance contingency, stimulus substitution, or appetitive behavior? *Journal of the Experimental Analysis of Behavior, 13,* 391-394.

Tomarken, A. J., Mineka, S, & Cook, M. (1989). Fear-relevant selective associations and covariation bias. *Journal of Abnormal Psychology, 4,* 381-394.

Torgrud, L. J., & Holburn, S. W. (1990). The effects of verbal performance descriptions on nonverbal operant conditioning. *Journal of the Experimental Analysis of Behavior, 54,* 273-291.

Truax, C. A., (1966). Reinforcement and non-reinforcement in Rogerian psychotherapy. *Journal of Abnormal Psychology, 7,* 1-9.

Ullmann, L. P. & Leonard, K. (1969). *A psychological approach to abnormal behavior.* Englewood Cliffs, NJ: Prentice Hall.

Umbreit, J. (1995). Functional analysis of discriptive behavior in an inclusive classroom. *Journal of Early Intervention, 20,* 18-29.

Van Houten, R. (1984). Setting up performance feedback systems in the classroom. In W. L. Heward, T. E. Heron, J. Trap-Porter, & D. S. Hill

(Eds.), *Focus upon applied behavior analysis in education* (pp. 112-125). Columbus, OH: Merrill.

Vyse, S. A. (1991). Behavioral variability and rule generation: General, restricted, and superstitious contingency statements. *The Psychological Record, 41,* 487-506.

Wagner, G. A. & Morris, E. K., (1987). "Superstitious" behavior in children. *The Psychological Record, 37,* 471-488.

Wasserman, E. A., & Neunaber, D. J. (1986). College students responding to and rating of contingency relations: The role of temporal contiguity. *Journal of the Experimental Analysis of Behavior, 46,* 15-35.

Watson, J. B. (1919). *Behaviorism* (rev. ed.) Chicago: University of Chicago Press.

Watson, J. B. & Rayner, R. (1920). Conditioned emotional reactions. *Journal of Experimental Psychology, 3,* 1-14. (197-198).

Weisberg P. & Waldrop, P. B. (1972). Fixed-interval work habits of Congress. *Journal of Applied Behavior Analysis, 5,* 93-97.

Wells, G. L. & Bradfield, A. L. (1998) "Good, you identified the suspect.": Feedback to eyewitnesses distorts their reports of the witnessing experience. *Journal of Applied Psychology, 83*(3), 360-376.

Wells, G. L., Small, M., Penrod, S. Malpass, R. S., Fulero, S. M. & Brimacombe, C. A. E. (1998). *Eyewitness Identification Procedures: Recommendations for Lineups and Phtosprreads,* APLS Scientific Review Paper.

Whaley, D. L. & Malott, R. W. (1968). *Elementary Principles of Behavior.* Kalamazoo, MI: Behaviordelia.

Wilson, R. (1984). A review of self-control treatments for aggressive behavior. *Behavior Disorders, 9,* 131-140.

Young, K. R., West, R. P. Morgan, D. P., Smith, D. J. Glomb, N.,Haws-Kuresa, S. (1987). *Teaching self-management strategies to adolescents: Instructional manual.* Department of Special Education. Utah State University. Logan, Utah.

Zametkin, A. J., Nordahl, T. E., Gross, M., King, C., Semple, W. E., Rumsey, J., Hamberger, S., & Cohen, R. M., (1990). Cerebral glucose metabolism in adults with hyperactivity of childhood onset. *The New England Journal of Medicine, 323,* 1361-1366.

Zimmerman, D. W. (1957). Durable secondary reinforcement: method and theory. *Psychological Review, 64,* 373-383.

Zimmerman, D. W. (1959). Sustained performance in rats based on secondary reinforcement. *Journal of Comparative and Physiological Psychology, 52,* 353-358.

Index

PUBLISHER DISCLAIMER